1981

EDGAR ALLAN POE:
The Design of Order

EDGAR ALLAN POE:
The Design of Order

edited by
A. Robert Lee

VISION
and
BARNES & NOBLE

Vision Press Limited
Fulham Wharf
Townmead Road
London SW6 2SB
and
Barnes & Noble Books
81 Adams Drive
Totowa, NJ 07512

ISBN (UK) 0 85478 146 3
ISBN (US) 0 389 20647 4

Library of Congress Cataloging-in-Publication Data

Edgar Allan Poe: The Design of Order

    (Critical Studies)
    1. Poe, Edgar Allan, 1809–1849. Criticism and
Interpretation. I. Lee, A. Robert, 1941–
II. Series: Critical Studies Series.
PS2638. E36 1986   818', 309   86-10708
ISBN 0-389-20648-2

Printed and bound in Great Britain by
L.R. Printing Services Ltd.,
Crawley, W. Sussex.
Phototypeset by Galleon Photosetting,
Ipswich, Suffolk.
MCMLXXXVII

Contents

Introduction:

by A. ROBERT LEE

Poe, prophet of a civilization buried alive....
— Ishmael Reed, *Flight to Canada* (1976)

So, with typical bravura, Ishmael Reed adds an Afro-American ingredient to the stock of legend about Edgar Allan Poe (1809–49). His is yet further testimony to the fascination, for good or ill, that Poe continues to exert, and wonderfully stylish and witty testimony at that as those who have read on in his novel would be quick to confirm. Even in a culture as eager as America to mythify its writers and artists, Poe stands out as the singular case, a source of controversy and a call to arms either as the supreme genius or the charlatan and fraud.

Who, after all, has been more identified for his 'horror', the supposed Gothic maestro in whose prolific stories and poetry virtually every nightmare and fear or phobia found expression? Who, too, just as supposedly, more led a life which might have been a page from his own work, Poe the dweller among the undead and their crypts, the would-be necrophiliac or vampire, the madman, the drug-taker, the alcoholic, the husband of a child-bride, the gambler and celebrant of 'the perverse', in effect none other than his own tormented figure of Roderick Usher? And who, in all of this, and whether read in childhood or later as an adult with the memory of those first enthralled encounters still in mind, has been more hedged about with half-truths, good and bad guesses, the absorption of his art into his life and reputation? Poe, it has been observed with justice, belongs as much to the history of publicity as to the American literature in which he played so distinctive and strange a founding part.

Not that, as invariably the case, the legend or myth of Poe does not contain its elements of truth. He did, in many ways, write from beyond, or below, a unique designer of images and narrative for our shared feelings of hysteria, fear, dislocation, the sheer randomness of things, each recurring plunge into self-fright and imagined powerlessness. The very sites of his best-known stories, indeed, call up domains to the far side of rationality, fantasy or dream worlds in which the inmost reaches of sensation are transformed into configurations of order. Why else do we remember as well as we do Poe's fissured House of Usher, his pitch-black inquisitorial dungeon in 'The Pit and the Pendulum', his whirling maelstrom, or his different entombments and immurations? Why else, to bring in his poetry, do we remember his croaking raven, his deathly city in the sea, his manic and tintillating bells? Poe, at his most Poe-esque as it were, refers us to those states of feeling where the usual rational props are put under suspension and we feel summoned to face ourselves in all our shaping anxieties and panic. Behind Poe's horror, then, though not for a moment to everyone's taste, lies his claim to altogether more consequential status, that of a visionary and artificer in the line of Blake, Rilke, Verne, Valéry, and latterly, Borges.

But sorting out Poe from his legend, his best work from his dross and ephemera, is not new. It began almost immediately with the publication of his first slim verse collection, *Tamerlane and other Poems*, in 1827. At the outset, thus, it does no harm to recall one essential Poe above all the others, that of the painstaking, hard-pressed magazine editor and contributor, who published more than seventy stories in total, a novel the length and ingenuity of *The Narrative of Arthur Gordon Pym of Nantucket*, the poetry, the wide variety of literary and philosophical essays, the endless reviews, the miscellany he called his *Marginalia*, and the 'cosmological prose poem' he believed underpinned all his efforts and which he first delivered as a lecture in New York in 1848 entitled 'The Universe', *Eureka*. It is the Poe inside this writing, a perhaps less glamorous figure than that passed down in legend, who serves as the main focus for this new collection of essays, Poe as carried in his prose and poems.

Poe did not, despite the myths, spring full-shaped out of some swampy and Southern Gothic estate. Quite the reverse in fact. Nearly all his life was spent in the workaday world of American Grub Street, rarely in funds, fraught, harried for copy, only on occasion able to resist the bullying and exploitation of unsentimental journal proprietors and editors. It was the search for an income from his work which caused his frequent shifts from city to city, whether the Richmond where he had been first raised, or New York, or Philadelphia, or Baltimore, where he died a troubled, almost freakish, death. Despite the writing that came out in book form under his own name, Poe in this respect was always the creature of the early nineteenth-century American magazines, be it as contributor, editor, reviewer, or even on occasion as fund-raiser and type-setter. Among the best-known of the magazines which at different times bore his imprimatur are the *Southern Literary Messenger*, *Burton's Gentleman's Magazine*, *Graham's Magazine*, the *Pioneer* and the *Broadway Journal*. Little wonder that through all his labour for these and other publications, he harboured the lifelong dream of a definitive literary journal, the *Stylus*, the harbinger of a Southern renaissance of letters to counter the cultural dominance as he saw it of New England and the Yankee north in general.

There is, too, a personal and domestic Poe, the Boston-born Southerner, whose own life indeed did go through extra-ordinary convulsions. His well-known proneness to excitation and nervousness no doubt had its origins in his early orphaning and the fostering out to the Allans of Richmond. The child-hood interlude spent in Stoke Newington, in north London, where his stepfather went about his business interests from 1815–20, clearly also dwelt long and unsettlingly in his mind—to be used later in his classic *Doppelgänger* story, 'William Wilson'. At the University of Virginia, in 1826, he was quickly expelled for debt, though not without a reputation as a scholar of languages, a versifier, a prankster and a habitué of the card-table. His stay in the army (as 'Edgar A. Perry') in 1827–28, and at West Point as a cadet in 1830, were similarly brief, the uncertain false starts of a writer still to find his true metier. In the 1830s, however, his career did take off, first as the winner of literary competitions, then through his association with the *Messenger* and its successors. But he took on, too, a menage of sorts, his aunt Maria Clemm, and teenage cousin Virginia, whom he most likely married in 1835. Their itinerant life, makeshift homes, Poe's own frequent ill-health, the endless shabbiness and cash worries, and even at this stage, the gathering if largely misfounded rumours as to Poe's drinking and general reprobate behaviour, did nothing to ease matters. When Virginia died a premature and invalid's death in 1847, it marked but one more set-back in a history where set-back had become the norm. Against conditions such as these, it remains a triumph of will as much as talent on Poe's part that he managed to put his always volatile energies to the literary purposes he did.

Poe seen only under his Gothic mantle does yet another disservice; it obscures his genuine diversity and range. As to his story-telling, for instance, to call 'The Fall of the House of Usher', 'The Pit and the Pendulum', 'The Masque of the Red Death', 'The Black Cat' or 'The Cask of Amontillado' simply 'Gothic' is to leave out the whole tone and texture of Poe's art, the carefully insinuated acknowledgements of his own artifice. Then, too, there is the 'ratiocinative' Poe, the Poe to whom logic, deduction, the meticulous working-out of problems and ciphers, plays into a story like 'The Gold Bug'. That interest finds its incarnation, too, in Poe's metaphysical sleuth, C. Auguste Dupin, no mere Holmes or Poirot, but Poe's poet-mathematician and cosmologist—at least on the evidence of his three classic Dupin pieces, 'The Murders in the Rue Morgue', 'The Purloined Letter' and 'The Mystery of the Marie Roget'. Alongside these stands Poe the hoaxer, the writer of, say, 'The Unparalleled Adventure of One Hans Pfaall' or 'Some Words with a Mummy' or the still more whimsical and comic 'How to Write a Blackwood Article' and 'The Man that was Used Up'. There have to be reckoned in, equally, Poe's visionary 'dark lady' stories, his fictions which envisage in their title-name heroines the witness to other worlds, 'Ligeia', principally, but also 'Berenice' and 'Morella'. To these must be added Poe's 'ideal landscape' pieces, his imagined magic gardens where all the dislocation and fright described in his other stories can be held in abeyance, 'The Domain of Arnheim' or 'Landor's Cottage'. Who, too, would deny Poe his place in the tradition of Science Fiction, a unique futurologist? His speculative intelligence shows particularly to advantage in, again, 'The Unparalleled Adventure of Hans Pfaall', as well as later pieces like 'The Balloon Hoax',

'Mesmeric Revelation' and 'Mellonta Tauta'. This latter, told
as a Letter to a Friend, also links to his conversation stories,
metaphysical and political Poe taken up with ideas of cosmic
utopia and dystopia, culture and anarchy, as, notably, in 'The
Colloquy of Monos and Una' and 'The Conversation of Eiros
and Charmion'. In any and all of these Poe's intricacy of
first-person narration, his utter and enclosing irony, look to a
subtlety of eye and ear in the reader which on past evidence
has not always been sufficiently granted him.

Implicit in his stories, as in *The Narrative of Arthur Gordon Pym
of Nantucket* (1837–38) and his essays and poetry, is Poe's
'cosmology', as finally evolved in *Eureka*. Not unlike Yeats, Poe
craved a unifying theory of all things, positing Unity and
Diffusion as twin impulses—his own and our world suffering
maximum diffusion. At one reach, thus, Poe indeed saw as a
visionary, a maker of cosmic myth. But if his visions were first
those of the poet, they were also to be approached and understood through 'logic'; hence, more than anyone, Auguste
Dupin, not to mention Poe himself, in his fascination as mentioned above with cipher, cryptogram, crime, puzzlement, the
very cat's cradle of language itself. This same mix of vision and
logic applies to his essay-work, especially the three landmark
enquiries into the aesthetics of literary composition, 'The
Poetic Principle', 'The Philosophy of Composition', and 'Letter
to B—'. There, an early New Critic and formalist, he argued
for pattern over 'life', poetry and the tale as superior by dint of
their 'concentration' over all longer verse forms—Poe's much
cited and controversial example was 'Paradise Lost'—and the
novel.

As to Poe's poetry, for all that in his own lifetime it won him
as much fame and attention as his story-telling, it has had the
most dramatic fall in fortune. Poe stands accused of ethereality,
inertness, pose, an unintended bathos. Even his celebrated
'musicality' fails to get him off the hook. And yet, to take up a
point made earlier, we remember if not the poetry as such then
Poe's invented icons and landscape. He surely did create the
most memorable of images in 'The Raven', or 'The City in the
Sea', or 'The Bells'. What, too, of visionary work like 'Ulalume—
A Ballad' or 'Annabel Lee'—simple incantation and no more?
Poe, to be sure, hardly gains in any serious comparison with

Keats or Shelley, but to dismiss him as simply an overwrought metrist does an unfairness.

One other Poe asks for attention, that is the figure conjured up by his fellow-authors, especially those of his native country. In part, after his death, that meant negotiating the strange calumny committed on Poe by his ill-chosen literary executor, the Rev. Rufus W. Griswold. He, more than anyone else, both in his obituary and a subsequent memoir, put into play the nineteenth-century daemonic version of Poe, the writer truly given to madness and dissolution. Almost as persistent, in its own time and subsequently, has been the couplet written by the New England Brahmin and poet, James Russell Lowell, in his *A Fable For Critics* (1848):

> There comes Poe, with his raven, like Barnaby Rudge,
> Three fifths of him genius and two fifths fudge.

More intriguing than both, because subtler, are the accounts offered by Herman Melville and Walt Whitman. In Melville's case, the picture of Poe as given in *The Confidence-Man* (1857) has to be taken somewhat provisionally as Poe is never actually named. In addition, Melville was indeed writing fiction, a 'masquerade' as he calls it. But as a portrait of Poe in both his shabbiness and grandeur, *Eureka* in hand, wrapt and with his gaze upon the distances ahead, has this been bettered?

> a haggard, inspired-looking man now approached—a crazy beggar, asking alms under the form of peddling a rhapsodical tract, composed by himself, and setting forth his claims to some rhapsodical apostleship. Though ragged and dirty, there was about him no touch of vulgarity; for, by nature, his manner was not unrefined, his frame slender, and appeared the more so from the broad, untanned frontlet of his brow, tangled over with a disheveled mass of raven curls, throwing a still deeper tinge upon a complexion like that of a shriveled berry. Nothing could exceed his look of picturesque Italian ruin and dethronement, heightened by what seemed just one glimmering peep of reason, insufficient to do him any lasting good, but enough, perhaps, to suggest a torment of latent doubts at times, whether his addled dream of glory were true.

Whitman's recollection of Poe is a reprint of his 'Edgar Poe's Significance', published in January 1880, but citing his own words at the dedication of a monument at Poe's graveside in Baltimore in 1875. Whitman, too, discerns a strange grandeur to Poe, the precarious balance in his creative make-up of 'dream' and unhingement:

> In a dream I once had, I saw a vessel on the sea, at midnight, in a storm. It was no great full-rigg'd ship, nor majestic steamer, steering firmly through the gale, but seem'd one of those superb little schooner yachts I had often seen lying anchored, rocking so jauntily, in the waters around New York, or up Long Island sound—now flying uncontroll'd with torn sails and broken spars through the wild sleet and winds and waves of the night. On the deck was a slender, slight beautiful figure, a dim man, apparently enjoying all the horror, the murk, and the dislocation of which he was the centre and the victim. That figure of my lurid dream might stand for Edgar Poe, his spirit, his fortunes, and his poems—themselves all lurid dreams.

To both these acts of witness, many more can be added, a quite dizzying historical spiral of favour and disfavour. One thinks of Hawthorne's correspondence with Poe in 1843 and his mention of 'your force and originality'. Or conversely of Emerson's dismissal of Poe as 'the jingle man' (as reported by Oliver Wendell Holmes in 1860). Or even, refreshingly, of Emily Dickinson's 'Of Poe, I know too little to think', in a letter to Thomas Wentworth Higginson in 1879. More magisterially, there is Henry James on Poe, both in his essay 'Charles Baudelaire' (1876)—'An enthusiasm for Poe is the mark of a decidedly primitive stage of reflection'—and in his *Hawthorne* (1879).

For the present century, to give matching examples, there has been D. H. Lawrence's necrophile Poe of *Studies in Classic American Literature* (1923), the Poe in the 'terror of his isolation' of William Carlos Williams's *In the American Grain* (1925), the 'subway', spectral Poe of Hart Crane's *The Bridge* (1930), the addled aesthetic theorist of Yvor Winters ('Edgar Allan Poe: A Crisis in the History of American Obscurantism', 1937), the imaginative 'Southern' kin of Allen Tate ('Our Cousin, Mr. Poe', 1949, and 'The Angelic Imagination: Poe and the Power of Words', 1952), and the essentially juvenile Poe of T. S. Eliot—the Poe with 'the intellect of a highly gifted young person before puberty' ('From Poe to Valéry', 1949). Latterly, and exemplarily, there has been the Poe developed in the essays of the poet Richard Wilbur (foremost 'The House of Poe', 1959), a Poe whose subject is 'psychic conflict', the 'civil war in the palaces of men's minds'. Wilbur's Poe also compares interestingly with the Freudianized reveller of his fellow-poet Daniel Hoffman in his showy but never unintelligent *Poe, Poe, Poe, Poe, Poe, Poe, Poe* (1972). This latter, in turn, conjures up Marie Bonaparte's influential *Edgar Poe: Etude Psycho-analytique* (1933), Poe as the like of other 'disturbed' artists, an Edvard Munch, say, or Gustav Klimt. Alongside these has to be invoked an earlier French Poe, 'Edgarpo', the *symboliste* figure and *poète maudit* imagined and translated by Baudelaire and Mallarmé and applauded by Valéry. In their hands, Poe might be said to have undergone an almost Ligeia-like rebirth, a Gallic second coming and identity. And to these, there is, inescapably, 'pop' Poe, the unpaid script-writer of films by Roger Corman and Freddie Francis (and the Hammer entourage of Vincent Price, Christopher Lee and Peter Cushing *et al.*) and the cult presence in a flourishing cartoon, poster and fashion art.

The present essay-collection opens with two complementary modes of reading Poe. The first, by Mark Kinkead-Weekes, looks at perhaps the best-known story in the Poe canon, 'The Fall of the House of Usher', in terms of reader-response, Poe's education of his reader as to the means as much as the substance of his drama. The second, by Harold Beaver, deploys an altogether more Barthesian, structuralist manner in its unravelling of 'MS. Found in a Bottle', a 'hieroglyphic' story-within-a-story. In turn, Arnold Goldman ponders a recurrent and generic interest in Poe's story-telling, his obsession with premature burial, the self enwalled and trapped. Poe as a comic writer, a wit at least, is explored by James Justus, Poe's indebtedness to inherited frontier tall-tales and 'black' humour. Robert Giddings, for his part, looks at yet another dimension of Poe's story art, the Dupin 'detective' stories, each an enactment of our deeply human desire to have mystery or derangement or things thrown out of order definitively resolved. In these, as in other stories, Poe shows himself not simply taken up with Parisian street and domestic crime, but with an altogether more important metaphysics of order.

My own account of *The Narrative of Arthur Gordon Pym of*

Nantucket argues for a Poe again aware of his own procedures, a reflexive writer to the core and a spirited creator of mock-documentary Antarctic exploration. In his account of Poe's poetry, David Murray moves on from the received condemnations of Poe's jingliness and deadness of idiom. He sets out a suggested new lexicon of 'allegory' by which the poetry can be read as it has not been previously. Eric Mottram takes on a broader perspective, Poe as reflecting a deep current of insecurity and vulnerability in an American republic seeking to hide its apprehensions within codes of civil and political law. Poe the Southerner—and what story more inaugurates 'Southern' writing than 'The Fall of the House of Usher'?—is given fresh attention by Richard Gray, Poe the creature of racial phobia, the ghosts of history, and his dream of a Southern palace of art and culture. Finally, John Weightman returns to French Poe, the trans-Atlantic *alter ego* of American Poe, a fascinating but invented literary double if ever there were.

Poe will never satisfy all tastes. To the one side he remains the vulgarian, the mere dabbler in sensation, a fraudulent and frequently tiresome maker of effects. Whether in his prose, his poetry, or his cosmology and essay work, he never rises above himself, ever a provincial and juvenile mind. To the other side, he beckons as a great custodian of inner unease and doubt. His writing at best shows him a canny, wonderfully alert and agile imagination, full of the most startling feats of invention. Which is to acknowledge that Poe goes on sponsoring a range of responses, dismay at his flatnesses, amazement at his genuine ingenuity and power. But whether we see him always inside his Gothic persona, a slightly crank-like American Walpole, or as the American *symboliste* cousin of Baudelaire and Mallarmé and thereby an inspired visionary of our own 'otherness', or as a master of irony who knows and signals his own artifice throughout, or as a literary-philosophical intelligence in the line of Coleridge and Emerson, or indeed as an uncertain but fascinating mix of all of these, will depend on personal conviction. But Poe cannot, in whatever way we place him, be denied his place, a writer who once lodged in the consciousness simply will not go away.

1

Reflections On, and In, 'The Fall of the House of Usher'

by MARK KINKEAD-WEEKES

> And all should cry, Beware! Beware!
> His flashing eyes, his floating hair!
> —Samuel Taylor Coleridge, 'Kubla Khan'

What is immediately impressive about 'The Fall of the House of Usher' is the care with which it sets out to establish the kind of reader it requires. As opposed, it turns out, to Coleridge's notion of an aeolian lute,[1] which resounds to every capricious gust of feeling or idea, there is to be scruple and discrimination, a challenge to put imagination, and feeling, and critical intelligence to work, in controlled harmony. The mode then is not merely Gothick,[2] but rather a 'Gothick' which at every turn signals a consciousness of its own operation, its own language and vision. From the outset we have before us, too, a narrator we must both respond to, and carefully watch responding:

> During the whole of a dull, dark, and soundless day in the autumn of the year, when the clouds hung oppressively low in the heavens, I had been passing alone, on horseback, through a singularly dreary tract of country, and at length found myself, as the shades of the evening drew on, within view of the melancholy House of Usher. I know not how it was—but with the first glimpse of the building, a sense of insufferable gloom pervaded my spirit.

This could be the opening script for a thousand 'horror' stories and films: the adjectival atmospherics, the *compositio loci* as the titles come up, the dreary landscape, the gathering darkness, the melancholy house, the lonely horseman, the preternatural feeling of gloom.

But just as the sense of something worked-up becomes conscious, becomes overdone with the word 'insufferable'— we are made aware of it as a word through a scruple, made to stand back and *look*, at both the Gothick and the motives of its audience. In other words, Poe keeps a controlling distance on what the opening paragraph terms 'that half-pleasurable, because poetic, sentiment with which the mind usually receives even the sternest natural images of the desolate or terrible'; this story will be no mere sensationalist exercise in 'horror'. Still less are we offered that darker romanticism which seeks in hallucination or drug some goading or torturing of the imagination into the sublime—but rather something more like the aftermath of that: the hideous awakening from illusion into sick depression and hangover, so that everyday reality seems poisoned and bitter. The narrator is both suspect and comes through. If there is a touch of 'romantick' or even decadent expertise, of one who has known the pull of the Gothick theatre and the opium den, nevertheless the outcome is a clearing away, from what we are to attend to, of those self-pleasing but necessarily falsifying and even sickening kinds of veil. We can hope for good Poe when the temptations to what can be bad in him are so clearly renounced.

From beginning to end in 'The Fall of the House of Usher' Poe requires of us a peculiarly double kind of reading response, at once attuned to the depressive qualities of the story, yet aware that we are being asked to think and to feel more than simply 'sensation'. That double note can be felt simply in looking

> upon the mere house, and the simple landscape features of the domain—upon the bleak walls—upon the vacant eye-like windows—upon a few rank sedges—and upon a few white trunks of decayed trees—.

Something is there, both in and behind the detail of the passage, a horror certainly but a horror conscious of its own effect, its own elusive power. Something. . . .

'What was it—I paused to think—what was it that so unnerved me . . . ?' Again the narrator anticipates by a split second the thoughtful (not Gothick) reader; but only to discover that rational 'analysis' cannot explain the strange 'power' of that 'combination of very simple natural objects'. Indeed it is that inability that can cause 'shadowy fancies' to accompany the realization of being out of one's depth. But just as there was a challenge to a different quality of imagination from the falsely 'romantick', so now the narrator tries a different kind of 'thought': contemplation, or more exactly, *reflection*. This shares with 'analysis' (i.e. taking to pieces) a kind of objectivity, an ability to stand outside an experience to see whether by deliberately rearranging its elements and shifting perspective, the experience can be made clearer. But this 'reflection' is unlike analysis in that it seeks not to dissect or explain but to re-cognize, seeing again but more whole, because mirrored against greater and darker depth. The lake suggests the bowl of the mind, in which reality can be not only reflected but reflected on, in a medium whose depth is not merely rational but holds darker and even ominous fathoms of consciousness below the surface, giving deeper focus to the image on the retina. In such reflection (it seems) imagination can join mind and what we now call the subconscious, in a wholeness of cognition.

The immediate effect however is to increase disturbance. In the dark medium the reflection of sedge and trees has become greyer and more 'ghastly', though still without explanation. It is nevertheless clearer. About now, if not before, the nature of what was caught in the original seeing and the inverted image ought to be graspable. Was it not an intimation of something deathly?—because what is in itself merely bleak and vacant, inorganic, becomes deathly if you see it as what has happened to a face and eyes?—and what is organic, still growing, is even more deathly if you see it as rank grey or ghastly white like mortifying flesh and bone? What we glimpsed was no mere seasonal decay, but death-in-life or living deathliness, further confirmed and increased by the sense of life inverted, perceived in reflection, though not yet articulated by more than a shudder.

Then, through a process of association, the narrator's mind

produces the further fathoming for his reflection to work more fully: the intuition of the connection between his response to the scene before him, and what he has learned of the state of Roderick Usher, disordered in body, nerves and mind, inheritor of a whole process of dynastic life and growth now withering into a last death-in-life—the connection between the 'family', its last representative, and the 'house', that is implicit in the name the locals have given it. So that, returning to his 'reflection', the narrator not only feels his apprehension heightened to a kind of terror, but is able to pin down more precisely three of its causes. He is frightened that he is about to encounter, indeed is already encountering in the House of Usher, an atmosphere not only deathly but infectious; a disintegration already almost complete beneath what still feels whole; and worst of all, that he himself may be already implicated in that infection and disintegration, entering the House. The atmosphere peculiar to the family mansion, and almost palpable like a miasma reeking up, is not merely death-in-life but 'pestilent', and evil, with 'no affinity with the air of heaven'. The extraordinary combination of total decay ('Minute fungi overspread the whole exterior') with still 'perfect adaptation of parts', becomes threatening with the discovery of the 'barely perceptible fissure', which can nevertheless be seen to run from top to bottom and into the tarn below the surface. The concealed threat of the comparison with 'the specious totality of old woodwork which has rotted for long years in some neglected vault, with no disturbance from the breath of the external air' is that the first breath of air from outside will bring instant disintegration—and there is the narrator entering. But most sinister of all is the possibility that it may not, after all, be a matter of the outsider risking infection or introducing an alien element.

For the House of Usher seems terribly *familiar*, a world he is used to, as well as producing unfamiliar and frightening fancies. If what seems living can be deathly, and what seems whole be about to disintegrate, might this not be true of the narrator?—it is his mind, after all, that is mirrored in the tarn. There is another but also possible irony in the evil physician he meets on the stair; for the narrator, too, purports to be coming to heal. Yet his scruple and capacity for self-examination do seem reassuring; this man who keeps accusing himself of childish-ness, superstition, fancy, dream, surely shows a sane mind and a good heart as well as imagination and intuition? But it is also true that, having renounced false forms of imagination and feeling, his language keeps trembling near the brink of indulgence in them[3]; the tarn in which his reflection is mediated is 'lurid' as well as deep, and may be poisoned. And most disturbing of all is his own sense of disturbance, and of recognition, much exceeding ours—suggesting that he does feel peculiarly implicated and threatened, as though he some-how belonged to the 'House' and the 'Family', as more than just a childhood friend. We cannot tell yet how to feel, but one thing is more and more certain: the questioning or response is not only continuous, but increasing.

However, our introduction to Roderick Usher (though of course we see him only through the narrator) begins to clarify the difference between them. He is the protagonist of the Gothick/Romantick which the story began by distancing: at the centre of its 'intricate' passageways; its dark spaces and recesses beyond inspection; its in-turned enclosure; its 'encrim-soned light' from windows not meant to see out of, but rather to transform the daylight artificially into a richer atmosphere of inner sensation. Indeed Roderick is the *artist* in these modes, the culmination of a long line—but both the narrator and Usher himself proceed to clarify what that development of imagination and sensibility may cost, in the loss of vitality and the reduction of fully human being:

> Many books and musical instruments lay scattered about, but failed to give any vitality to the scene. I felt that I breathed an atmosphere of sorrow. An air of stern, deep, and irredeemable gloom hung over and pervaded all.

We soon discover why. The one-sided development of that kind of artist clearly involves a loss of physical vitality, indeed an atrophy of the body, so that the narrator can hardly recognize the 'wan being' Usher has become. Intuitions about the House are reinforced and diagnosed in the impressions made by its owner. His extraordinary luminous eyes may seem very different from the vacancy of the house-face (though we have just had a hint of how they might look from outside in the daylight) but the 'cadaverous complexion' and hair 'of a more than web-like softness and tenuity', floating about the high temples—everybody remarks on the resemblance to Poe himself—also irresistibly and horribly remind one of the previous sense of grey substance and floating fungoid growth, living but corpse-like, a death-in-life now located in the poet and musician as well as in his House. Moreover the delicate mouldings of lip and nostril, bespeaking beauty and sensibility, are at odds with the lack of moral energy betrayed by the chin. The cost of lustrous eye and Arabesque expression is a radical splitting of 'simple humanity': a deep division of personality betrayed by inconsistency and incoherence of behaviour, attitude, voice. Roderick's 'cordiality' is both 'overdone' and sincere; he both deeply needs and deeply rejects human contact and relation:

> His action was alternately vivacious and sullen. His voice varied rapidly from a tremulous indecision (when the animal spirits seemed utterly in abeyance) to that species of energetic concision . . . which may be observed in the lost drunkard, or the irreclaimable eater of opium, during the periods of his most intense excitement.

Apathetic hangover and drugged excitement appear again—and it becomes clear that it is the willed and unnatural over-development of the senses in the artist that has caused his 'malady'. As his capacity for sensation has become more acute, it has also become not only 'unnatural' but 'morbid'. Alexander Pope imagined how a more-than-human sense of smell might become fatal, so that one might 'die of a rose in aromatic pain'[4]. In Usher the artist's over-developed senses have indeed made him helplessly vulnerable—like the lute which cannot help resounding—to all their objects in the sensible world, so that, in self-preservation:

> the most insipid food was alone endurable; he could wear only garments of certain texture; the odours of all flowers were oppressive; his eyes were tortured by even a faint light; and there were but peculiar sounds, and these from stringed instruments, which did not inspire him with horror.

Moreover, the over-development not only defeats itself, but strikes Usher as certain to be fatal. The trembling nervous agitation, which had seemed partly excitement at communicating himself to his friend, reveals itself more deeply as terror: terror of *anything* 'other', not in itself, but in its deadly impact on his own excitability, so that responsiveness has become the risk of self-annihilation.

> I shudder at the thought of any, even the most trivial, incident, which may operate upon this intolerable agitation of soul. . . . I feel that the period will sooner or later arrive when I must abandon life and reason together, in some struggle with the grim phantasm, FEAR.

Still worse, it is dawning on Usher, in the guise of 'superstitious impressions' about the influence of the 'mere form and substance' of the grey house and dim tarn upon him, that things which seem merely in the dimension of '*physique*' (of the body) can actually affect the '*morale*' of existence (of the soul). He has begun to suspect that the Gothick/Romantick habitation, 'by dint of long sufferance' of its influence, may not only have produced physical deterioration, morbid over-sensitivity, and nervous agitation, but an effect upon his spiritual being.

And finally in this catalogue of gloom—confessed with the greatest hesitation—is the dying of his 'tenderly beloved sister' which will leave him the last of the Ushers—the most 'natural' and 'palpable' sorrow of all, as it seems.

At this point the narrator seems wholly vindicated. His first intuitions have been confirmed, not only by what he finds in Roderick Usher, but also by what Usher himself has made explicit. And however he may have been familiar with and even tempted by Usher's world in the past, his perception of its disastrous consequences is now clear, and keeps him clear of it. But just here we find a paradox. At the moment of the reader's greatest confidence in the narrator's power of 'reflection', he suddenly produces a wholly inexplicable response, as never before. As the Lady Madeline

> passed slowly through a remote portion of the apartment, and without having noticed my presence, disappeared. . . . I regarded her with an utter astonishment not unmingled with dread; and yet I found it impossible to account for such feelings. A sensation of stupor oppressed me, as my eyes followed her retreating steps.

23

There is some kind of intuition at work; but why 'dread'? and 'stupor'? Moreover the strangeness of response is immediately followed by a mystery of event; and one which recalls the previous suspicion about the possible effect of the narrator's intrusion into the House of Usher. 'Post hoc' may not be 'propter hoc', but on the very evening of his arrival the Lady Madeline takes finally to her bed. 'For several days ensuing, her name was unmentioned by either Usher or myself'— which seems highly peculiar, from both sides. Again, why? Before we know where we are, the news comes 'abruptly' that she is dead . . . but even before that, the mystery has deepened by our sense, along with the narrator, that the blackness which 'pours' like a fountain from Roderick Usher must spring from some source darker than we have yet fathomed. For:

> as a closer and still closer intimacy admitted me more unreservedly into the recesses of his spirit, the more bitterly did I perceive the futility of all attempt at cheering a mind from which darkness, as if an inherent positive quality, poured forth upon all objects of the moral and physical universe in one unceasing radiation of gloom.

There is no explanation. Just as we determine that we can trust the narrator, we are left to ourselves.

Or rather, we are given Roderick Usher's *art* as our clue to the deeper source of such darkness. The narrator imparts only vague suggestiveness: 'An excited and highly distempered ideality threw a sulphureous lustre over all'—'a certain singular perversion and amplification of the wild air'— 'vaguenesses at which I shuddered the more thrillingly, because I shuddered knowing not why'—'there arose out of the pure abstractions . . . an intensity of intolerable awe, no shadow of which felt I ever yet in the contemplation of the certainly glowing yet too concrete reveries of Fuseli'. He is obviously out of his depth; both his language and in the last instance his syntax have gone soggy. He clearly intuits something 'distempered', 'sulphureous', 'perverted' and shudderingly awful behind what he insists is ideal and abstract—the adjectives are very telling when one looks. But he is clearly unable to pin down what that *is*. Or perhaps he is subconsciously unwilling to do so, feeling that vagueness is safety and preserves the glow; the remark about Fuseli being too concrete may be significant.

It is all the more striking after this that Roderick's poem and his picture should be so specific; even, in what the narrator admits is 'the nakedness of their designs', an exposure, demanding interpretation. The poem is only superficially disguised in allegory and very quickly unlocks itself into explicitness, as soon as one recognizes that once again the 'building' is a way of bodying forth the inner nature of the human being within. It is a confession of the inner corruption and perversion of a human being. We first see the 'Haunted Palace' in its Eden-state, a green and fertile valley, a fair palace-of-man where, because 'the monarch Thought' is on the throne, there is also always spiritual power and protection, radiant light, golden movement and liveliness, sweet fragrance. How different from the dreary country, the ruined and fissured house, the most ungolden fungoid-hair, the reeking pestilential tarn where the Artist of Sensation has ruled! The contrast is further underlined in terms both of consciousness and the art that springs from it. Here the 'luminous windows' of the eyes are clear and open to the day, and one can see into an interior behind them where spiritual energies move musically to 'a lute's well-tuned law'—as opposed to the automatism of the aeolian lute resounding to every impetus of sensation. Where Mind/Spirit, born to the purple, rules, the song that comes through the pearl and ruby of the mouth is both an ever-flowing of 'surpassing beauty' and also specifically a celebration of wit and wisdom. (We are to imagine Usher's song, conversely, as performed with 'fervid facility' and, in the notes of accompaniment, as a 'wild fantasia'.) But in the Haunted Palace the monarch has been overthrown and is dead, the old times are 'entombed', and the palace has been transformed to the House of Usher. There, in the final stanza, are the 'red-litten' windows of Roderick's Gothick habitation, eyes still luminous, but behind which portentous fantasies spring in discordant melody; there, the 'ghastly' spate of speech and hysteria of the man close to mental and nervous breakdown. The narrator cannot but recognize 'in the under or mystic current of its meaning . . . a full consciousness on the part of Usher of the tottering of his lofty reason upon her throne'. The

25

diagnosis of Usher's malady has come a step further; the hypertrophy of the senses comes about *through* atrophy of the High Reason (which includes both the rational and the spiritual), so that there has not only been a splitting apart of faculties which belong in harmony when the hierarchy is right, but an overthrow of the highest part of the self followed by its death and burial. But what the narrator fails to recognize is that Usher is exposing his awareness, not only of mental breakdown and the growth of sorrow, but of having given domination to *evil* things in sorrow's garb, a 'hideous throng'. That apprehension has been touched on once or twice, but it is becoming more and more explicit; we have to attend to more than physical and nervous breakdown, more than mental breakdown, to the growth of something redder-litten in the Red-man of Usher, something infernal. Moreover, as the Romantic is always aware that the human being creates, or at least partly creates the world, so that 'sentience' flows between him and a living rather than inorganic universe, so Usher has come to believe that his line of development has indeed created in their House—which we can now define as Gothick/Romantick art—an almost palpable 'atmosphere' of artifice and reflection which has an 'importunate and terrible influence' on any inhabitant. The 'darkness' we have to see into is blacker than mere sorrow.

We are yet however to seek for the nature of what (to use the words the narrator is unwilling to follow up) might be 'sulphureous', or 'perverted'. What could have filled him with such stupefying dread that he will not even make enquiries? Suddenly we are reminded of his strange response to the Lady Madeline . . . and then discover that we too know more than we thought we knew, when we confront her brother's picture. For if we once imagine that the picture might be 'about' the relation of the brother with the sister, it becomes far from 'phantasmagoric' let alone 'abstract'. We already know that Roderick and Madeline are the last representatives of a family which had for generations no 'collateral' branches; that is, had only the most minimal relations and connections with other people. This chimes with Roderick's terror of anything 'other': a terror both physical and psychological which would be bound to affect the possibility of any relationship, unless with someone who felt least 'other'. If it is something 'perverted' we are looking for, the possibility exists in the ambiguity of 'his only *relative*'.

We turn to the picture to guess at the resonances of the 'vault or tunnel', the smooth whiteness, the intense light, which have no access to the outside world but are buried far underground. The suggestions are (are they not?) of intense possessiveness or even imprisonment, and of intense secrecy or repression; and it seems to be the enclosure that makes the light, so intense and splendid in itself, seem 'ghastly and inappropriate'. (The vault or tunnel may also be a sex-symbol—though that might be Freudian stock-response, and 'rectangular' is discouraging!)

But as the word 'incest' forms as a possibility in one's mind, it would be as well to be careful, since the most interesting part of the chain of deduction is the psychological explanation rather than any Gothick sexual frisson. And we have established nothing about the Lady Madeline herself, or *her* malady. The only clue to the nature of the Lady is her name—but fortunately that says a great deal. For if Usher represents an overdevelopment of the senses at the expense of High Reason and Spirit, the Magdalen who lies behind all forms of the name is the archetype of the refining of the fleshly into saintliness—she is, although of the same flesh as her brother, the opposite kind of development. (It should be no surprise to learn, a page or two later, that they 'had been twins, and that sympathies of a scarcely intelligible nature had always existed between them'.) If we think of the story as monodrama like the poem in it—as it seems increasingly useful to do[5]—we could see them as the twin dimensions of human being which require to be harmonized in the Fair Palace of an integrated personality. But then, incest really is a perverter of the psyche and the soul, since, far from the higher faculty being enthroned, far even from its otherness being respected, it is usurped, possessed, pent in and submerged, kept from relating to the world or even existing in its own light, and made complicit in Usher's own sensationalism. The Magdalen, too, might be made mad-line.

We begin to sense what the effect on the Lady might be, and catch the resonances of first 'apathy', and then 'catalepsy'. But this is to bring out a second 'horror' metaphor: the vampire, who bleeds his victim's life-blood away until she becomes passive, devitalized, paralysed, and dies. If the narrator, who is sensitive to the Gothick, intuited anything remotely of this nature from the apparition of the lady and its effect on Usher, it is hardly surprising that he—who betrays a distant resemblance to the House of Usher and a familiarity with their kind of habitation—should dread and repress what he will not dare to think. Only (one repeats) the point is not to create Gothick frisson, but to diagnose the evil that its one-sided development has brought about by deranging the psyche of its habitués, and the art which it produces. Since the story clearly is about a kind of art, its protagonists can be seen as three dimensions of an artist's self-inquisition, in order to grasp its consequences. The narrator will be the daylight self, but still attached to the others below the surface, and likely to repress knowledge of what they have been up to, that is 'insufferable'.

All this of course is sheer speculation as one reads—the evidence is only what fits with the details that have gone before. As the story now goes on, with the abrupt news of the Lady's death and the plan to entomb her in the dungeon (which the narrator readily accepts, to guard against the sinister doctor who might try to dig her up and conduct an investigation), the only thing that will perhaps strike every reader is the uneasy reminiscence of the vault in the cellarage to the vault in the picture, though this one is far more confined and there is no light in it whatever. The body of the Lady also creates disquiet because of 'the mockery of a faint blush upon the bosom and the face' but especially because of the 'suspiciously lingering smile upon the lip which is so terrible in death'. It is appropriate enough to her character, since the final mark of the Fair Palace is that its 'pale door' should 'smile'; but it is not at all appropriate in what is supposed to be dead, and being buried.

Moreover the effect of the death and burial on Usher is disastrous. The luminousness in his eyes, which seemed the one compensation for the bodily decay and the incipient nervous and mental breakdown, goes out altogether. The division in the self seems to have disappeared, but only because he is possessed altogether by an even more extreme terror than before. He seems 'labouring with some oppressive secret', or like a madman 'gazing upon vacancy for long hours, in an attitude of the profoundest attention, as if listening to some imaginary sound'. The narrator begins to feel 'infected'. 'I felt creeping upon me, by slow yet certain degrees, the wild influences of his own fantastic yet impressive superstitions.' Then suddenly we are plunged into the full Gothick experience: the sleepless night, the gloomy furniture, the tattered draperies swaying fitfully in the draught, a tempest brewing outside, the awakening—with uncontrollable and inexplicable shuddering—to mysterious sounds in the intervals of the storm. After being held at a distance for so long, the full Gothick flesh-creeping seems to have taken over, with the narrator leading the required response, as the door opens to reveal the Gothick protagonist in a state of 'restrained *hysteria*'. (Usher himself of course had predicted a 'species of mad hilarity' as the end of the process described in his poem.) As he now throws open the window to the storm, it is clearly a reflection of the inner tumult now reaching its climacteric, and an admission of both its beauty and its terror. If it images a psychological state, the significant feature would seem to be that the densely oppressive cloud-cover is now being visibly disintegrated by 'frequent and violent alterations in the direction of the wind' to produce a contention in which, with 'life-like velocity' the warring energies 'flew careering from all points against each other, without passing away into the distance'. Not only can the clouds no longer 'prevent our perceiving', but the 'under surfaces' of the issue-less war are 'glowing in the unnatural light of a faintly luminous and distinctly visible gaseous exhalation which hung about and enshrouded the mansion'—an electric manifestation of what one might call spiritual energy turned lurid. The whole universe seems to be at war, and Roderick Usher, throwing the window open, seems to insist on the correspondence of 'outside' with 'inside'.

But the narrator will have none of this. He tries to insist that the storm is a merely physical phenomenon with natural causes, or at worst the result of miasmas from the tarn; and that 'You must not—you shall not behold this.' The daylight self, shuddering, insists that the cover-up continue. He even thinks that a milder form of romantic experience could be

useful therapy; and reads from the 'Mad Trist' of Sir Launcelot
Canning in the 'vague hope' that, however little its 'uncouth
and unimaginative prolixity' may interest 'the lofty and
spiritual ideality' of his friend, it may act as a kind of inocula-
tion, a mild dose of the disease of folly, to calm his fevered
excitement.

Now there is an entirely new note; and critics who find the
'Mad Trist' a lapse in what they take to be a truly Gothic
offering, tend to miss both its meaning and its comedy.[6] For
this is the point at which the attentive reader passes decisively
beyond the narrator's limitations, indeed begins to convict
him of short-sighted complacency. He failed before, by not
daring to enquire about the Lady Madeline and Usher's art;
but now a blind optimism makes his self-assurance comic,
though we only see this fully on a second reading. For the
'Mad Trist' is just what its title suggests, a crazy trust or
confidence misplaced. Its kind of Gothick depends on the
belief that the knight-errant can safely engage with the powers
of evil and come off, magic-shielded and victorious, rescuing
the Maiden of Innocence in the end. Sir Launcelot is a secular
author, not Sir Galahad or even Sir Perceval. Waxing doughty
on wine—the note of self-intoxication again—his errant knight
does not bother to come to any understanding with the
'obstinate and maliceful' reclusiveness that imprisons the
Lady, but with sturdy confidence merely breaks the door
down. He is just as confident in dealing with the evil dragon
that takes the hermit's place, guarding the treasures and the
Maiden—again he bluffly knocks it on the head.

Is there not a parallel with the assurance of the narrator
that he can open up, control, and cure, the House of Usher
and its owner, and his refusal, now, to heed the sinister warning echoes which accompany each stage of Sir Launcelot's
story? He feels superior to its 'uncouth and unimaginative
prolixity'—but he exactly shares and mirrors it. He fails
altogether to identify the hermit, and the dragon, because he
persists in a fiction of Usher's 'lofty spirituality' against all the
evidence: the poem, the picture, the self-diagnosis, and the
hysterical affinity with the dark tempest. But insofar as he
does recognize something of his friend's 'mental disorder'
(though he persists in trying to think it 'hypochondriac') he

has Sir Launcelot's utterly misplaced belief in his ability (with 'gentle violence') to control, shield, and cure it. He is, and has been, blundering into a situation he does not in the least understand; unaware especially how each move makes things worse, as the dragon is worse than the hermit, and the next manifestation will be more dangerous still. When one re-reads, there will be a grotesque comedy of complacency in the language—as against the sinister echoes which comment on each phase of the 'Mad Trist' and its reading of the situation. Of the first sinister sound of breaking open in the House of Usher he remarks:

> It was, beyond doubt, the coincidence alone which had arrested my attention . . . the sound, in itself, had nothing, surely, which should have interested or disturbed me. [There is no question mark.] I continued the story. . . .

After the 'most unusual screaming or grating sound' he congratulates himself that he

> retained sufficient presence of mind to avoid exciting, by any observation, the sensitive nervousness of my companion. I was by no means certain that he had noticed the sounds in question; although, assuredly, a strange alteration had, during the last few minutes, taken place in his demeanour. . . .

In fact the utter fear of Usher, the turning of his whole body to face the door, the hysterical rocking, betoken somebody in the last extremity of terror; but simply do not register with the voice that can say 'I knew he was not asleep', or describe the agonized rocking as 'a gentle yet constant and uniform sway'.

Moreover the narrator, and Sir Launcelot, have also quite mistaken the nature of the 'shield'. Far from enabling anybody to rescue the Lady Soul from enchantment, the dropping of the shield is the falling of the last scale of protection from *their* eyes, to reveal a condition unrescuable and incurable, a psychological disaster reaching its inevitable end in total destruction. Far from rescuing the Maiden, it is necessary to recognize that she has been dangerously, fatally transmuted, and for ever.

Now the secret comes out, in the 'distinct, hollow, metallic and clangorous, yet apparently muffled, reverberation' which cannot be ignored, and the gibbering confession which accompanies the Lady's approach up the stairs and into the open.

> Ethelred—ha! ha!—the breaking of the hermit's door, and the death-cry of the dragon, and the clangour of the shield!—say, rather, the rending of her coffin, and the grating of the iron hinges of her prison, and her struggles within the coppered archway of the vault! Oh whither shall I fly?

What followed incest and vampirism was attempted murder. The coming of the narrator (we may deduce) so greatly increased Roderick Usher's anxiety—partly desiring cure, but mostly terrified of exposure—that he hastened, on the Lady's latest catalepsy, to bury her, alive. Both his poem (about not only the overthrow but the evil death of the monarch) and his picture (imagining the means) show some premeditation and awareness of how repression could become final burial. His confession, now, proves that even if he only subconsciously knew what he was doing at the time, he knew beyond question soon afterwards and did nothing. And now:

> Have I not heard her footstep on the stair? Do I not distinguish that heavy and horrible beating of her heart? . . . 'MADMAN! I TELL YOU THAT SHE NOW STANDS WITHOUT THE DOOR!'

It is not quite clear whether 'Madman' is addressed to himself or to the narrator, but it does not matter, it will do very well for both (especially if both are sides of the same person). Usher's madness is beyond question. The narrator's consisted in imagining that he could control or cure such disintegration: of relationship on one level; or on the other, monodramatically, such preying on one side of the psyche by another, with the inevitable reaction. In case one had forgotten . . . the last result of vampirism is the creation of another vampire. The red one has tried to devitalize, paralyse, bury the white one—and there she stands now, with 'blood upon her white robes', in a doorway that opens like jaws. As she falls 'heavily inward upon the person of her brother, and in her violent and now final death-agonies, bore him to the floor a corpse . . .', we watch the inevitably destructive reaction of that which has been buried alive against its repressor; an appalling parody of the sexual act by what had been the saintly Lady; and the ineluctable movement back into unity of that which had been split. (As Poe was to write in *Eureka* a decade later, 'in the original unity of the first thing lies the secondary cause of all things, with the germ of their inevitable annihilation'—though here the splitting of the soul has been so unnaturally violent that the return to unity is correspondingly appalling.)

There can be no cure or compromise as death-in-life completes itself—only the narrator's headlong flight in self-preservation. As he crosses the causeway his final glimpse of the Fall of the House of Usher exactly images how, after such splitting, unity can only be regained in annihilation. As the zig-zag fissuring opens wider and wider, the radiance that comes through and sheds its 'wild light' along the narrator's path is that of a blood-red and setting moon: red-and-white in a moment of fusion but at the price of annihilation. The House disintegrates and the deep tarn closes over its fragments—the last 'reflection', the last conscious act of the narrator precipitately fleeing back to his daylight world, is to cover a ruinous process in unconsciousness.

But because Poe is so much more than the narrator and the actors (those sides of himself who play out his deliberate nightmare of disintegration), it is possible for the reader to become more fully *conscious*—so as neither to evade, nor to succumb to, the Fall of the House of Usher. The story itself tells us how to read it: not as an indulgence in the Gothick, but as an imaginatively critical exploration into the implications, the fascinations, and the price of the Gothick artist's over-development of imaginative sensationalism at the expense of body, thought and spirit. Poe was fascinated by the genre, and its exaggeration of certain aspects of 'the romantic poet' offered a persona that clearly had its appeal. But what is the real distinction of this story above all his stories, is the capacity for self-scrutiny with which he set out both to explore, and to understand and criticize, that appeal, to grasp what was deathly and dehumanizing in it through admitting, but also examining, its fascination. I can think of no story which offers its author, its narrator, or its reader more opportunity for Gothick indulgence and frisson. But it is not only meticulously made, so that every detail counts, but also, and on a much deeper level, it has real psychological penetration. I take it that it is the House of *Usher* because it is also a prophecy, of what uncritical indulgence in that kind of imaginative over-development would usher in, and cost. Here (as not always in Poe or his critics) it is clear that art must be more than a sounding-board for gusts of 'feeling' or 'idea' masquerading as inspiration; must make more intelligent, aware, and more deeply humane and spiritual music than

> The dull sobbing draft, that moans and rakes
> Upon the strings of this Aeolian lute,
> Which better far were mute.[7]

And the artist needs to be intelligent and self-critical too; able to peer into the abyss of his own psyche, but also to build a Coleridgean Fair Palace, not merely a haunted one.

NOTES

1. See 'Dejection: An Ode'. The appropriate lines are quoted at the end of the essay. Poe added the opening quotation from Béranger in 1842 after the first three printings of the story, see Burton R. Pollin, *Discoveries in Poe* (Notre Dame, 1970), Chapter 4—who does not, however, see the application of the quotation as the placing comment I believe it to be, cf. p. 69.
2. I use the spelling to distinguish the late-eighteenth-century genre of fiction pioneered by Walpole and Mrs. Radcliffe. Poe himself insisted that he wrote 'a Gothic not of Germany but of the soul'.
3. E.g. 'with a shudder even more thrilling than before' . . . a note that persists.
4. *Essay on Man*, Epistle 1, 200.
5. Finally, I think, the 'monodramatic' reading is the most illuminating one; but there are advantages in holding it back, for the implications of 'incest' and 'vampirism' are much less disturbing if one is thinking purely in terms of the relations of different sides of the same psyche. The best way of reading may be to see the story in terms of its three human protagonists first, before allowing the monodrama to well out of that.
6. I take it that the same combination of jokey teasing and underlying suggestiveness is to be found in the booklist. The only certainty in my mind is that I would not wager money as to any title being either true or fictitious, but I also imagine that there might be a higher proportion of suggestiveness than 'phantasm', irrespective of their truth or falsity. I take it also that the first association that springs to mind with 'Ethelred' is 'Unready' . . . or, unready in what is significant, but over-ready in his mad trist?
7. Samuel Taylor Coleridge, 'Dejection: An Ode'.

2

Doodling America: Poe's 'MS. Found in a Bottle'

by HAROLD BEAVER

> *Pascal avait son gouffre, avec lui se mouvant.*
> *—Hélas! tout est abîme,—action, désir, rêve,*
> *Parole!*
>
> —Baudelaire, *Le Gouffre* (1862)

In July 1833 the *Baltimore Saturday Visiter* announced an open competition: with a prize of $50 for the best short story and of $25 for the best poem. Poe submitted a whole series of stories (possibly six in all) under the general title, *Tales of the Folio Club*. Not only did 'MS. Found in a Bottle' win the main prize, but his entire entry received the judges' accolade:

> We cannot refrain from saying that the author owes it to his reputation, as well as to the gratification of the community, to publish the entire volume. These tales are eminently distinguished by a wild, vigorous, and poetical imagination, a rich style, a fertile invention, and varied and curious learning.

His literary bottle had been miraculously retrieved. That prize marked the beginning of Poe's career.

The judges were right to insist on the 'curious learning'; and 'poetical imagination' was to remain the hallmark of all his future endeavours. Like Keats, Poe put an absolute trust in 'the truth of imagination'. But the retrieval of such truth, he realized, was far more complex than the ridiculous contrivance of a bottle. It might entail the breakdown of all rational

35

methodology and so put at risk even commonplace norms of communication. Moving beyond all fixed codes, in search for the origins of language itself, it involved the discovery of something that might not, in the last analysis, be capable of being shared. As the manuscript's narrator, among his closing insights, puts it: 'It is evident that we are hurrying onwards to some exciting knowledge—some never-to-be-imparted secret, whose attainment is destruction.' In the realm of the imagination it was perpetual night.

An oblique narrator was to become an essential ploy of all Poe's fictions. 'MS. Found in a Bottle' must literally be read *as if* it were a manuscript. The title operates as a stage-direction, framing theatrical imagery. For what closes in a whirl, 'round and round the borders of a gigantic amphitheatre', opens (on second publication) with a quotation from *Atys* (1676), a *tragédie-opéra* written by Philippe Quinault as a libretto for Lully. This was 'curious learning' with a vengeance. 'He who has but a moment to live' the text runs, 'has nothing left to dissimulate':

> *Qui n'a plus qu'un moment à vivre*
> *N'a plus rien à dissimuler.*

Presumably this is a comment by Poe, as editor, unless the narrator's 'education of no common order' acquainted him with the obscurer operas performed at the court of Louis XIV. What it unequivocally points to is the status of the narrative, which turns out (true to an alternative name for fiction) to be 'utterly novel'. For the fictional manuscript dissimulates that it has nothing to dissimulate. It methodizes the unmethodical, furthermore, by embracing science ('physical philosophy', the 'habits of rigid thought') for expounding what the narrator calls an 'eloquent madness' or, more precisely, 'the raving of a crude imagination'. Such are the paradoxes of art, as we shall learn: to 'name' the nameless; to define the 'indefinite'; to analyse that 'which will admit of no analysis'. The prologue, or opening paragraph, rightly presents a self-portrait of the narrator who will be cornered into presenting such paradoxes.

Not surprisingly he turns out to be more than somewhat paradoxical himself. An extreme form of scepticism, as taught by Pyrrho of Elis, is his explicit model. Yet he prides himself on his empirical, scientific, reductively 'positive' education and temperament. That pursuit of 'some exciting knowledge' (of his closing paragraphs) is thus undermined by his initial belief that the 'attainment' of certain knowledge was impossible, since the contrary of every proposition can be maintained with equal plausibility:

> Beyond all things, the study of the German moralists gave me great delight; not from any ill-advised admiration of their eloquent madness, but from the ease with which my habits of rigid thought enabled me to detect their falsities. I have often been reproached with the aridity of my genius; a deficiency of imagination has been imputed to me as a crime; and the Pyrrhonism of my opinions has at all times rendered me notorious. Indeed, a strong relish for physical philosophy has, I fear, tinctured my mind with a very common error of this age—I mean the habit of referring occurrences, even the least susceptible of such reference, to the principles of that science.

At the same time this curiously wealthy, anonymous narrator (without explicit antecedents) is some kind of Byronic outsider, 'having no other inducement than a kind of nervous restlessness' which haunts him 'as a fiend'. It is this that prompted him to take passage on a ship sailing from Java through the Indonesian archipelago. We know nothing else about him except his height (five feet eight inches) and his profession; as 'a dealer in antiquities', he tells us, he had already travelled throughout the Middle East (through modern Lebanon, Syria and Iran). Yet his cool, deliberate style is closer to that of Defoe, or of Swift's ship-surgeon, Gulliver (in his rôle of traveller, observer, geographer), than Byron. His scientific instinct, at moments of crisis, is always to the fore: whether on first glimpsing the gigantic ghost-ship ('of, perhaps, four thousand tons', he meticulously adds) about to crush him; or when rushing southward to the pole on that Flying Dutchman, he adds:

> I am led to attribute these frequent escapes to the only natural cause which can account for such effect.—I must suppose the ship to be within the influence of some strong current, or impetuous under-tow.

Or again:

> As I imagined, the ship proves to be in a current; if that
> appellation can properly be given to a tide which, howling and
> shrieking by the white ice, thunders on to the southward with a
> velocity like the headlong dashing of a cataract.

Imagination for this narrator remains strictly a matter of
scientific hypothesis. It can have nothing to do with the
mysterious and inexplicable nature of his experiences; nor, for
that matter, with the 'few cases of opium' that happened to be
on board. Yet it is to this narrator that Poe deviously entrusts
the task of propounding his philosophy of art, or, more exactly,
his art of fiction. It seems a desperate act. As the narrator
turns to his empirical training to expose the eloquent 'falsities',
that is to say the fictions, of idealist philosophy, we must turn
to the imaginative 'raving' which he presents to test the limits
of his scepticism.

Poe's ultimate plot (or hoax), then, is to present a fiction
that denies its own imaginative status by means of an art that
would deny its own roots in the imagination. The narrator,
that is, invokes a very definite hierarchy that would always
privilege 'truth' (in other words, 'positive experience') over
fiction (snubbed as 'crude imagination'), just as it self-
evidently extols method ('my habits of rigid thought') at the
expense of 'madness' ('raving', 'the *ignes fatui* of superstition',
'the reveries of fancy'). Yet the narrator himself, by his very
relish for 'eloquent madness' (of 'the German moralists',
admittedly) implies that such a hierarchy may be reversible:
that it may be possible to privilege fiction over truth, and
'raving' over scientific method. His own 'Pyrrhonism', after
all, with its claim that the contrary of any proposition can be
maintained with equal plausibility, attests to that reversal. His
own manuscript, as fiction, neatly plays out that reversal.

Of course it is Poe, the ultimate manipulator, who plays out
that reversal. Poe, to use Derrida's vocabulary, deconstructs
the hierarchical status of 'truth' (as immanent and natural)
and 'fancy' (as artificial and contrived) by showing that the
qualities predicated of 'fancy', as a dependent term, are in fact
a condition of 'truth' or 'science', as a spontaneous or
immediate term, until the narrator's whole linguistic system is

decentred and the autonomy of what is considered by him ideologically serious is exposed as sham. For all writing, claims Poe, is theatre; all is paradox. There are no 'severe precincts of truth' whose data have a superior fullness or weight. All codes are unstable, like Ship I itself which (freighted with 'a few cases of opium') 'consequently crank': zigzagged, that is, twisted and turned. The narrator himself soon begins to speak in oxymorons: 'I could not help feeling the utter hopelessness of hope itself.' For just as his reason is haunted by 'a kind of nervous restlessness', he turns out to be the forerunner of a familiar Poe persona: the neurasthenic as sceptic, or rather the sceptic as neurasthenic.

The exact moment of reversal, in narrative terms, is exactly pivoted at the centre: when the narrator is catapulted from Ship I into the 'rigging' of the mysterious Ship II. Such rigged contrivance is itself a hoax. But the universal nature of that hoax is not made clear until Poe explores further possibilities in that rigging:

> An incident has occurred which has given me new room for meditation. Are such things the operation of ungoverned Chance? I had ventured upon deck and thrown myself down, without attracting any notice, among a pile of ratlin-stuff and old sails, in the bottom of the yawl. While musing upon the singularity of my fate, I unwittingly daubed with a tar-brush the edges of a neatly-folded studding-sail which lay near me on a barrel. The studding-sail is now bent upon the ship, and the thoughtless touches of the brush are spread out into the word DISCOVERY.

For the act of writing itself and chance are compounded; 'thoughtless touches', or doodling in other words, can produce amazing discoveries. That very sail, inscribed (in caps) with the word 'DISCOVERY', acts, as we might say, like a concrete poem: it typographically enacts the very concept that it stages. But if such tar-brush daubings form a kind of legible doodling, what about this very 'MS' (found in a bottle) in which that doodle is recorded? Might it not too be a kind of doodle, opening with its 'spiral exhalations' and closing in a vortex? The whole tale reels and unreels in whirlpools and revolutions. Poe himself admitted to this aleatory quality of his own fiction when, in 1845, he added a note which claimed that the story 'was originally published in 1831' (itself a fiction) and continued:

> it was not until many years afterwards that I became acquainted with the maps of Mercator, in which the ocean is represented as rushing, by four mouths, into the (northern) Polar Gulf, to be absorbed into the bowels of the earth; the Pole itself being represented by a black rock, towering to a prodigious height.

So the writer, taking his imaginative chances, both anticipates verification (of a kind) and is confirmed by it.

But of equal importance to the sail is the ship which it so boldly labels. If the narrator is apparently without origins (with nothing to report of his country or family), Poe himself was very much the Virginian and patriotic American. What ship is this? Not an American ship clearly. Yet clues abound: it is built of wood which has 'every characteristic of Spanish oak'; in its hold are piled 'decayed charts of navigation' and its deck is scattered with 'mathematical instruments of the most quaint and obsolete construction'; its captain pores over a royal 'commission'. Could it be anything but a Spanish ship from the golden age of discovery? Could there be any doubt (as Burton R. Pollin was the first to argue) 'that the language was Spanish and that this was Christopher Columbus'?[1] Like the Princes of Serendip, Columbus too had a way of finding things for which he was not looking. Sailing westward across the Atlantic as a short cut, he reckoned, to Marco Polo's Indies or Cathay, Columbus discovered—what? Something 'new'. Land so 'utterly novel' that it had 'no name'. Literally it was a New World. Columbus did not discover 'America', as in retrospect it was called. Like Poe's narrator, rather, he might have said:

> A feeling, for which I have no name, has taken possession of my soul—a sensation which will admit of no analysis, to which the lessons of by-gone times are inadequate, and for which I fear futurity itself will offer me no key. . . . Yet it is not wonderful that these conceptions are indefinite, since they have their origin in sources so utterly novel. A new sense—a new entity is added to my soul.

From a physical, therefore, Poe turns to a metaphysical 'discovery'; or from literary chance to the chance 'discovery' of

America. For that very American continent on which he lived, looming haphazard and unexpected in the path of European expectations, was the very paradigm of what might be called Poe's psychology of composition. This entailed at least three operations: the observant or inductive (on which the manuscript's narrator prides himself); the deductive hunch (of which Poe's investigator, C. Auguste Dupin, is a master exponent); and finally that open capacity to incorporate chance, or aleatory, elements. Poe's psychology was remarkable in its attention to such plays of chance, whether in the realm of aesthetics or of morality. For such meaningless scribblings, which turn out to be meaningful, have their moral counterpart in Poe's 'Imp of the Perverse'. All Poe's principal discoveries were in this shadow-land of the unconscious whose moral extension, in terms of decision and social action, he named the 'perverse': that paradoxical undertow of semi-conscious desires, the urge to repudiate accepted norms, cross boundaries, jump from cliff-tops, violate procedures. (The shock values of both the moral and aesthetic components of Poe's psychology have been explored and recombined, in our own day, by William Burroughs whose scissored cut-ups of miscellaneous books and newspapers, as *objets trouvés*, have become a prime source for contemporary theories of aleatory art.)

Again and again Poe relied on such devices. 'The Gold-Bug' (1843), for example, depends on the conjunction of a symbolic accident and accidental symbol. The resolution of a mystery there too is wholly dependent on a 'rough sketch' and a chance discovery:

> Well, as I was in the very act of crumpling it up, my glance fell upon the sketch at which you had been looking, and you may imagine my astonishment when I perceived, in fact, the figure of a death's-head just where, it seemed to me, I had made the drawing of the beetle. . . . My first idea, now, was mere surprise at the really remarkable similarity of outline—at the singular coincidence involved in the fact, that unknown to me, there should have been a skull upon the other side of the parchment, immediately beneath my figure of the *scarabaeus*, and that this skull, not only in outline, but in size, should so closely resemble my drawing. I say the singularity of this coincidence absolutely

41

stupified me for a time. This is the usual effect of such
coincidences. The mind struggles to establish a connection—a
sequence of cause and effect—and, being unable to do so,
suffers a species of temporary paralysis.

What paralyses is the rational attempt to grasp such
coincidence. The need to accept and play with and transform
coincidence is the very essence of Poe's art. The matching of
scarabaeus and skull produces a kind of hieroglyphic fit. The
interpenetration of death's-head and gold becomes the visible
signature of a hidden meaning. A series of chance interventions by the gold-bug (its initial bite, its skull-like appearance, its reverse image on the parchment) leads to the
discovery of buried treasure:

> Do you observe how mere an accident it was that these events
> should have occurred on the *sole* day of all the year in which it
> has been, or may be, sufficiently cool for fire, and that without
> the fire, or without the intervention of the dog at the precise
> moment in which he appeared, I should never have become
> aware of the death's-head, and so never the possessor of the
> treasure?

Accidental interventions must never be dismissed out of hand.
Symbolic clues, or decoys, lurk everywhere for logical resolution. But reason, left entirely to its own devices, is helpless. In
Dupin's phrase from 'The Purloined Letter' (1845): 'As poet
and mathematician, he would reason well; as mere mathematician, he could not have reasoned at all. . . .'

So the hierarchy of fact over fancy, or truth over fiction,
insisted upon by the narrator, is reversed by the story itself. It is
not fact that leads on to fancy, as the progress from Ship I to
Ship II seems to imply, but fancy that leads to fact. That is the
'DISCOVERY'. That is the 'key' to 'sources so utterly novel'.
It is not coincidence that is dependent on logic, but logic on
coincidence, as truth is ultimately dependent on imagination.
With Keats, in his letter to Benjamin Bailey, Poe might exclaim:

> I am certain of nothing but the holiness of the heart's affections
> and the truth of imagination—what the imagination seizes as
> beauty must be truth—whether it existed before or not.[2]

This new hierarchy of imagination over truth asserts the
primacy of art or myth. For imaginative order (of Flying

Dutchman and Ancient Mariner, even of the pseudo-science of John Cleves Symmes[3]) transcends logical order and linguistic order and semantic order. Without that overarching psychological and metaphysical structure, there could be no such thing as science, as 'positive experience' even, at all.

The manuscript's own explicit movement from Ship I to Ship II is 'polarized' (to use Poe's own word) by a series of reversals: a 'dusky-red' moon turned to a 'sickly yellow' sun; transparent water, to a turgid sea; breathless calm, to a furious blast; heat to cold; light to pitchy dark. Such 'rapid revolution' is controlled by the figure of the spiral, in air and water, at both the beginning and the end. What is a spiral but a circle that extends through time, by a series of antitheses or contracting U-turns, to a point of no return beyond observation? It is an infinite extension of energy into the void, like the rainbow likened elsewhere to the Muslim 'pathway between Time and Eternity'.[4] This is Poe's realm where he longs to hover, without 'calculating time', continually 'upon the brink of Eternity, without taking a final plunge into the abyss'. It becomes the very scenario of 'The Pit and the Pendulum' (1843), of an abyss below the sweeping scythe of time. It is transformed into 'The Facts in the Case of M. Valdemar' (1845), whose very name (literally *val-de-mar*) spells his agonizing descent into the maelström.

The 'Simoom' itself, that blows Ship I into the path of Ship II, is a suitably Afro-polar paradox: a dry desert wind howling off the Australian coast. For everything swings to its contrary. Even the polar latitudes are at first without 'the usual impediments of ice'. What began by castigating 'superstition', ending with a cry 'oh God!'; what had opened in mortal fear, ending reconciled to 'the most hideous aspect of death'. Not surprisingly 'silent wonder', 'great amazement', 'astonishment' and 'awe' are the narrator's controlling moods, all commingling at the climax when he sees the captain (of Ship II) 'face to face':

> Although in his appearance there is, to a casual observer, nothing which might bespeak him more or less than man—still a feeling of irrepressible reverence and awe mingled with the sensation of wonder with which I regarded him.

For in that transition from Ship I to Ship II the ultimate reversal has taken place. This Byronic narrator, who prides himself on the rational scepticism of a Gulliver, finds himself driven instead into the polar latitudes of the Ancient Mariner, gasping 'for breath at an elevation beyond the albatross'. It is as if a Swift, mockingly aware of Coleridge, had turned into a Coleridgean dreamer with the inherited skills of Swift.

It is in 'a hiding-place in the hold', of a black-hulled ship, in the blackness of eternal night (where nothing beyond 'twenty paces' could be seen) that the narrative mysteriously pivots. For the narrator, who had alluded without comment to the original crew of Malays and the old Swede (sole survivor of the first disaster), is overwhelmed by this new experience:

> A man passed by my place of concealment with a feeble and unsteady gait. I could not see his face, but had an opportunity of observing his general appearance. There was about it an evidence of great age and infirmity. His knees tottered beneath a load of years, and his entire frame quivered under the burthen. He muttered to himself, in a low broken tone, some words of a language which I could not understand, and groped in a corner among a pile of singular-looking instruments, and decayed charts of navigation. His manner was a wild mixture of the peevishness of second childhood, and the solemn dignity of a God. He at length went on deck, and I saw him no more.

It is then that a 'sentiment ineffable', a 'feeling, for which I have no name', a 'sensation which will admit of no analysis' takes hold of him. He is uncentred by these emotions: this incomprehensible language (beyond language), this obsolete science (beyond discernment), this nameless feeling (beyond analysis). Little does the narrator, unlike his author, realize that the 'mental features discoursed of as the analytical, are, in themselves, but little susceptible of analysis.'[5] He was lost in a whole visual and oral semiology without a 'key'. At the crux of his tale, that is, he had slipped into Lacan's matrix of linguistic consciousness, that unvoiced source of speech where the ties between signifier (S) and signified (*s*) may become unattached and broken. His signified, that is, were devoid of signifiers (a 'feeling, for which I have no name') and signifiers devoid of signified (the captain's 'language which I could not understand'). In repression, according to Lacan, when the ties between S and *s* are broken, permitting S free metaphoric and metonymic association and exchange, the subject will eventually fail to grasp signs, either when he asserts them (in speech) or when they assert themselves (in symptoms). Thus he is alienated from his own thought (which he does not recognize) and from his own speech (which he misunderstands).

For Poe imagination makes accessible this dissociated and floating language of dreams, of the intermittent REM (Rapid Eye Movement) phases of sleep with their jumbled, compacted metaphors and puns. It is art alone that can re-appropriate the source of language itself in all its fluid potential for renewal. Poe kept a pillow-book for such marginal awareness 'upon the very brink of sleep', where 'the confines of the waking world blend with those of the world of dreams',[6] as the concealed narrator now keeps a journal:

> Concealment is utter folly on my part, for the people *will not* see. It was but just now that I passed directly before the eyes of the mate—it was no long while ago that I ventured into the captain's own private cabin, and took thence the materials with which I write, and have written. I shall from time to time continue this journal.

'One is tempted to speculate', John T. Irwin comments, 'that the manuscript's fictive origin in the theft of writing materials . . . is meant to invoke the invention of writing as a transgression against the father.'[7] Certainly after giving up concealment (or repression) and committing that Oedipal theft (or transgression), the narrator is again able to compose coherently. He can retrace the signs (with pen and paper) just as the reader retrieves the bottle (with the manuscript) on the very 'brink of Eternity'. Oddly enough, he does not try for stylistic innovations, in symbolist fashion, to accommodate the nameless into his text. He continues to use his essentially eighteenth-century style and devices (including that of the journal); for he had discovered the figure of the double.

In Lacan's terms, the narrator remains tied to the Imaginary stage (*stade du miroir*) of his development en route for the symbolic. As Poe is to the narrator, so the narrator is to the captain. All are of exactly the same height: 'that is, about five feet eight inches'. It is a triple mirror image. Poe, the narrator and the captain form a *mise-en-abîme*, capable of extension into an 'indefinite' and ultimately infinite recession of forms. What on one view may seem narcissistic, on another presents the necessary triplication of the act of writing: incorporating the writer himself (Poe), his 'written self'[8] (the narrator as writer of the manuscript), and his text as hieroglyph (the God-like, aged, but peevishly incomprehensible captain). Of Poe, the man, there is no need to speak here. The mark of his 'written self' is, as we have seen, a scientific 'curiosity' whose momentum, maintained to the end, is 'to penetrate the mysteries' of those awful polar regions, even at the expense of death. But this 'written self' cannot read; above all, it cannot read its mirror-image, the captain; that grey hair, those greyer eyes, that royal 'signature' even (though the narrator is an antiquarian, versed in the ruins of Baalbec, Tadmor and Persepolis) remain inscrutable. For the captain not only speaks an incomprehensible language, he is surrounded by 'iron-clasped folios', or incomprehensible texts. His very figure is indecipherable, evoking 'records of the past' (his hairs) and sibylline prophecies of the future (his eyes). Those multiplied ancient mariners, his crew, too have eyes with 'an eager and uneasy meaning'. But to the narrator all such meaning is meaningless. Such hieroglyphic mysteries lead him merely to hover, as Ship II had originally hovered over Ship I, upon the brink of the abyss.

That abyss ('whose attainment is destruction') is 'Eternity', or the infinite, at the origin of all meaning. The manuscript, in its puzzled perusal of the indecipherable, can be jettisoned and salvaged. But what cannot be written and what cannot be said are, in Wittgenstein's phrase, beyond the limits of our world. In his eager quest for 'some exciting knowledge—some never-to-be-imparted secret', the narrator scarcely realizes that he is rushing to decode the meaning of meaning itself, the origin of all language, in that whirling fusion of polar opposites, at the edge of the spinning amphitheatre of icy white and eternal night. 'Writing in search of its origins', Irwin concludes, '*is* the self-dissolving voyage of the abyss.'[9]

But Baudelaire took a less desperate view. The end of *Le Voyage* exactly echoes the exuberance of the manuscript's narrator:

Doodling America: Poe's 'MS. Found in a Bottle'

Nous voulons, tant ce feu nous brûle le cerveau,
Plonger au fond du gouffre, Enfer ou Ciel, qu'importe?
Au fond de l'Inconnu pour trouver du nouveau![10]

And perhaps that matched Poe's vision too. His tales were to move beyond Death-in-Life (as the angelic dialogues show[11]) to Life-in-Death; perhaps as the narrator escaped from certain death on Ship I by the miraculous descent of Ship II, so there remains (in Poe's eyes) the possibility of a further transition, via a descent into the vortex, from those icy ramparts 'like the walls of the universe'. Perhaps as fiction transcends fact, so there is a metaphysical realm, where all meaning becomes transparent, transcending fiction. Perhaps there, after all, 'futurity' will offer the narrator a 'key'. Perhaps it is for this reason that the captain's eyes had so mysteriously seemed 'Sybils of the future': since they alone could foresee the whirlpool extend its circling beyond the vanishing-point; since they alone could imagine infinity spiralling outward, as in a mirror image, beyond the vortex.

NOTES

1. *Romance Notes*, Vol. 12 (1971), p. 336.
2. Letter to Benjamin Bailey, 22 November 1817.
3. For Poe had been reading not only *The Rime of the Ancient Mariner*, but *Symzonia, A Voyage of Discovery* (1820) by one Captain 'Adam Seaborn', possibly the eponymous Symmes himself. 'I declare the earth is hollow and habitable within ... that it is open at the poles' pronounced a manifesto in 1818 to 'all the world'. John Cleves Symmes, its author, had studied the confused mariners' reports of warmer water and contrary migration of birds near the poles to promote one overriding idea: that the earth, formed by rotation, consisted of five concentric spheres with access through 'holes at the Poles'. Whether Poe really believed in 'Symmes's Hole', as it was popularly called, he liked to make play with this idea of the globe as a series of spheres with open drainage, as it were, passing from the outer rim of one down the inner side of another. Though the allusion to Mercator tries to put us off the trail, that final vertiginous plunge must be into 'Symmes's Hole'.
4. 'A Descent into the Maelström' (1841).
5. Opening of 'The Murders in the Rue Morgue' (1841).
6. 'Marginalia', No. 5, *Graham's Magazine* (March 1846).

7. John T. Irwin, *American Hieroglyphics* (New Haven: Yale University Press, 1980), p. 69.
8. Irwin, *American Hieroglyphics*, p. 120.
9. Irwin, *American Hieroglyphics*, p. 91.
10. 'This fire so scorches our brain, that we wish/ To plunge into the depths of the gulf, Hell or Heaven, who cares?/ To find something *new* in the depths of the Unknown!'
11. 'The Conversation of Eiros and Charmion' (1839); 'The Colloquy of Monos and Una' (1841); 'The Power of Words' (1845).

3

Poe's Stories of Premature Burial: 'That Ere Kind of Style'

by ARNOLD GOLDMAN

It may appear invidious in me, Miss Psyche Zenobia, to refer you to any article, or set of articles, in the way of model or study; yet perhaps I may as well call your attention to a few cases. Let me see. There was '*The Dead Alive*', a capital thing!— the record of a gentleman's sensations, when entombed before the breath was out of his body—full of tact, terror, sentiment, metaphysics, and erudition. You would have sworn that the writer had been born and brought up in a coffin.

> —Mr. Blackwood, in Poe's 'The [Signora] Psyche Zenobia'
> (1838; later titled 'How to Write a Blackwood Article',
> with 'taste' for 'tact')[1]

1

Difficulties multiply when Poe's stories are grouped. Attempts have been made at different kinds of categorization, sometimes based on or developed from terms Poe himself used, for example 'grotesque' and 'arabesque'.[2] Often, however, the dynamism of interpretation falters and category pigeonholes become superficial, so that collections of Poe's 'tales' of 'mystery and imagination', for example, are segregated from the 'comic Poe'. The problems which arise when one reads across these groupings and finds common topics, themes or subjects must be faced. The variety of Poe's treatments of comparable topics can be bewildering. How can he be straight-faced to obsession about a subject, attention to which he has *earlier* satirized? Is he engaging in deliberate (and reverse) self-parody? Does the variety of handling cast doubt on both the comic and the 'serious'—the one disguising committed obsession, the other commercial exploitation, together cancelling one another out? Alternatively is there a significant development in these apparently so different treatments? In 1958 Harry Levin suggested that the only 'integration' Poe ever attained may lie in his 'retelling a sequence of overlapping anecdotes'.[3] In this essay I will be taking Poe's stories involving premature burial as the exemplar of such a sequence, and I will explore the extent to which they contain a natural history and describe a development across his career.[4]

2

One of the earliest of the abortive *Tales of the Folio Club* is 'A Decided Loss' (1832), a comic extravaganza about a bridegroom who, while upbraiding his bride 'on the morning after the wedding', inexplicably suffocates—though he carries on living with everything but 'breath'. Loss of breath (the story's later title) proves only a temporary inconvenience to speech as the protagonist soon finds an alternative method, but the world turns against, and then hounds and punishes this 'breathless' man. At this point in the story, the narrator-protagonist's condition becomes a comic vehicle for the expression of the anticipation and embodiment of social prejudice. Splenetic and indomitable, however, Mr. Lacko'breath (to use the name he bears in revised versions of the story) expresses a certain relish for his circumstances, as when his crowded coach becomes so airless that others risk extinction: 'Happily the state of my respiratory faculties rendered suffocation an accident entirely out of the question.' Later, hung for a thief—a case of mistaken identity—he does not die: 'I stood in no danger.' If 'breathlessness' is an inconvenience and worse (though not for the expected reason), it is also advantageous, and twice saves Mr.

Lacko'breath from death, though he dies at the end of the story, in its initial version, from an over-enthusiastic galvanic experiment—an unexpected way of concluding a first-person narrative. As an early parody of a *Blackwood's Magazine* story, 'A Decided Loss' answers as well to the prescriptions laid down in 'How to Write a Blackwood Article' as does 'A Predicament', which Poe produced specifically by way of illustration.

In a second version of the story, carefully refurbished three years later for Poe's *Southern Literary Messenger*, and subtitled 'A Tale Neither In nor Out of Blackwood', Mr. Lacko'breath's hanging is handled very differently. 'The rapid determination of blood to the brain', unlike the earlier pulmonary failure, actually threatens his life. Lengthy passages describe the horror of the event, at times in a manner wholly different from the story's previous outlandish unpleasantries: 'the veins in my hands and wrists swelled nearly to bursting . . . and I felt that my eyes were starting from their sockets.' Only then comes the Blackwood-parody touch: 'Yet . . . my sensations were not absolutely intolerable.' While the 'determination' does not actually kill him, it renders him unconscious, which combined with the titular 'loss of breath' convinces his fellows that he is a candidate for interment. (Earlier, immobility had not been a requirement.) A 'public sepulchre' is introduced, and Poe now adds an extended episode of premature burial not present in the 1832 original. As the epigraph to this essay shows, a case of premature burial is the first example that comes to 'Mr. Blackwood's' mind to cite to the aspiring writer of sensational stories. But just at this point both the comicality of the absurd premises of the original story and the punctured extravagance of the revised hanging fall away.

Without the deflating humour, let alone the patent absurdity of previous episodes, the extensive passages about premature interment are impressive. Mr. Lacko'breath at first believes himself actually to *be dead*, believes his sensations to be those of the dead. He finds mentally painful the sensation that though he has been at first placed in a small chamber, 'much encumbered with furniture—yet to me it appeared of a size to contain the universe'. Paradoxically, it is the impression 'of abstract magnitude—of infinity' which appalls him, not the confined, enclosed space. His fingers feel 'swelled to a size according with the proportions of the Antoeus [*sic*]. Every portion of my frame betook of their enormity.' He claims the same extension for 'sentiments' as for physical impressions. If these unexpected feelings leave him less than horrified, almost even entertained, it is not with the effect of an earlier Panglossian inability to recognize or admit the threatening. Poe will later develop the paradox of increased enclosure accompanied by an access of freedom. For all the horror of 'premature burial', there is also an evanescent if undeveloped recognition of renewed strength in the experience; it is like Antaeus who, touching his mother Gea, the Earth, precisely at the point when his opponents seem to have mastered him, regains his powers.

Of course it turns out that Mr. Lacko'breath's speculations about life after death are only that, because he is not dead, but about to be buried alive. When men come to encoffin him, he senses that he is still alive, but being immobile (and still without 'breath') he cannot convince them otherwise. En route to the cemetery, his sensations 'assumed, all at once, a degree of intense and unnatural vivacity', whose detailing endows the prose with a preternaturally precise realism. After 'a deep and deathlike sleep', he awakens to find he can now move. Unable to signal his condition to the outside world, he 'endeavored to lighten the tedium of my hours'; by now, and though he is properly entombed, he has passed beyond the worst horrors of the place and even of the anticipation of death. Here is the touch beyond comedy, that facing the worst horror, however unwillingly and accidentally, may result in freedom from horror and release from obsession. (There is a similar release in 'A Descent into the Maelstrom' (1841), and it too facilitates the protagonist's solution and escape.)

At this point the story returns to quasi-comic reflections on the mortality of the other inhabitants of the tomb and in this version Lacko'breath does not die but comes upon his rival in love, Mr. Windenough, and the two attract attention to themselves. The theme had momentarily extended to foreshadow two other developments which would outlive in Poe even the most horrific exploitation of 'living death' in 'The Fall of the House of Usher' (1839), that is the ability to imagine existence from the hither side of death, as in 'The Colloquy of Monos and Una' (1841), and to project self-cure through experience of that which is most feared, as in 'The Premature Burial' (1844). Poe excised these new passages subsequent to their appearance in *Tales of the Grotesque and Arabesque* (1840), which therefore provides the fullest and most intricate version of 'Loss of Breath'. He may have thought it best to remove them to make room for (or not trespass upon) the territory of 'The Premature Burial'.[5]

The comic premises of 'A Decided Loss'/'Loss of Breath' are continually violated and shifted, less by an author flogging a worn-out jest than by the extravagant delight Poe found in making conceptions and language dance to his will. He may have returned to the story not simply to pad out an issue of the *Southern Literary Messenger* but to touch base with a remembered creative surge.[6] The suffering of the prematurely buried and the wider reaches of speculation about it threaten to burst the anarchic comedy and were removed after 1840 and placed where they could be contained. At the same time, they constitute a trial run for other uses of the theme, as in *The Narrative of A. Gordon Pym* (1838).

There, Pym, Dirk Peters and another discover a 'fissure in the soft rock' which 'extended back into the hill some eighteen or twenty feet'. Some filberts, growing from 'stunted shrubs' therein, take Pym's curiosity. He, followed by the others, enters the chasm; then they make as to leave but are suddenly buried alive by a 'concussion' so startling that it seems 'that the whole foundations of the solid globe were suddenly rent asunder and that the day of universal dissolution was at hand' (Ch. XX). If the episode begins apocalyptically enough, the narrative which follows is remarkable for its search for an appropriate language:

> As soon as we sufficiently recovered from our fright and surprise to be capable of conversing rationally, we both came to the conclusion that the walls of the fissure in which we had ventured had, by some convulsion of nature, or probably from their own weight, caved in overhead, and that we were consequently lost for ever, being thus entombed alive. For a long time we gave up to the most intense agony and despair, such as cannot be adequately imagined by those who have never been in a similar position. I firmly believed that no

incident ever occurring in the course of human events is more adapted to inspire the supremeness of mental and bodily distress than a case like our own, of living inhumation. The blackness of darkness which envelops the victim, the terrific oppression of lungs, the stifling fumes from the damp earth, unite with the ghastly considerations that we are beyond the remotest confines of hope, and that such is the allotted portion of *the dead*, to carry into the human heart a degree of appalling awe and horror not to be tolerated—never to be conceived. (Ch. XXI)

Some of the initial coolness of tone may derive from the stance of the retrospective narrator, who after all survived, even if it makes Pym and Peters sound like comic *philosophes* on the 'Loss of Breath'/*Blackwood's* model. But the sculptured first sentence, which swallows up 'fright and surprise', clangs down on 'entombed alive'. A second sentence almost gives up without trying, a third stakes out a claim without delivering proof, though both allow a vocabulary of 'agony and despair', 'distress' and 'living inhumation' to trouble the rhetorical pace. By the 'blackness of darkness', Pym/Poe is willing to try to describe what he has said he could not—or has he only said that others cannot imagine what he can? A ghastly catalogue then progresses from outside to inside ('fumes . . . unite with . . . considerations'), merging the victim and his environment. What is worst in this 'appalling awe and horror' seems to be the mere physical condition of '*the dead*', their 'allotted portion', the grave in which the body becomes amalgamated with its environment. The *gestalt* is crucial—the identification and commingling of the individual with the earth. And it is this which is most insupportable.[7]

That Poe has had his purpose from the ambivalently apocalyptic, coolly observed and yet agonizing and distressful entombment is demonstrated by the risible calm and speed with which it is set aside. Despite Pym and Peters being purportedly poleaxed by the horror of their position:

At length Peters *proposed that we should endeavour to ascertain precisely the extent of our calamity*, and grope about our prison; it being barely possible, he observed, that some opening might yet be left us for escape. . . . Hardly had I advanced a single step before a glimmer of light became perceptible, enough to convince me that, at all events, we should not immediately perish for want of air. [Ch. XXI, emphasis added]

Five sentences more bring the two to 'little doubt of finding . . . a clear passage into the open air'.

The passage is one of a number which punctuates *Pym* and creates a rhythm as the story progresses through three of the categories Levin, in the passage earlier cited, proposed for the protagonists of Poe's tales: the observer, the actor, and the sufferer or agonist (p. 111). Earlier, as a stowaway, Pym had experienced his 'thorough concealment' in 'an iron-bound box' turn from a snug 'little apartment', metaphorically a 'palace', to a 'dungeon' and nearly to a tomb. At first, reference to his being 'buried' causes no concern. Then he awakens confusedly from sleep, finds his watch has run down, part of his food-store putrified, begins to fancy breathing is difficult, falls into a stupor and has 'terrific' dreams. One such is of being menaced by a 'fierce lion'. Waking, he realizes that an animal is indeed on his bosom, but it is, unaccountably, his Newfoundland dog Tiger. Discovering at length, after much difficulty, that the egress from his hiding-place is now blocked, he begins to experience sensations 'of extreme horror and dismay'. He is 'entombed' and imagines 'suffocation and premature interment' as his lot. Eventually he is rescued. Such enclosure in a ship's hold, as in 'MS. Found in a Bottle' (1833), is succeeded in *Pym* by the putatively worse enclosure of the chasm, which is itself a step in a phased succession whose final term merges images of enclosure and freedom: a 'materially increased' darkness, a 'white curtain before us', 'the embraces of the cataract, where a chasm threw itself open to receive us', and in the path 'a shrouded human figure . . . the hue of [its] skin . . . of the perfect whiteness of the snow' (Ch. XXV).

3

The obsessed narrator of 'Berenice' (1835) violates the fresh grave of his beloved to extract her teeth. We learn this retrospectively—as he does,[8] for he cannot remember having (earlier that same night) perpetrated the horrendous deed. It is discovered because 'a wild cry' has been heard by 'the household'—Berenice had been buried alive, her 'epilepsy' having counterfeited the appearance of death. What has offered the opportunity for her rescue and possibly actively awakened her is paradoxically the very act of violation, the bizarre dental extraction, though whether the narrator has knowingly left her for dead thereafter we cannot know. It is possible; in paragraphs which were part of the story in its initial publications (1835 and *Tales of the Grotesque and Arabesque*, 1840), the narrator has sight of Berenice encoffined before burial: 'There had been a band around the jaws but, I know not how, it was broken asunder. The livid lips were wreathed with a species of smile. . . .' On seeing her teeth, the narrator bolts from the room and, we may suspect, refuses to entertain the possibility that Berenice is still alive. (Though he had apologized for these paragraphs to T. W. White in 1835, Poe did not delete them until the 1845 *Broadway Journal* republication.) In this refusal there are suggestions of 'The Fall of the House of Usher' and of the predicament of the narrator of 'The Raven' (1845), who despite his 'dreaming dreams no mortal ever dared to dream before' remains unable to credit that it is 'the lost Leonore' who is 'gently rapping, rapping at my chamber door'. His 'fearing' and 'doubting' overcome his 'wondering' and 'dreaming'—we do not know who or what it is that 'echoes' the name 'Leonore'—and from that point the raven with its message of 'Nevermore' succeeds the bereaved lover's more 'fantastic terrors'.[9]

In 'The Fall of the House of Usher', Roderick Usher, suspicious of 'certain obtrusive and eager inquiries' from his sister Madeline's 'medical men', confides to the narrator his 'arrangements for [her] temporary entombment'. This apparent attempt to frustrate potential grave-robbers of a more scientific/mercenary intent than the protagonist of 'Berenice' strikes the narrator of 'Usher', who finds the doctor 'sinister', as 'a harmless, and by no means an unnatural, precaution'. The place chosen to receive the coffin lies 'at great depth', and is entered through a 'door, of massive iron' and 'immense weight'. The coffin lid is 'screwed down' and the door 'secured'. Though Madeline's illness had been 'cataleptical', which leaves her in death with 'the mockery of a faint blush upon the bosom and the face' and a 'suspiciously lingering smile', nothing untoward *is* suspected.

Usher of all men has, however, the sensibility to experience his sister's plight on revival and apparently does so. The narrator comes to consider that Usher 'was laboring with some oppressive secret, to divulge which he struggled for the necessary courage'. It is not the fact of her premature entombment which is in question with Usher, but his ability to reveal it. This displaces the theme or rather makes it the emblem of a condition in Usher, whose nature will reveal more of the sources of the theme's interest than have previous treatments.

The facility of speaking interchangeably of 'the House of Usher' as family, individual and building is one which the story is at pains to establish. Half a long and careful paragraph is required to pull matters round to the point where 'the quaint and equivocal appellation . . . seemed to include, in the minds of the peasantry who used it, both the family and the family mansion.' For 'a family including ancestors and descendants; a lineage, a race' (*O.E.D.*, 6) to merge not only with 'The persons living in one dwelling; the inmates of a house collectively; a household, family' (*O.E.D.*, 5), but with 'a building for human habitation; esp. a building that is the ordinary dwelling-place of a family' (*O.E.D.*, 1), it is necessary to elide collateral branches. Poe eliminates all but 'the direct line of descent' of the Ushers: 'the stem of the Usher race . . . had put forth, at no period, any enduring branch.' All the family has thus inhabited this building and none has lived outside it. The equivocality of the 'appellation' will be brought out as the narrator first anticipates, then hears directly of and finally shares Roderick Usher's deepest fear, that he *is* his 'House', that he has no separate existence from it—that is, that he is buried alive in it.

The careful establishment of both building and family as, against expectation if not paradoxically, comprehended in the 'House' permits the introduction of the ground upon which the narrator will develop his 'sense of insufferable gloom', his 'utter depression'. Considering the 'deficiency' of collateral branches, he speculates on 'the perfect keeping of the character of the premises with the accredited character of the people [the

Ushers], and . . . the possible influence which the one, in the long lapse of centuries, might have exercised upon the other . . .'. (The conflation by the peasantry is its version of expressing 'the possible influence'.)

As he looks up from the image of the house in the tarn, the merely 'shadowy fancies' materialize into 'a strange fancy', that of 'an atmosphere peculiar' to 'the whole mansion and domain', 'which had reeked up from the decayed trees, and the gray wall, and the silent tarn'. Why this 'atmosphere' should be so 'ridiculous' a fancy will only become clear as it is elaborated by Roderick Usher himself; Usher's version of the 'atmosphere' will confirm suspicions which the narrator has tried unsuccessfully to dismiss, replace and (when he cannot) repress.

When Usher describes his 'malady' to the narrator, he mentions, in order, a 'morbid acuteness of the senses', an 'anomalous species of terror' which is 'the grim phantasm, FEAR' and 'certain superstitious impressions in regard to the dwelling which he tenanted':

> an influence which some peculiarities in the mere form and substance of his family mansion, had . . . obtained over his spirit—an effect which the *physique* of the gray walls and turrets, and of the dim tarn into which they all looked down, had, at length, brought about upon the *morale* of his existence. (M, 2.403)

Usher 'dread[s] the events of the future', he 'shudder[s] at the thought of any, even the most trivial, incident', for their 'results' and 'effect' presumably upon himself. That is, it is the 'thought' rather than the 'effect' that appals him. This puzzling paragraph introduces Usher's 'superstitious impressions in regard to the dwelling which he tenanted', its 'influence' and 'atmosphere'.

The 'shadowy fancies' have become a 'strange fancy' and now Usher's own 'superstitious impressions' of 'an influence'. Its *'morale'* is his. (The narrator had earlier experienced, and attempted to reject, his impression that the influence of the physical site 'had moulded the destinies of his family, and . . . made *him* what I now saw him—what he was'.) This is further elaborated when Usher discourses upon 'suggestions arising from' 'The Haunted Palace', the rhapsody or ballad he has just sung, and which itself identifies the palace and its ruler/monarch by, among other things, windows/eyes. (The narrator has earlier recoiled from the House of Usher's 'vacant and eye-like windows'.) Not only does Usher evince belief in 'the sentience of all vegetable things', he extends the idea until it 'trespassed, under certain conditions, upon the kingdom of inorganization'.[10] The narrator refers Usher's opinion back to a previous hint—it must be to the impression of 'an influence ... over his spirit'. Now it is located in 'the method of collocation' of the grey stones of the house,

> in the order of their arrangement, as well as in that of the many *fungi* which overspread them, and of the decayed trees which stood around—above all, in the long undisturbed endurance of this arrangement, and in its reduplication in the still waters of the tarn. (M, 2.408)

Usher experiences himself not as an individual but as an object, 'un luth suspendu; /Sitôt qu'on le touche il résonne'. (Poe found the lines for his epigraph in a book he reviewed in 1841, and added them to the text for the 1845 *Tales*.) The self is indistinguishable from the other. The individual cannot maintain equilibrium, but experiences absorption. Usher feels suffocated, prematurely buried by his growing and finally confirmed discovery. As he is his House, he is his sister and her premature burial is the symbol of *his* condition. Perception of this paralyses his will and he cannot intervene to deny her living death (which is his own). The spring of action is removed. When he reveals that he is helpless in his knowledge, the symbol of it attacks and embraces him and he falls, 'a victim to the terrors he had anticipated'. The House disappears into the black tarn, taking its mirror image with it into nothingness. A decade later, in *Eureka*, Poe projects the death of the universe itself; then in a leap of faith he speculates a resurrection, a new creation.[11] 'The Fall of the House of Usher' stops short of that, and it epitomizes the horror at the heart of the image—life itself experienced as premature burial. Poe's treatments henceforth can diverge into the spiritual and the psychological, and most significantly the fearful element is banished. Awakening from apparent death can in Poe subsequently be awakening into an afterlife, as in 'The Colloquy of Monos and Una'—'there came upon me . . . a breathless and motionless torpor; and this was termed *Death* by those who stood around me', says the narrator, without any trace of apprehension, even remembered apprehension. Or, in sublunary existence Poe's treatment will reach distanced and rationalized conclusions.

4

It is not until 'The Premature Burial' is half over that it declares itself a tale, and then only by the reader's not taking the first person narrator as the veritable author. To that point Poe's frontal treatment of the titular subject moves from a discursive, essayistic posture to affected reportage. Its sequence of four anecdotes, though in fact bearing a variety of relationships to fiction, suggests an author methodically exhausting a card-file; indeed the story will ultimately bid farewell to and dismiss a topic it initially postulates as obsessively and interminably interesting.

The author begins by promising to identify 'certain themes of which the interest is all-absorbing'. 'Prominent and unjust calamities' best fit this bill, but only if 'true', for they are 'too entirely horrible for the purposes of legitimate fiction'. In any case 'vast generalities of disaster' are less affecting than 'individual instances'. The extreme of misery in the sufferer and the affective power of the account are being conflated. Thus by apparent 'logic' the author arrives at, 'To be buried while alive is, beyond question, the most terrific of these extremes which has ever fallen to the lot of mere mortality.' The extended anecdotes which follow successively approximate the ultimate 'type' of the story, where event and affect converge on the person of the writer.[12]

The first anecdote is sited 'in the neighboring city of Baltimore' (we imagine ourselves New Yorkers or Philadelphians). A Congressman discovers his wife's skeleton at the door of 'her family vault' three years after her coffined body was placed in it. In France, a distraught lover, 'a poor *littérateur*, or journalist', unearths his mistress's body (she had rejected him for 'a banker, and a diplomatist'). His grief-maddened caresses awaken her, and the two flee to America. Thirdly, a peasant feels 'a commotion of the earth' when 'sitting upon the grave' of an artillery officer, who is thereafter revived. Poe's consistent tone appears to desert him when, in a throwback to the original version of 'A Decided Loss', experimental galvanic shock sees the officer well and truly off. The resemblances to Poe's previous treatments of the topic here and elsewhere in 'The Premature Burial', however, suggest not accidental repetition but deliberate résumé.

Finally, in an anecdote whose alleged date of occurrence Poe would shift forward in subsequent printings, 'a young attorney of London', dead of typhus, is unearthed by resurrectionists and accidentally revived by the same application of a battery. The account is in fact taken from a story in *Blackwood's Magazine*, 'The Buried Alive' (1821), which Poe had referred to jocularly earlier in 'How to Write a Blackwood Article' (though with an incorrect title), and which I have used as an epigraph. Here, there is no parody and the notion is exploited—'Mr. S. himself asserts . . . that at no period was he altogether insensible—that, dully and confusedly he was aware of everything which happened to him'—as the bridge to a generalized passage on the presumptive horrors of premature interment:

> *no* event is so terribly well adapted to inspire the supremeness of bodily and mental distress, as is burial before death. The unendurable oppression of the lungs—the stifling fumes of the damp earth—the clinging of the dark garments—the rigid embrace of the narrow house—the blackness of the absolute Night—the silence like a sea that overwhelms—the unseen but palpable presence of the Conquerer Worm. . .—that our hopeless portion is that of the really dead—these considerations, I say, carry into the heart . . . a degree of appalling and intolerable horror. (M, 3.961)

Having asserted, and having built by anecdote and rhetoric, the claim that there is 'nothing so agonizing upon Earth' or in Hell as live burial, Poe proceeds to install a narrator to evince 'my own positive and personal experience'. Except that the conclusion of the narrator's tale, if it does not make light of the terrors of anticipation, casts an altogether different light on the nature of the story being told. We now learn of the narrator's own susceptibility to 'catalepsy' and the growth of this fear that he would be buried alive during one of his trances: 'My fancy grew charnal [*sic*]. I talked "of worms, of tombs, and epitaphs". I was lost in reveries of death, and the idea of premature burial held continual possession of my brain.' '[T]he one sepulchral Idea' possesses him entirely, waking or in unwilling and tormented sleep. The narrator relates how he became a kind of Roderick Usher:

> My nerves became thoroughly unstrung, and I fell a prey to perpetual horror. I hesitated to ride, or to walk, or to indulge in any exercise that would carry me from home. . . . I doubted the care, the fidelity of my dearest friends.

He attempts to outwit his fate by 'elaborate precautions' for ready means of escape from a bespoke coffin and tomb. (Mabbott and others reckon Poe's story to have been precipitated by an article on a 'life-preserving coffin' by N. P. Willis in 1843; M, 3.971.) Despite these preparations, the narrator's fears persist, even increase, and then one day seem to be realized. He wakes, but all is dark, he feels the sides of a coffin not his own and he shrieks in agony (it is not a cry for help he believes will not come).

Immediately, instantly, rustic voices disabuse him of his utter conviction of entombment: 'What do you mean by yowling in that ere kind of style, like a cattymount?' He had *not* been buried alive, he had been asleep in the bunk of a sloop, in conditions that permitted his confusion and error, an error to which his 'ordinary bias of thought' had carried him. The vernacular-borne revelation dispels mandarin, exquisitely self-honed 'tortures . . . quite equal . . . to those of actual sepulture'. The Antaean narrator, who has in imaginative experience touched the earth, is restored to strength. He finds himself mysteriously cured:

> [The] very excess [of the 'inconceivably hideous' tortures] wrought in my spirit an inevitable revulsion. My soul acquired tone—acquired temper. . . . I breathed the free air of Heaven. I thought upon other subjects than Death. I discarded my medical books. 'Buchan' I burned. I read no 'Night Thoughts'—no fustian about church-yards—no bugaboo tales—*such as this*. In short, I became a new man, and lived a man's life. From that

memorable night, I dismissed forever my charnal apprehensions, and with them vanished the cataleptic disorder, of
which, perhaps, they had been less the consequence than the
cause. (M, 3.969; Poe's emphasis)

A haunting last paragraph, adapted from H. B. Wallace's
Stanley (1838), reminds the reader that 'the grim legion of
sepulchral terrors cannot be regarded as altogether fanciful'
and rescues the story's ending, and the story itself, from the
comic auto-destruction of 'no bugaboo tales—*such as this*'.
What 'The Premature Burial' has done is not to consign to
oblivion Poe's own treatments of 'charnal apprehensions' but
to *review* them, from comic versions—where, for example,
galvanic shocks resurrect and then kill—to anticipations of
living interment (*Pym*), to a surrogate confrontation ('Usher'),
to release from the bondage of obsession, mysterious and
permitting balance where that had been lost and unimagin-
able. 'The Premature Burial' embodies the whole sequence of
Poe's 'buried alive' tales, does them in their different voices,
and brings them to a co-incident conclusion. It recapitulates
the sequence of which it is itself the last term, and which it
supersedes. It suggests and demonstrates that the comic and
the deadly serious, and all the postures between and combining both, can coexist and take their places in a super-
ordinate formula. And it makes it the more plausible that the
universal grave, which is the grave of us all, could cease to
hold a disenabling terror for the author-to-be of *Eureka*.

NOTES

1. *Collected Works of Edgar Allan Poe*, ed. Thomas Ollive Mabbott (Cambridge, Mass., and London: Harvard University Press, 1978), 2.339.
   Henceforth all references to this edition, in three volumes (1969, 1978,
   1978), are in the form M, 2.339.
2. See David Ketterer, *The Rationale of Deception in Poe* (Baton Rouge and
   London: Louisiana State University Press, 1979), pp. 35–8 *et passim*.
3. Harry Levin, *The Power of Blackness* (London: Faber and Faber, 1958),
   p. 110.
4. That interest in this theme is current can be seen from Karl Miller's
   judgement, 'His journeys embody the search for a mother, and an effort

to regain the mother he had lost, and his "depart, yet live" [in 'Hans Pfaall'] may be matched with the tension in his writings between an impulse to guard against the horrors of premature burial and an impulse to be interred with the maternal remains' (in *Doubles: Studies in Literary History* (Oxford: Oxford University Press, 1985), p. 164).

5. He had earlier (21 September 1839) written to an enquirer who questioned the ending of 'Ligeia' (1838) that he could not end that story as he should have, with a final relapse of Ligeia's hold over Rowena, because he had already used that ending in 'Morella' (1835). Both, in having an apparently dead woman alive again—or attempting to come alive—in the body of another, touch on the topic of premature burial.

6. Mabbott, however, felt that Poe 'laboured over ["Loss of Breath"] . . . with a zeal worthy of a better cause' (M, 2.51).

7. In 'Hawthorne's Old Home', I have offered a comparable treatment of this theme in Hawthorne. See *Nathaniel Hawthorne: New Critical Essays*, ed. A. Robert Lee (London: Vision Press, 1982), pp. 148–70, esp. p. 158.

8. This narrative strategy is still being found useful: see Norman Mailer, *Tough Guys Don't Dance* (London: Michael Joseph, 1984).

9. This reading, of course, needs comparing with Poe's comment: 'The idea of making the lover suppose, in the first instance, that the flapping of the wings of the bird against the shutter, is a "tapping" at the door, originated . . . in a desire to admit the incidental effect arising from the lover's throwing open the door, finding all dark, and thence adopting the half-fancy that it was the spirit of his mistress that knocked.' But 'originated . . . in' can refer to a conception later superseded, and in the poem the 'half-fancy' takes the narrator *before* the door is opened. See 'The Philosophy of Composition' (1846), in Edgar Allan Poe, *Essays and Reviews* (Library of America, 1978), p. 21.

10. Herbert Smith noted that Poe's cited source for vegetable sentience, Watson, may also have suggested 'the organic relatedness of *all matter*', 'the kingdom of inorganization' being the mineral kingdom. See M, 2.149n.

11. 'When, I say, Matter, finally, expelling the Ether, shall have returned into absolute Unity,—it will then (to speak paradoxically for the moment) be . . . Matter without Matter—in other words, again, *Matter no more*. In sinking into Unity, it will sink at once into . . . that Material Nihility from which alone we can conceive it to have been evoked. . . .

   'But are we here to pause? Not so. On the Universal agglomeration and dissolution, we can readily conceive that a new and perhaps totally different series of conditions may ensue—another creation and radiation, returning into itself—another action and reaction of the Divine Will. . . . [A]re we not, indeed, more than justified in entertaining a belief—let us say, rather, in indulging a hope—that the processes we have here ventured to contemplate will be renewed forever, and forever, and forever . . .' (*Eureka*, in *The Science Fiction of Edgar Allan Poe*, ed. Harold Beaver (Harmondsworth: Penguin Books, 1976), pp. 306–7).

12. Compare 'the death . . . of a beautiful woman is, unquestionably, the

most poetical topic in the world—and equally it is beyond doubt that the lips best suited for such topic are those of a bereaved lover' ('The Philosophy of Composition', op. cit., p. 19). The same 'logic' characterizes the assertions in both 'The Premature Burial' and 'The Philosophy of Composition'.

4

Poe's Comic Vision and Southwestern Humour

by JAMES H. JUSTUS

> The papers read every Saturday evening were characterized less by depth than buffoonery. They were all whipped syllabub. There was no investigation of first causes, first principles. There was no investigation of anything at all. There was no attention paid to that great point the 'fitness of things'. In short there was no fine writing like this.
>
> —'How to Write a Blackwood Article'

1

If one begins with an extract from Poe's most explicit comic piece—'How to Write a Blackwood Article' and its mock-sequel 'A Predicament'—it is in part because of all his first-person narrators few speak more congenially than Signora Psyche Zenobia. Despite her highfalutin name ('I'm all soul' she confides) and her apprenticeship to two 'literary' mentors, Dr. Moneypenny and Mr. Blackwood, she reveals herself from the outset as wonderfully humourless, obtuse and literal-minded. Her overblown costume (a crimson frock studded with green *agraffas* and orange *auriculas*), like her overblown name, puts before us a dedicated seeker of literary fashion, a seeker after style. In having her seek to escape the 'whipped syllabub' of her bluestocking society, Poe opens up a satire on literary fashion itself, the quest for 'show', 'display', all the puffery and formula writing of his day.

66

Not that Poe excluded himself as his own butt. His irreverent two-part story targets for satire much of his own fiction of sensation-and-analysis—often enough read with a straight face by readers of the magazines and quarterlies. Its undermining transaction is thus as self-directed (Poe as sensation-monger and Poe as transcendentalist) as it is directed against those disparate high-thinkers that he elsewhere called *'Believers in everything Odd'* whose only common link was 'credulity'.[1] The Psyche Zenobia story is one of Poe's better comic efforts—indeed, the only explicitly humorous Poe that is ever anthologized—but its salient ingredients are those that characterize his satire in general: an already extravagant situation pushed to absurd, even grotesque, extremes; flamboyant verbal wit embedded in the usual rhetoric of excess; an urban temperament accustomed to coterie humour involving professional and other specialized groups—in this case, popular journalists.

Poe's comic sense can be both curiously old-fashioned and presciently fashionable. If he sometimes resembles a collegiate humorist in naming an editor 'Scissors' or in playing rhyming games with a law firm ('Bogs, Hogs, Logs, Frogs & Co.') and a gentleman's ancestry on the distaff side (Froissart-Croissart-Voissart-Moissart), at other times Poe sounds like a trendy philosopher; he likes the peculiarly jocular manner of story-telling in one novel he reviews 'inasmuch as to say "I know I am writing nonsense, but then you must excuse me for the very reason that I know it."' In that same novel, *Sheppard Lee*, Poe delights in its author's *bizarreries* by which nine of the hero's siblings die within six years 'by a variety of odd accidents—the last expiring in a fit of laughter at seeing his brother ridden to death by a pig'.[2]

2

In the preface to his first collection of fiction, *Tales of the Grotesque and Arabesque* (1840), Poe would seem to invite us into a region not exclusively Gothic. By this time he had already gained the reputation he would continue to have for the next century: as the author of 'the wild—unnatural and horrible!'— the result of a fatal 'German enchantment'. Poe acknowledges the Germanic flavour of some of his tales, but then remarks curiously: 'Tomorrow I may be anything but German, as yesterday I was everything else'—a playful statement that semantically seems to deny *any* German taint or, alternately, that congenially projects himself into whatever categories his critics prepare for him. Poe's first book of fiction contains twenty-five tales, at least eleven of which are wholly comic in intent. The forms and moods range widely. While the satiric burlesques of popular genres most decisively reveal Poe as the wide-awake and competitive magazinist, one suspects that the broader, more farcical tales reflect a truer side of the man, the Poe who extracts grim humour out of physical discomfiture, violence, and death.

The two drunk sailors of 'King Pest' are caricatures more than characters: Legs is six-and-a-half feet tall, stooped, thin, hawk-nosed, chinless; Hugh Tarpaulin is four feet tall, bow-legged, small-eyed, thick-lipped, purple-faced. With the gestures of stage comedians they dominate their literally dead environment, plague-ridden London streets, and their kinetic highjinks propel them down some stairs and into the circumscribed space that Poe usually reserves for his Gothic tales: a wine cellar, abandoned except for six victims in the latter stages of disease. Against the simple drunken appetitiveness of the sailors Poe juxtaposes the pettiness and vanity of a mock-court playing at illusory life. The grim carousal, amid skeletons and still unburied corpses, of a gaunt company soon to be both erupts in slapstick rebellion and violence. For all its repulsive subject matter, 'King Pest' is marked by its creator's usual fondness for puns, literary allusions, and mock-allegorical names. As T. O. Mabbott shows, Poe liked it well enough to revise meticulously.

Poe's artistry in the revising of his comic tales generally is more striking than his originality. For all the individualizing effects that go to make these tales indisputably Poesque, their origins—in continental literature, English romanticism, American writing, and contemporary newspapers—range from the classical to the ephemera of popular journalism. Two of his most good-natured thrusts at human pride are free adaptations of ancient narrative forms. An early sketch, 'Four Beasts in One', is a variation on the fairy tale about the emperor's new clothes; and a later story, 'The Spectacles', is based on the old joke about the man who discovers that his beautiful wife is an old hag artfully disguised. The latter situation allows Poe to use the practical joke as moral corrective: a young man who out of pride refuses to wear needed eyeglasses is easily tricked into courting and marrying his great-great-grandmother. For the king who dresses in the hide of a beast 'for the better sustaining his dignity as king', the reversal of the hierarchical status of man and beast is willed in madness: 'With how superior a dignity the monarch perambulates on all fours!' His subjects dutifully hail him Prince of Poets and Glory of the East, but when in a sudden mutiny the kingly fortunes change, human instinct reasserts itself and the Prince of Poets is 'upon his hinder legs, running for his life'. This droll exercise reveals a Poe fully participating in such mainstream literary themes as the vagaries of power and fame, the beast within the man, and the thin line separating the flattering public and the raging mob.

The human urge of a perverse king or a foolish young man to reshape reality to suit a more idealized vision always comes to grief in Poe's humorous pieces. In some ways that lesson, repeated in various narrative combinations, paradoxically underscores a darker vision of the nature of man than his outright tales of terror, clotted as they are with such esoterica as metempsychosis and diabolism. In his serious assaults on the mysteries, Poe's fascination with one of the ultimate questions—What is Man?—is obsessive, but his answers, approached from diverse perspectives, remain exploratory, tentative. In the comic pieces Poe's mind is settled. They may dramatize his view of man-as-beast, a bundle of biological attributes that the ego foolishly elevates to something higher; or, just as often, they depict man-as-mechanism—a collection of cogs, pumps, conduits. In either instance, the famous yearning for supernal ideality that we so often associate with Poe is conspicuously missing.

It is doubtless true that Poe's comedy is primarily satiric, trimmed here and there with turns from vaudeville and the theatre of farce. Important to this formulation, of course, is a not-so-hidden indignation at the spectacle of life itself. One scholar asserts that the function of Poe's brand of satire is 'the exposure of a society in which heroes and rulers are shown to be deluded or irresponsible and their subjects a dehumanized, sycophantic mass'.[3] Such specificity explains the cautionary 'Four Beasts in One', the grim gallows humour of 'Hop-Frog', and that more genial exercise in turned tables, 'The System of Doctor Tarr and Professor Fether'. And although explaining a writer's sense of humour is only a little easier than explaining a joke, it would seem that in addition to the social motive of exposure, Poe's forays into comedy are often self-revelations of the most personal kind.

The pseudo-biblical prose of 'A Tale of Jerusalem', for example, is an over-elaborate dressing for a simple ethnic joke, a faintly scatalogical tale of discomfiture in which the besieging Romans respond to the Jewish request for a sacrificial Sabbath lamb by substituting 'a *hog* of no common size'. There is no reason to think that Poe in his maturity did not continue to think this extended joke funny; like other lesser efforts he carefully revised this one. Another kind of self-revelation shows up in 'Thou Art the Man', a ratiocinative tale in which a good-humoured, neighbourly old gentleman turns out to be the murderer. The brutal handling of the victim's corpse for the purpose of extracting a confession narratively and morally justifies the dénouement, but it does not explain the gusto with which the detective-narrator thrusts a stiff whalebone down the throat of his friend, now a 'bruised, bloody and nearly putrid corpse', transforming it into a jack-in-the-box that will pop up at an expeditious moment.

What is both publicly exposed and privately revealed is human fallibility in a vision of man that seems darker in its comic versions than in its serious, partly because of a technique of cheerfully indiscriminate pastiche. Though Poe may begin with conventional satiric purposefulness, he dilutes it with exaggeration, caricature, puns and other wordplay, farce, literary burlesque, even private jokes. The comic sense in Poe often emerges from the very proliferation of such devices, and though they may be funny in themselves, they crowd and nudge each other to the point where satiric intent is smudged. In the serious tales, we may quarrel over the meaning of 'Ligeia' or 'The Fall of the House of Usher', but we tend to accept the author's boast that nothing in them is extraneous, no detail that does not contribute to the unity of his chosen effect. But only someone who is haunted by separation and disjunction could make so much of the principle of unity. The harmony of parts coalescing into the whole is finally more important than what the whole means. The famous tales of death are themselves dead—intensely coherent constructions featuring marionettes posturing against painted backdrops. In his theoretical essays his tortured metaphors—the steady pressure of the stamp upon the wax, the dropping of the water on the rock—celebrate the mechanical process by which Poe thinks proper literature gets written.

In certain respects we get a more transparent, less mediated Poe in his comedy, where the psychic aggression is more open, because there is no pretended harmony of their units. Mabbott once remarked that Poe believed 'all wholly inappropriate combinations comic'.[4] Indeed, the mismatched parts and crude rivets help to shape the jerry-built structures into symbolic artifacts of Poe's vision, and their message reads: there is no harmony in man or society. The sheer juxtaposition of pratfalls, mock-Gothicism, wit, parody, buffoonery, and personal pique points to a reality ununified and an actuality of disproportion. In an early sketch, 'The Assignation', the stranger-hero shapes his environment to accord with his insight into the absurdity of life; the interior of his palazzo, a riotous hodgepodge of incongruous styles and embellishments, is almost a pre-parodic version of those harmonious and extravagant interiors so lovingly detailed in the mature fiction. 'Some things are so completely ludicrous that a man *must* laugh or die', says the Byronic protagonist. He does both.

In his relentless exploration of man, Poe finds convenient the available and conventional scientific assumptions about the human body; when he literalizes them, they invariably dramatize the deflation of man, and the process of human reductiveness becomes comic. The Brevet Brigadier General of 'The Man that was Used Up', formerly a famous Indian fighter, is introduced as the most imposing personage in Philadelphia society. Poe first telegraphs the real ordinariness of his hero by naming him John A. B. C. Smith before he finally reduces him to a nondescript bundle over which the narrator nearly stumbles. The hero with an *air distingué* turns out to be a human fragment with assorted mechanical devices to fill him out: artificial leg, arms, shoulders, bosom, wig, teeth, eye—all capped with an ingenious palate, a contrivance that turns the general's natural squeaks into sonorous booms. The narrator of 'Loss of Breath' searches in his *boudoir* for his lost breath, finding instead 'a set of false teeth, two pairs of hips, an eye, and a bundle of *billets-doux* from Mr. Windenough to [his] wife'. Although this story begins as a verbal joke—the literalization of a common expression—it develops, like the modern cartoon, through a series of debilitating physical encounters. In Mr. Lackobreath's declension, a surgeon cuts off his ears, two cats fight over his nose, he suffers a fractured skull and broken arms, and, mistaken on a stagecoach for an object of convenience, he is finally used as a makeshift mattress. The corporeal stripping away is also a psychological reduction, and the curiously deadpan tone of the first-person narrator intensifies this masochistic fantasy.

Allen Tate once recalled the pride of his ancestors in being able to claim Poe as one of their own because 'nothing that Mr. Poe wrote, it was said soon after his death, could bring a blush to the cheek of the purest maiden.'[5] Perhaps mid-nineteenth-century maidens were more doughty than their late nineteenth-century legend, or perhaps they were merely selective. The kind of tastelessness that made Victorians blush—corporeal explicitness—is usefully forestalled in Poe's lyrics by obfuscation and esoteric allusion, but in the fiction the potential offence of the bad taste is pre-empted by surprise, the *frisson* of revelation: bloody cerements, infused gore of corpses, simian indelicacy with a woman's body. If the visceral emphasis in Poe's fiction did not cause maidens to blush, did it ever make them sick? Gross visceral actuality even informs some of those pieces based on Poe's fascination with scientific discoveries of his day.

In 'The Case of M. Valdemar', the serious experiment of extending life to the dying by mesmeric trance is undercut by a grim relish in its inevitable and messy failure. By tinkering, Valdemar's bodily degeneration is slowed until nature asserts itself over the artificial and speeds up the processes. It is an experiment conducted without regard for the victim's distraught pleas: 'quick!—quick!—put me to sleep—or, quick!—

waken me!—quick!—*I say to you that I am dead!*' Valdemar is denied the dignity of his own death: 'his whole frame', reports the narrator, 'crumbled—absolutely *rotted* away beneath my hands. Upon the bed, before that whole company, there lay a nearly liquid mass of loathsome—of detestable putridity.' The final detail, towards which this otherwise indifferent tale moves, is of course meant to be shocking. But the horror of visceral transformation—a too-too solid flesh reduced in the twinkling of an eye to disgusting jelly—is also linked, I think, to what Henry James and T. S. Eliot saw generally as Poe's arrested development at the pre-adolescent stage.[6] The Valdemar dénouement is a displaced child's joke, suggesting that period when the young, after years of private absorption and training in their own bodily mechanisms, socialize the fascination, converting the most natural functions into the most elemental humour. Ingestion, digestion, evacuation— with all that the nose smells and the ear hears—become public phenomena to be appreciated as comedic spectacles. This linkage of gross corporeality and childish humour does not comport well with the image of Poe the metaphysical yearner, but it grimly supports the underlying seriousness of Poe's dark view of the human species; to be mindful of man is to be mindful of how a seemingly stable solid is really a fragile envelope of gases and liquids into which the entire organism finally dissolves.

More explicitly, the feat in 'Some Words with a Mummy', bringing Count Allamistakeo back to life, disintegrates into childish oral competition between the scientists and the now-voluble mummy. The satire in this tale is directed against nineteenth-century progress as represented by the voltaic pile and the galvanic battery, but Poe's vaudeville imagination constantly threatens to submerge the satire. Dandifying the mummy into an acerb snob in order to dismiss progress is a recognizable variation on Poe's eighteenth-century models in which visitors from exotic lands visit and evaluate modern civilization, but allowing the mummy to give a swift kick to his resuscitator's groin is slapstick business borrowed from the farcical theatre and the practical jokes of the frontier humorists.

3

Clearly the mordant purposefulness of satire is not the only impulse behind Poe's comedy. As one critic recently observed, Poe 'sometimes simply enjoyed being silly or foolish or playful'. He signals his fondness for such generic humour by constructing his own Joe Miller jest book—'Autography', a series of character readings based on the signatures of well-known figures. Compared to the solid presence of such signatures as Washington Irving, J. Q. Adams, and W. E. Channing, the indefatigable collector of autographs himself has no stable identity ('the Miller family are indigenous every where, and have little connection with either time or place'); he appears successively as Joseph A. Miller, Joseph B. Miller, Joseph C. Miller and so on, alphabetically. This is the Poe who rarely resists the opportunity to pun, even in the most puerile way, or to exploit the language and situations of specialized groups. The names of the trio of literary fakes in 'The Literary Life of Thingum Bob, Esq. '—Mrs. Fibalittle, Mrs. Squibalittle, and Mademoiselle Cribalittle—are one device that makes this example of coterie humour, a breezy attack on the inflated reputations of Poe's rivals, available to the ordinary reader. Another example, 'X-ing a Paragrab', is only an extended visual joke in which a compositor substitutes an *x* for each use of *o* because in the rivalry between two newspaper editors the entire *o* font has been stolen.

In some of his reviews, too, Poe could be fresh and funny. If the work of those writers he considered his serious competition brought out his slasher instincts, he was considerably more genial in exposing Indian epics, prairie sagas, forest romances, and other dismal works written as patriotic responses to the numerous calls for a native American literature. It may be that even in such uncomplicated sallies Poe struck his contemporaries as something of an eccentric. The editor of the *Broadway Journal* confided to James Russell Lowell that he thought Poe had 'an inconceivably extravagant idea of his own humor'.[7] And the year after the writer's death, one reviewer of Griswold's edition of Poe's *Works* declared the humorous pieces unfunny; like his other stuff they were 'pure *grotesque*', resembling only fantastic aperies,—the grimaces of some unknown species of goblin monkey, twistings and quaint gesticulations which we cannot understand at all. It is too far removed from fleshly sympathies to excite the nerves of laughter.[8]

In an 1836 review of *Georgia Scenes*, a book not at all removed from 'fleshly sympathies', Poe would seem to agree with those who thought him deficient in humour; his high praise suggests that only an extraordinary example of somebody else's 'nerves of laughter' could excite his own. Poe admires the accuracy of A. B. Longstreet's depiction of 'Scenes, Characters, Incidents, &C, in the First Half Century of the Republic' even as he succumbs to its primary appeal: 'Seldom—perhaps never in our lives—have we laughed as immoderately over any book as over the one before us.' He admits the anomalous effect on him:

If these *scenes* have produced such effects upon *our* cachinnatory nerves—upon *us* who are not 'of the merry mood', and, moreover, have not been unused to the perusal of somewhat similar things—we are at no loss to imagine what a hubbub they would occasion in the uninitiated regions of Cockaigne.[9]

Poe's response is noteworthy for several reasons. Most obviously it shows the magazinist at his competitive best; Poe sees the potential impact of frontier American humour on a British periodical audience, while simultaneously discounting its novelty to American readers. But more significant than Poe's alertness to the literary marketplace is what the statement reveals of his curious relationship to the mode itself. His enthusiasm for a métier that would seem to be so alien to his own is specifically centred on those aspects that dramatize that difference: both social accuracy and humour.

Poe finds 'joint humor and verisimilitude' in 'The Horse-Swap'. 'The Fight', though it dramatically focuses on the 'horrible and disgusting details of southern barbarity', is nevertheless worthy for the 'vivid truth to nature' of its characters. Such experiences, he asserts, are 'to be found sparsely in Georgia, Mississippi and Louisiana, and very plentifully in our more remote settlements and territories'. With 'The Gander Pulling', he assumes an insider's stance and recreates for the novice reader the rules and circumstances of this 'unprincipled barbarity not infrequently practised in the South and West'. And he praises 'The Shooting Match' for its portraiture of 'the manners of our South-Western peasantry'.

Like many of the southwestern humorists, Longstreet professed his allegiance to social history more fervently than his desire to make readers laugh; sometimes explicit in their aims, sometimes not, these authors wrote from the assumption that the people, customs, and language of the newly settled backwoods should be memorialized before they disappeared. Poe's own literary interest was of course not in verifiable American history and geography but in highly stylized art in which arcane figures moved melodramatically across synthetic landscapes and interiors. And despite a lifelong fascination with the southwestern frontier and the demotic style with which its literature was associated, Poe's own occasional efforts could never be confused with those of William Gilmore Simms; his most notorious attempt to create a dialectal character, Jupiter in 'The Gold-Bug', is neither funny nor accurate. Yet we have no reason to doubt the excitement with which Poe entered into the spirit of *Georgia Scenes*—partly, I suspect, because Longstreet's sketches confirmed the popular image of life in the backwoods while at the same time it was depicted from a perspective that was genteel, sophisticated, spectatorial. In effect Poe judges the book from the same point of view as the author's; there is no confusion of author and subject, no equating the genteel narrators with the barbarians they delineated with such verve. The Hall and Baldwin personas of *Georgia Scenes*, like many pseudonymous raconteurs in the southwestern sketches, are too serenely confident of their superiority to the raucous goings-on of 'our South-Western peasantry' ever to be more than bemused.

Georgia Scenes was the only volume of what we now call southwestern humour that Poe formally reviewed. He gives no further hint of the 'somewhat similar things' that in 1836 he is 'not unused to', since in the retrospect of literary history Longstreet was the first in a long line of amateur writers who were 'importuned' by friends to collect the sketches they had previously allowed to be published in regional newspapers. But uncollected sketches, amusing 'communications' or 'correspondence' from the hinterland, would have been familiar fare because of the exchange system in which scissors was nearly as important as a press; and the figure of the backwoodsman as both hero and oral comedian, symbolized by David Crockett in his varied avatars on the popular stage and in the Crockett *Almanacs*, was culturally unavoidable in the 1830s.[10]

At one point in his review of *Georgia Scenes* Poe praises its author's penetrating understanding of 'that class of south-western mammalia who come under the generic appellation of "savagerous wild cats" '. With the possible exception of Billy and Bob, the village stallions of 'The Fight', there are no figures in Longstreet that could justly be described as 'savagerous wild cats', but Poe is responding to the most celebrated literary representation of the Old Southwest even when it is but faintly represented: the frontiersman as half-horse-half-alligator, made famous by the actual Colonel Crockett and his theatrical brother, Nimrod Wildfire, in Paulding's popular *Lion of the West*. Poe uses one of the colonel's more celebrated feats—grinning a squirrel from a tree—as a calculated comparison in his attack on Theodore Fay's *Norman Leslie*. When he discovers that the smile of the handsome lover reduces the heroine to a swoon, Poe exclaims:

> Alas! Mr. Davy Crockett,—Mr. Davy Crockett, alas!—thou art beaten hollow—thou art defunct, and undone! thou hast indeed succeeded in grinning a squirrel from a tree, but it surpassed even thine extraordinary abilities to smile a lady into a fainting fit![11]

For all their transformations, Poe would have recognized in *Georgia Scenes* his own literary ancestors, Addison and Irving, and the evolution of its flexible genre, the sketch, from the more stable forms, the 'character' and the essay. Though he admires the rendering of the bluff fighters, he also likes the scene-stealers at the edges of the main event—the squires and dirt-eaters who are emotionally refreshed by violence; and he is particularly fond of Longstreet's characterization of the nags in 'The Horse-Swap'. As he knew from his own practice, humans, animals and creatures in between are all possible for the gifted writer. Those sketches that Poe singles out for appreciation are generally those that we think of highly today—those reflecting a masculine world of trading, joking, and fighting—but there is enough of Irving in Poe to draw him to some of the gentler pieces in which Longstreet delineates the awkwardness of human intercourse.

Poe explicitly perceives the presence of Addison in 'The Ball', an account of a soirée in the backwoods; and while admitting that 'The Song' is a 'burlesque somewhat overdone', he nevertheless quotes a passage from the broadly conceived satire of French and Italian vocal music, a fashion that had penetrated even to Georgia. Miss Aurelia Emma Theodosia Crump, with an eye to the gentlemen in the room, is readily persuaded, first, to play the piano piece she has learned from 'Seignor Buzzifussi', then to sing a song she has been taught by 'Madam Piggisqueaki, who was a pupil of Ma'm'selle Crokifroggietta'. For a writer who unfailingly succumbed to such names as Mr. Moneypenny, Mr. Touch-and-go Bullet-head, and the Arch Duchess Ana-Pest, Poe would have understood this kind of occasional indulgence in *Georgia Scenes*. But Longstreet and his fellow frontier humorists in fact rarely allowed themselves to invest as heavily as Poe in such numbing satiric conventions. The names that fill their stories are pungent and direct—and, in view of the actual demography of the yeoman settlers they used as their subjects, plausible as well as appropriate. To make names resonant and connotative is to keep within the reasonable boundaries of realistic reportage; to extend their function to the allegorical, for all its comic possibilities, threatens the verisimilitude these authors used as their excuse for writing in the first place. Hence the suggestiveness of Sut Lovingood and Ovid Bolus and Ransy Sniffle. Rance Bore-'em and Mr. Bobolink are among those at the very upper limits of usefulness. More common—and more removed from the *Spectator* tradition— are the bluntly felicitous Jim Doggett, Daddy Biggs, Mike Hooter, Simon Suggs, Ham Rachel, Squire Loggins, Brother Crump.

The aptness of names used by the southwestern humorists for their own pseudonyms as well as their characters ('Sugar-tail', 'The Turkey Runner', 'Solitaire') required a skill equal to the kind of comic allegorizing practised by Poe. The difference lay in Poe's professionalism, his commitment to the tradition of high art. One aspect of his genius was that he could address himself with competence and often brilliance to almost every kind of prose—philosophical inquiry, narratives of exploration and adventure, tales of mystery, gothic romances, reveries, meditations, critical theories, scientific expositions, folktales, journalistic scoops—and with breath-taking reversals, mocking his own practice and his highly trumpeted principles of literary order, transform them all into comic pieces. The Poe who loved to solve riddles, puzzles, and cryptograms was also the Poe who loved to play hoaxes. He found useful comic forms that aped reason, order, ratiocination, logic, and those that celebrated energy, indeterminacy, dream, incongruity—forms of imagination as free of stable anchors as Hans Phaall's balloon fashioned of dirty foolscap. The most comprehensive genre for Poe's humour, the only container capacious enough to hold its divergent impulses, is the old Irvingesque *salmagundi*, or the newer *ollo podrida* of Willis Gaylord Clark—incongruous edibles metamorphosed into a literary stew, a miscellany.

But, interestingly, for all their variety and profusion, his forms, like the *salmagundi* itself, are always urban exercises, extensions or reversals of patterns out of the same models of high art that Poe always acknowledged. Partly because of his particular temperament and partly because of his sustaining commitment to literary tradition, Poe could go no further than appreciate the rural-backwoods-village matter on which the comic forms of the southwestern humorists were based. The very profession of amateurism instantly provided these writers the maximum latitude for divergence from the patterns of traditional art. Most of them move beyond the conventional satire of their literary sources into more fluid, open-ended, and ill-defined modes, but their common thread is the non-urban character. Even as amateurs, these authors were creating their own *olla podrida*, responding to the genially accommodating editors of dozens of newspapers in the Mississippi valley. The best in the Old Southwest—the St. Louis *Reveille* and the New Orleans *Picayune*—competed with smaller and more local papers to make theirs the most lively purveyor of humorous anecdotes reflecting the tumultuous life of the region. And the very subtitle of *The Spirit of the Times*, 'A Chronicle of the Turf,

Agriculture, Field Sports, Literature, and the Stage', suggests something of the happy generic impurity of its characteristic pieces; by encouraging the variety of contributions and nourishing his disparate authors in the South and West, William T. Porter fashioned his New York paper into the most famous outlet of non-genteel literature before the Civil War.

Just as backwoods life was always viewed by urbanites as colourful but distasteful, so the literature that mirrored it came to be regarded as amusing but unrespectable—reading matter, like off-colour jokes, fit only for all-male audiences. The sketch's very appearance on the page—dialectal accounts of horse-swaps, gander-pullings, courtings, fights, and practical jokes—confirmed eastern readers in their notion about actual life in the frontier settlements. The sketches are filled with physical embarrassments—the loss of trousers and petticoats, cruel punishment in which eyes, noses, cheeks, and buttocks suffer prominently, chases by bears and panthers in which the human is forced into inglorious postures of escape. They are also marked by verbal extravagance—self-proclaimed exceptional men identified by their bravado of speech if seldom of actual deed, vernacular yarn-spinners whose style is as explosive and grotesque as the substance of their tales. Though Poe never knew first-hand the kind of life that nourished such vernacular literature, he had witnessed some of the 'barbarities' associated with the lower South at the University of Virginia, where biting and gouging were almost as common as the more genteel *code duello*.

4

Good taste is a frequent topic in Poe's criticism, especially when a particularly wretched writer violates it, but in his review of *Georgia Scenes* the infamous 'tomahawk' slasher is indulgent and admiring of the repeated violations. Perennially soft on southerners, Poe felt obliged to encourage any sign of genuine literary activity, and he accepted the native Georgian's claim for sociological accuracy. More importantly, however, Poe is drawn to *Georgia Scenes* because he finds reflected in its picture of human life his own fears about the fragility of man and society. The world of southwestern humour is just as frightening, just as tentative, as the urban one that Poe depicts in most of his humorous pieces. Longstreet features either colourful characters operating within a context of economic opportunism in the only kind of relationships available— bargains, trades, swindles, and impersonations the better to carry them off—or commonplace characters caught in the colourful circumstances of their makeshift society—games, jokes, athletic and sporting contests, camp meetings, court- ings, militia exercises, court cases. In all instances the organized social structure is wobbly, its loyalties expedient, its institu- tions usurped by anarchic individualism.

For a man of Poe's temperament the buoyant chaos of the backwoods would be only an uncultivated version of his own dark vision. His only tale set in a frontier community, 'Thou Art the Man', is a grimmer reading of frontier life than even that of Johnson Jones Hooper, but it suggests the same weak coherence of social and familial life. Its hero, a cross between a vernacular Dupin and a frontier practical joker, never gives a second thought to his dubious methods for bringing a murderer to justice; the logic of the story says that manipulating human putridity is what even good men must do, since that is what all men are. 'Thou Art the Man' is another of Poe's hoaxes, and the moral end for which it is effected cannot disguise the grim personal triumph of the narrator. The urban equivalent of the practical joke, the hoax is an act of revenge that forces public acknowledgement of the perpetrator's superiority. Like the practical joke, it is an act of aggression disguised as fun, the point of which is the naming of the 'best man'.

In view of Poe's great reputation for his charming of older women, it may not do to question too closely the psychic motivation behind his little squib in the Philadelphia *Public Ledger*:

> If there be an old, infirm lady in the omnibus, do not move your feet as she endeavors to pass, but if you well nigh trip her up, it will be serviceable in reminding her of her declining years and strength, and thus help to reconcile her with fate.[12]

If here Poe summons a mock moral for his aggression, he sometimes drops even that. The virtue of 'The Business Man', a first-person account of how a genial small-time entrepreneur stays afloat in the city, is its straightforward assumption that the con-man mentality is the moral norm; the humour arises from the contrast between the narrator's insistence on the rigour of his methods and the only limited and temporary success of his trivial schemes. The norm is more explicit in a companion piece, 'Diddling Considered as One of the Exact Sciences', in which the cool narrator takes pleasure in analysing the true swindle. He begins with a definition—'Man is an animal that diddles, and there is *no* animal that diddles *but* man'—before listing nine requirements: minuteness (when a diddler is tempted into ambitious speculations he becomes a financier), interest ('his pocket—and yours'), perseverance, ingenuity ('He invents and circumvents'), audacity, nonchalance, originality, and grin. The final requirement, the seal of the transaction, is perhaps the most telling; since material gain in the tricks he catalogues is so modest, only internal satisfaction, the fattened ego, makes the game worth while.

If 'The Man of the Crowd' is one side of Poe's urban vision, the existential bleakness of man who has no identity except in the impersonal company of sidewalk humanity, 'Diddling' is the other, a lighter, cynical view that celebrates some of the very qualities that made Jackson-era Americans so distinctive. There are no large schemes in the southwestern sketches, either. When frontier man diddles, it may be for a horse (either one with an incurable saddle sore or one that is blind), for a free champagne-and-oyster supper, or for miscellaneous cash collected in a hat at a camp meeting. When the frontier diddler is tempted into 'magnificent speculations' be becomes a banker or a land-shark, and such real predators are never the direct subject of southwest humour.

One of the implications of the jokes, con games, fights, and other contests that recur in frontier humour is that the backwoods necessarily nourishes a coarseness of sensibility in its denizens. The formal correspondence in the sketch is rhetorical: the necessity for the well-defined, sharply differentiated narrator to distance himself from the jokesters and victims who manifest cultural coarseness even as they justify the very existence of the sketch. Poe says the author of *Georgia Scenes* adopts the two narrators, Hall and Baldwin, because he wants his identity kept secret; but the rigorous separation of Longstreet and his subject is also a measure not merely of social finickiness but of moral uneasiness—the sincere expression of a man of decent instincts and humane learning sporadically appalled by the brutality he generally finds amusing.

In his comic pieces Poe the professional took greater risks than Longstreet the amateur, not only because his invention was richer but also because the artistic control of his chosen materials was less self-conscious. Unlike that of the south-western humorists, Poe's work betrays no anxiety about authorship or about the pragmatic interchangeability of fact and fiction. Despite his touchy pride in the way he regarded himself as a southern gentleman—Boston is made to suffer because he sees it as a kind of inadvertent birthplace—Poe never worries that his fictional 'I' might sully the good name of Edgar A. Poe. That first-person narrator is variously raconteur, friend, sleuth, madman, hoaxer, cynic, dreamer. His comic narrators range from the cynical free spirit who lays down the rules for 'Diddling' to the foggy innocent of 'The System of Doctor Tarr and Professor Fether' who, when faced with a bizarre spectacle, proudly maintains 'the *nil admirari*' and for his credulity gets a thorough beating. His fondness for the hoax, as Edward Davidson suspects,[13] may express Poe's deep-seated resentment against a world that denied him the recognition and privileges that a Virginian and a genius had every right to expect, but his commitment to art was at least as strong as his theoretical hurt. The very profusion of fictional voices testifies to the aesthetic freedom of even a displaced gentleman.

Though the southwestern writers shared Poe's political sympathies for southern whiggery, their gentlemanly narrators never quite enjoy a freedom of tonal range and stylistic variety. Longstreet, Baldwin, Hooper, and most of the other humorists make no attitudinal concessions to their authority over the raucous and energizing life they describe. Their narrators realize that their voices are restrained, conventional, even anaemic compared to those of the tricksters, victims, and buffoons; but however attractively chaotic and anarchic the life they describe, the authorial control of the first-person observer is jealously guarded. Much of our interest in the frontier sketches lies in the interplay between styles, the pervasive tension between power and form. The author finds himself vacillating, pulled to the energy and open-ended freshness of his materials and pulled back to his innate sense of order; his emotional and aesthetic need is to contain as well as exploit an incoherent and plosive vitality. The shaping impulse is always towards the conventional forms that will celebrate him as well as his subject. What the sketches demonstrate is that however genial and amateurish these scribes regarded themselves, the power lay ultimately not in the robust figures cutting vernacular rusties all over the landscape, but in themselves; the hand of power is the hand that *composes*.

These writers achieve a certain distinction, however, by virtue of their very conservatism. The romantic glorification of the frontiersman by the 1820s did not wholly supplant the lingering eighteenth-century fears that the westering process necessarily meant the deterioration of civilized man. For both Poe and the southwestern authors, however, the philosophical basis of those fears was little more than a cultural predisposition, a tendency to regard the frontier spectacle with tolerant bemusement. The physical distance separating him and the frontier South, as well as an aesthetic bias that generally excluded its materials, meant that Poe could matter-of-factly accept the stereotype of the 'savagerous wild cats' that he professed to find in *Georgia Scenes*.

Because of their proximity to the sources of their art, the southwestern writers were open to a wider perspective. In their sketches an artless honesty prevails over both social distaste and aesthetic convention. It was their mission, they reasoned, to render the flavour of a life about which they were at best ambivalent, and the modest and familiar frame became a transparency allowing full disclosure. They knew at first hand, for example, the assumptions behind those self-celebrators who dismissed the easterner's valuation of them, who indeed reversed the terms of the discourse. In habituating themselves to their backwoods environment they actually *ascended* the scale of being. By first acknowledging the worthiness of beast as natural combatant and then by metaphorical fusion of man and animal (wild cat, bear, alligator, snapping turtle), usually in shrewd combinations, the frontiersman elevated himself over such ordinary humans as effete easterners and British travellers. Their amphibian chroniclers—whiggish outsiders drawn to and challenged by democratic natives—readily accepted the buckskin-clad backwoodsmen as iconographic reminders of that logic while temperamentally resisting the obvious power inherent in it.

If barbarism is the defining rubric of man-as-animal in the comic vision of the southwestern writers, inanimateness is that of man-as-machine in the comic vision of Poe. One is characterized by· an excess of accretion, the other an excess of diminution; both derive their strength from a conservative orientation that bravely posits order and harmony as an ideal for civilized man. Aggressive deviation from that ideal produces in both frontier and urban versions a humour flowing from the principle of disharmony, incongruity, extravagance, and disproportion. Common to both is a central concern, the indeterminacy of identity. If the 'snap' games for fleecing the unwary are the most interesting social interactions on the frontier, the ritualized fights are the most dramatic; in both cases, equivocal identity lies at the heart of the encounter. In marginal society methods of personal accreditation are as shaky as they are protean; the most stable referents are style and character, and because both are highly prized both are susceptible of profitable counterfeiting. The more civilized violence in Poe's comic fiction and the more cultured rationalism of his street-wise con-men cannot disguise the gloomy fact that urban society for Poe is in fact as marginal as the flush-times environment along the frontier. His masquerades and impersonations are in fact more tainted by evil than the rustic ones in 'barbaric' Georgia and Alabama. Like that of his fellow whigs in the Southwest, his comic world offers not merely a satiric model of democratic society but a vision of man; only in Poe, however, is the mordancy so bitter.

The southwestern writers managed to convince readers that *actual life* on the frontier, however vital *per se* and however necessary to the building of the nation, was cacophonous, extreme, inappropriate—and deserving of laughter on that account. Their modest literary representations, even when potentially shocking to a genteel audience, were consequently based on reader expectations, as we see in Poe's review of *Georgia Scenes*. And unlike the comedic structures of the southwestern writers, which in effect displace serious anxieties about personal identity, social hierarchy, economic stability, and accurate perception, Poe's underscore such anxieties. His humorous fictions never dissolve real worries in laughter but rather force the reader to face them on the author's own bleak terms. Poe revivifies human uncertainties by reintroducing the inherent savagery beneath the bland appearances of ordinary life.

Even in his own day Poe's humour asked readers to imagine more deeply than they were normally willing to do. To perceive the nature of man and society through Poesque spectacles was to see sanity in madness, the lifeless in the breathing, the corpse in the living body, the joker in the ordered universe—and to think of these paradoxes as funny.

For a writer who described himself as 'not of the merry mood', Poe produced a remarkable amount of 'unserious' fiction. As Mabbott's edition of the prose fiction shows, in terms of sheer bulk nearly half is overtly comic; and G. R. Thompson has argued persuasively that even the gothic fiction that we normally read as straight contains more than trace elements of the comic. In the last decade scholars have unearthed a writer of such monumental duplicity that the dominant image of Poe the exploiter of terror and sensation may eventually be replaced by that of the witty self-parodist and burlesque comedian.[14] How 'merry' his comic prose may be is another question, of course. Certainly the social reality in 'Doctor Tarr and Professor Fether' and 'Loss of Breath' is as imaginatively skewed as that in 'Berenice' and 'The Black Cat'—the laugher they generate is laced with mockery. Compared to Poe's outrageous liberties with social reality, those of Longstreet and his followers must have been received as scarcely more literary than the travel letter, the emigrants' guide, and the other 'communications' from the hinterland.

NOTES

1. *Collected Works of Edgar Allan Poe*, ed. Thomas Ollive Mabbott (Cambridge: Harvard University Press, 1978), III, 1099. All quotations from the prose fiction come from this edition.
2. *The Complete Works of Edgar Allan Poe*, ed. James A. Harrison (New York: Crowell, 1902; rep. New York: A.M.S. Press, 1965), IX, 138, 126. All quotations from reviews and criticism come from this edition.
3. Stephen L. Mooney, 'The Comic in Poe's Fiction', *American Literature* 33 (January 1962), 433.
4. *Works*, II, 83.
5. Allen Tate, 'Our Cousin, Mr. Poe', *Partisan Review* 16 (December 1949), 1209.
6. James's widely quoted remark on Poe's appeal to 'primitive' tastes appears in *French Poets and Novelists* (London: Macmillan, 1893), p. 60; Eliot, *From Poe to Valéry* (New York: Harcourt, Brace, 1948), p. 19.
7. Quoted in Mabbott, *Works*, II, xx.
8. Quoted in Donald B. Stauffer, *The Merry Mood: Poe's Uses of Humor* (Baltimore: Enoch Pratt Free Library, 1982), pp. 3–4.
9. *Southern Literary Messenger*, II (March 1836), 287. Harrison in his edition misprints the phrase 'have not been unused to' as 'have not been used to'. G. R. Thompson in his Library of America volume, *Edgar Allan Poe: Essays and Reviews* (New York: Literary Classics of the United States, 1984), p. 778, corrects the misprint.
10. For a survey of the reception of Crockett as hero and popular myth see Richard Boyd Hauck, *Crockett: A Bio-Bibliography* (Westport, CN: Greenwood Press, 1982).
11. Harrison, *Works*, VIII, 53.
12. *Works*, III, 1091.
13. Edward H. Davidson, *Poe: A Critical Study* (Cambridge: Harvard University Press, 1957), pp. 139–40, 210–11.
14. G. R. Thompson, 'Poe and "Romantic Irony"', in Richard P. Veler, *Papers on Poe: Essays in Honor of John Ward Ostrom* (Springfield, OH: Chantry Music Press, 1972), p. 30. A fuller treatment is Thompson's *Poe's Fiction: Romantic Irony in the Gothic Tales* (Madison: University of Wisconsin Press, 1973). For the 'duplicitous' Poe see the collected essays in Dennis E. Eddings (ed.), *The Naiad Voice: Essays on Poe's Satiric Hoaxing* (Port Washington, NY: Associated Faculty Press, 1983). Two of the finest studies are Terence Martin, 'The Imagination at Play: Edgar Allan Poe', *Kenyon Review* 28 (March 1966), 194–209; and Constance Rourke, *American Humor: A Study of the National Character* (New York: Harcourt, Brace, 1931), *passim* for both Poe and the Southwestern Humorists. See also Donald Weeks, 'The Humour of Edgar Allan Poe', *Maatstaf* 26, ii (November 1978), 75–89.

5

Was the Chevalier Left-handed? Poe's Dupin Stories

by ROBERT GIDDINGS

1

Edgar Allan Poe prefaces 'The Murders in the Rue Morgue' with the following sentence from Sir Thomas Browne: 'What song the Syrens sang, or what name Achilles assumed when he hid himself among women, although puzzling questions are not beyond *all conjecture*.'[1] The emphasis on *all conjecture* is significant, and the whole quotation is an apposite text for the Dupin stories. It signals not only the leading theme of these fictions—that conjecture in the hands of an expert may be a key which unlocks the most baffling mysteries—but also evokes associations with the author of *Pseudodoxia Epidemica* (1646) and *Hydriotaphia, Urn-Burial* (1658).

Browne's first volume was a demolition of the silly things which thousands of people believed—vulgar errors, travellers' tales, superstitions, fabulous animals, false opinions, common fallacies, pious myths, hoaxes, hexes and a gallimaufry of widely credited nonsense—while the second was a treatise on human mortality and ancient burial customs. Sir Thomas Browne was a successful and distinguished physician but also an eclectic scholar whose intellect was drawn as to the magnetic North towards all that was mysterious, arcane, the unthinkable and the semi-morbid. Browne thrived on paradox. He was intoxicated by unanswerable questions, fascinated by hieroglyphs, puzzles, cryptograms and the riddles of antiquity. But behind all his energetic ratiocination there was a rockbed of firm belief that a simple, clear and direct solution exists for each and every one of the mysteries we turn our minds to, could we but see it. His *Garden of Cyrus* (1658), for example, is a study of the quincunx and the appearance of the number five in a wide variety of phenomena; he believed that five was one of the mysterious numbers which held the universe together, that it pervades all the horticulture of antiquity and recurs throughout all plant life and the figurations of animals.

The emphasis on *all conjecture* in the sentence is Poe's, but it draws attention to the ineluctable seduction of the curious-minded by seemingly imponderable questions. Sir Thomas Browne himself is here echoing Suetonius, who recorded that Tiberius was devoted to Greek and Latin literature, and had a particular bent for mythology:

> ... and carried his researches in it to such a ridiculous point that he would test professors of Greek literature—whose society ... he cultivated above all others—by asking them questions like: 'Who was Hecuba's mother?'—'What name did Achilles assume when he disguised himself as a girl at the court of King Lycomedes?'—'What song did the Sirens sing?'[2]

Suetonius is celebrated for his gift of supplying curious biographical details, and he records of Tiberius that he was strong and heavily built and of more than average height:

> His shoulders and chest were broad, and his body perfectly proportioned from top to toe. His left hand was more agile than the right, and so strong that he could poke a finger through a sound, newly-plucked apple or into the skull of a boy or young man.[3]

The combination of left-handedness and the interrogation of the mysteries of the world is both striking and to the point.

It urges us further in our enquiries about the nature of Edgar Allan Poe in so far as it is revealed in the Dupin stories, further than the breezy dismissal of Poe's juvenile interests so famously made by his fellow American, T. S. Eliot. In *The Sacred Wood: Essays on Poetry and Criticism* (1920) Eliot writes:

> That Poe had a powerful intellect is undeniable: but it seems to me the intellect of a highly gifted young person before puberty. The forms which his lively curiosity takes are those in which a pre-adolescent mentality delights: wonders of nature and of mechanics and of the supernatural, cryptograms and cyphers, puzzles and labyrinths, mechanical chessplayers and wild flights of speculation.[4]

This has been a highly influential description of Poe's mind, and as for his art, Eliot did not leave it there. For in his essay 'Wilkie Collins and Dickens' (1927) he took occasion to comment on Edgar Allan Poe's contribution to the 'detective story' as a *genre*:

> The detective story, as created by Poe, is something as specialized and as intellectual as a chess problem; whereas the best English detective fiction has relied less on the beauty of the mathematical problem and much more on the intangible human element. In detective fiction England probably excels other countries; but in a genre invented by Collins and not by Poe. . . .[5]

But a careful reading of 'The Murders in the Rue Morgue', 'The Purloined Letter' and 'The Mystery of Marie Roget' can demonstrate quickly enough that Poe was engaged in far more than simply unravelling puzzles, cryptograms and labyrinths, and that these stories are steeped in an intangible human element. The fascination with questions which need answers, with riddles and mysteries—the very basis of Poe's Dupin stories—is never to be underrated. Mankind has a record of obsession with all manner of 'mystery', from the high-flown to the most humble. It is a fascination which appears fundamental in human narrative.[6]

Ancient examples of 'mystery' such as the story of Oedipus, thus continue to hold our interest and, it is claimed, hold essential clues to the explanation of human behaviour.[7] More modern examples, not least Shakespeare's *Hamlet*, are full of similar probes and attempts at detection. It is this irreducible human curiosity which unites Oedipus, Hamlet and Dupin, and places Poe's Chevalier in company to which Eliot (at least) thought he was scarcely suited.

When Oedipus solves the riddle of the Sphinx, he saves Thebes from a dreadful tyranny long endured. When Thebes is afflicted by a terrible plague, he attempts to seek out the cause, only to discover that Thebes is being punished for the crime of its King—unknowingly Oedipus has killed his father and married his mother. In Sophocles' drama the Chorus assure us that none can be called happy until that day arrives when we carry our happiness with us down into the grave in peace.[8] It is my guess that the tragedy of Oedipus fascinates us not because of its gloomy moral precepts, but because it involves the unravelling of a great mystery. Human beings have always loved riddles,[9] and Sophocles' great tragedy opens at the moment when King Oedipus, who seems so all-powerful and so secure, is asked the question: why is this happening? He is bound to seek the cause of the distress endured by Thebes in order to bring it to an end. The unravelling of this mystery constitutes the tragedy of Oedipus.

Hamlet further demonstrates how fascinating a really complex mystery can be. Sadly familiarity and the distortions of post-romantic criticism have dampened the sense of mystery, focusing far too much attention on the 'psychology' of the Prince of Denmark, but if we read the play properly we can see that essentially it is constructed on the basis of a mystery (the death of Hamlet's father in strange circumstances), a hypothesis which would explain the mystery (the revelations of the Ghost), and the testing of the hypothesis (the play scene and all which follows from it). This will all be plain enough if we consider *Hamlet* as a tragic drama, in terms of dramatic action, rather than in the light of a Coleridgean/Bradleyan character study of Hamlet himself. As the tragedy unfolds we learn, as Hamlet learns, that God did not abandon Creation after the Fall, that Providence is there to help good to triumph over evil, offering opportunities through the agency of Fortune. Man must exercise judgement, his right under Free Will, to help the workings of Providence. Horatio, always prosaic and down-to-earth, urges Hamlet not to go through with the duel with Laertes if he has any misgivings. Hamlet answers:

> Not a whit, we defy augury: there is a special providence in the fall of a sparrow. If it be now, 'tis not to come; if it be not to come,

91

it will be now; if it be not now, yet it will come—the readiness is
all. Since no man owes of aught he leaves, what is't to leave
betimes? Let be.[10]

Hamlet's resigned 'Let be' answers his previous 'To be, or not
to be'. He now knows that provided he exercises his judgement,
that faculty in which man is superior to the beasts, and is ready
to choose a course of action when Fortune offers it, he may trust
to divine Providence, which is omnipresent to oversee the will of
Almighty God. At the end of *Hamlet* Providence has prevailed—
evil has been exposed and punished, social order has been
restored, and those who nobly died shall rest in peace. The
riddle, the mystery and the numerous questions posed have all
been answered.

2

Oedipus, Hamlet and Dupin each epitomize an ideological
moment. Oedipus is quintessentially Hellenic. Hamlet truly
Elizabethan. Dupin is very American, despite his Parisian
location, or it may well be, *because of it*. In the Hellenic
conception of the tragic, man was pitted against the remorse-
less and capricious gods. Tragedy here had little to do with
reward or retribution; it was concerned—on the contrary—
with the spectacle of man pitted against an unreasonable
destiny which destroyed him. As George Steiner has written:

> the *Iliad* is the primer of tragic art. In it are set forth the motifs
> and images around which the sense of the tragic has crystallized
> . . . the shortness of heroic life, the exposure of man to the
> murderousness and caprice of the inhuman, the fall of the
> City. . . . the fall of Troy is the first great metaphor of
> tragedy. . . . Fate is given a name, and the elements are shown
> in the frivolous and reassuring mask of the gods. But mythology
> is only a fable to help us endure. The Homeric warrior knows
> that he can neither comprehend nor master the workings of
> destiny. . . . Call for justice or explanation, and the sea will
> thunder back with its mute clamour. Men's accounts with the
> gods do not balance.[11]

Hamlet enshrines the Elizabethan world-view. It portrays
man created in the form of an angel, but fallen from the state
of grace. Grace is always attainable through the intervention

of the Saviour. Providence is there to see that good triumphs over evil. The tragic sense is presented in the manner in which men must endure in the context of the resolution of tragic circumstance. In Shakespeare's world man is not alone in his predicament. The hand of God may reach out to help him, can he but see it. We are not as flies to wanton boys, who kill us for their sport; but we must endure our going hence, even as our coming hither. This is what such fellows as Hamlet should do, crawling between earth and heaven.

The basic assumptions on which the world of Dupin is constructed are quite different, and different in fundamental and revealing ways. In moving from the world view of the Oedipus dramas to *Hamlet* we shift from a conception of humanity as sport for the gods, to that of a benevolent and loving creator who seeks to help mankind save itself and regain a state of grace, offering his creatures providential warnings and stimulation to their divine reason so that they might seek solutions by exercising judgement. On 6 April 1580 there was an earthquake sensed quite strongly in England. The Queen and her council interpreted this as a sign that divine punishment was at hand for the nation's sins. A catalogue of fast days and prayers, including special prayers to be recited by the heads of households when families retired to bed, was proclaimed.[12] The defeat of the Spanish armada would seem to the Elizabethans fully to justify the measures prescribed after such portentous warnings.

The world of Dupin, significantly located by Poe in Paris, the centre of the Enlightenment, is one based on the divinity of human reason. Dupin solves mysteries in his own room. He works at night. He bases his solutions on evidence he reads in newspapers. His activities personify the free play of individual intellect. It is important to note that the narrator first meets him in a library; books are a powerful emblem of human knowledge. Dupin manifests that *hubris* which sadly is such a part of the legacy of the scientific enlightenment[13] and which Europeans take to be such a typical quality of modern North Americans. America itself was a product of the enlightenment, constructed, put together after the war with Britain in 1776, by human effort: it was not a nation organically developed

over the years in the course of various accidents of history. In
Anthony Burgess's words:

> When Europe, after millennia of war, rapine, slavery, famine,
> intolerance, had sunk to the level of a sewer, America became
> the golden dream, the Eden where innocence could be recovered
> . . . in America man could glow in an aura of natural goodness,
> driven along his shining path by divine reason. The Declaration
> of Independence itself is a monument to reason. Progress was
> possible, and the wrongs committed against the Indians, the
> wildlife, the land itself, could be explained away in terms of the
> rational control of the environment necessary for the building of
> a New Jerusalem.[14]

Dupin is the natural heir of that unmistakably Newtonian
confidence we find in such comments as that which Newton
wrote in a letter to Robert Hooke on 5 February 1675:

> If I have seen further than you and Descartes, it is by standing
> upon the shoulders of Giants. . . . I frame no hypotheses; for
> whatever is not deduced from the phenomena is to be called an
> hypothesis; and hypotheses, whether metaphysical or physical,
> whether of occult qualities or mechanical, have no place in
> experimental philosophy.[15]

Dupin's individualism is wholly American. He is also, be it
noted, a young man.

3

Writing in *The Atlantic Monthly* in December 1899 Hamilton
Wright Mabie asserted: 'Poe stands alone in our literature,
unrelated to his environment and detached from his time.'[15]
Lewis Mumford believed that Poe escaped into: 'a phan-
tasmal world which registers a complete divorce from his
environment'.[16] An examination of the character of C.
Auguste Dupin and the relationship between Poe-as-narrator
and the Chevalier Dupin will reveal that these opinions
require considerable qualification, if not rejection.

To begin with an absolutely basic condition—the means of
literary production and their effect on the nature of that which
is produced—Dupin is essentially a creature of the age of
print. The kind of narrative which gave us Dupin was only

possible in an age which had interiorized literacy. And the technology of paper manufacture, printing and transport had combined in creating an extended mass literacy, producing a new kind of narrative, which involves the temporal sequence of events, in which the situation at the end is subsequent to that which pertained at the beginning.[17] Economic and technical factors contributed considerably to the thought-processes which mark Dupin out as the first modern detective, the prototype of all those intellectual sleuths from Sherlock Holmes to Adam Dalgleish. The very ratiocination which is Dupin's hallmark, was also the product of a stage in the history of human culture, being, as it was, the effect of the impact of writing and printing on the way the human mind worked.[18] Walter Ong asks:

> Why is it that lengthy climactic plot comes into being only with writing, comes into being first in the drama, where there is no narrator, and does not make its way into lengthy narrative until more than two thousand years later with the novels of Jane Austen? Earlier so-called 'novels' were all more or less episodic. . . . The climactic linear plot reaches a plenary form in the detective story—relentlessly rising tension, exquisitely tidy discovery and reversal, perfectly resolved dénouement. The detective story is generally considered to have begun in 1841 with Edgar Allan Poe's *The Murders in the Rue Morgue*. . . .[19]

Walter Ong's discussion of the various answers to these questions is satisfactory at most levels, but leaves one or two important points unmade. He is surely correct in his interesting proposition that all lengthy narrative before the early 1800s was episodic, and that this was universally the case, and that no one had written a 'detective' story before 1841. Berkley Peabody's book *The Winged Word: A Study in the Technique of Ancient Greek Oral Composition as Seen Principally Through Hesiod's Works and Days* (1975) offers some useful pointers, and what he has to say about ancient Greek narrative song has a wide if not universal application, namely that there is a basic incompatibility between linear plot and oral memory, and what was communicated in ancient Greek epos drew its strengths from the remembered (often formulaic and traditional) stanzaic patterns, rather than in the singer's attempts individually to organize 'plot' in a particular way or fashion. In Peabody's words: 'A singer effects, not a transfer of his own intentions, but a conventional realization of traditional thoughts for his listeners, including himself.'[20]

The poet, the singer—call him what you will—did not directly convey to his audience a story-line, with characters, plot, situations, climax, etc. of his own imagining, but recalling, and embroidering as he recalls them, all the previous treatments of the same subject matter that he has ever heard, and the audience respond to his offering because their understanding, likewise, is conditioned hugely by what they have all heard and remembered before. The very word for this kind of performance—a rhapsody—means something stitched together.[21] The obvious parallels are to be found in modern popular culture, in the Westerns—say, of John Ford—where Ford draws on the situations, characters and iconography of all the Westerns he has seen, and the audience respond in large part by drawing on their collective experience of cinema Westerns.[22] The bard, singing epic material to the tribe, takes part in an act of public recollection or memory; he is in a situation which is not entirely under his own control. The resulting 'Work' is the final product of interaction between the singer, the tradition on which he draws, and the audience to whom he sings.

Literacy and print allow the 'author' to organize plot as never before, and to construct a sequence of events under his own conscious control. The 'text' is composed to be consumed by a distanced reader, often in solitude. Narrative develops tighter climactic structures:

> Print . . . mechanically as well as psychologically locked words into space and thereby established a firmer sense of closure than writing could. The print world gave birth to the novel, which eventually made the definitive break with episodic structure.[23]

The detective story is a fine example of the heavily structured plot, which builds up to a finely graded tension, climaxing in recognition, or explanation, or reversal or fortune, and in the dénouement of which all the fine details—clues, observations, pieces of evidence—are shown to be totally relevant. Such narrative was only possible in print. Print provided the immediacy of text in which the plot was presented. Print also plays another important part in the riveting success of Poe's Dupin tales; Poe obtained his basic material from the daily newspapers he read,[24] but also Dupin bases his investigations and hypotheses on evidence of cases that he reads in newspapers. He solves the mystery of the murders in the Rue Morgue by reading accounts of the crimes and the depositions of witnesses in the papers. Not only does this make the case much more of a 'closed-door' mystery, but it supports the credibility of the story. Newspapers are part of the daily and weekly ebb and flow of modern life, and having newspapers play such an important part in Dupin's expertise gives the story a contemporary *vraisemblance*. Even though the genius of C. Auguste Dupin is rare, eccentric and poetic, he clearly inhabits the same world as we do. In three important respects then, print technology influenced the very nature of these fictions: the technology created the means of literary production and distribution which Poe was able to exploit— 'The Murders in the Rue Morgue' appeared in *Graham's Magazine* in 1841, 'The Mystery of Marie Roget' was serialized in the *Ladies' Companion* in November and December 1842 and February 1843, and 'The Purloined Letter' appeared in *The Gift* in 1845—the very nature of the prose narrative itself, with its concentration on a sequence of events, accumulation of detail, unravelling of mysteries and the climax of dénouement— all this was made possible only by the impact of print on literacy, which meant that certain habits of reading become interiorized; and finally, the believable quality of the stories themselves, the manner in which Poe is able to insinuate the credibility of Dupin's genius, is the result of his being presented to us as a reader of newspapers.

4

Dupin is an epic character in so far as he epitomizes the spirit of his time and the character of his nation. He is very American, and very much a man of his period. The quoted passage at the opening of 'The Murders in the Rue Morgue', the story which introduces Dupin to us, is from Sir Thomas Browne's *Urn-Burial*, and associates Dupin immediately with

Achilles. His mental characteristics are given us as emphatically analytical, rational and reflective. But these qualities are harnessed to *usefulness*. This is a very American quality.[25] 'The Murders in the Rue Morgue' opens:

> The mental features discoursed of as analytical, are, in themselves, but little susceptible of analysis. We appreciate them only in their effects. We know of them . . . that they are always to their possessor . . . a source of the liveliest enjoyment. As the strong man exults in his physical ability . . . so glories the analyst in that moral activity which *disentangles* . . . . the higher powers of the reflective intellect are more decidedly and more usefully tasked by the unostentatious game of draughts than by all the elaborate frivolity of chess. In this latter, where the pieces have different and *bizarre* motions . . . what is only complex is mistaken (a not unusual error) for what is profound.[26]

Monsieur C. Auguste Dupin, though he may reside in Paris, presents some very American qualities. He is young, and though of good old family stock, the family fortunes have declined and he has to shift for himself in the world. He cares only for the basic necessities of life. His individualism shows itself in the way he abjures most social contacts. Although no less than Oedipus and Hamlet Dupin finds himself entangled in the resolution of mysteries, there are several important qualities which mark Dupin out as a new departure. Each of the three tales which feature Poe's analytic hero is unique unto itself, but there are some common features which are very important in qualifying the essence of Dupin, and establishing that there is much more to be yielded by examining them than simply demonstrable Freudianism.[27] One obvious difference is that Dupin is not personally involved in the problems he solves. They are not a matter of life and death to him. Nor does he set out—as Oedipus had—to solve a problem which affected the whole community. Nor, as was the case with Hamlet, does he wrestle with problems of kingship, succession, conscience, heaven and hell. The importance of the mysteries lies in the very fact that he is the one who solves them by exercising his particular gifts. This is one of the first points Poe makes about him.

The Dupin stories are studies of what Poe terms analytic

mental features. They are not susceptible to analysis themselves; he tells us this at the opening of the first one, 'The Murders in the Rue Morgue' (1841). We can only appreciate them in their effects. To those who possess them they are a source of 'the liveliest enjoyment'. They seem to consist in the ability to assemble all the known and verifiable factual elements of a puzzling situation, and then almost by a process of intuition infer a hypothesis from them, which explains that which is otherwise inexplicable. All three mysteries present a factual surface quality which seemingly cannot logically be explained.

In 'The Murders in the Rue Morgue' a young woman and her mother are foully done to death in a locked room, with the key inside the room. Who could have committed such a crime when there was no apparent means of entry or exit? 'The Mystery of Marie Roget' presents a murder case which baffles the Prefect G— of the Paris police; it seems an 'ordinary' murder and yet appears unsolvable. A young girl's body appears in the Seine. On the face of it, she had been violated and murdered by a gang of ruffians, who then disposed of her corpse in the river. But in the search for the gang, all the clues peter out. In the last Dupin story, 'The Purloined Letter', a vital document disappears. The police have every reason to suspect its having been taken by a particular individual, yet all attempts to find the letter come to nothing. It is correctly assumed that the letter can only be valuable to him who stole it if it can be produced at a moment's notice, and therefore he must have it near him—yet no one can find it.

In each case a baffling question is answered in the same way: Dupin, completely removed from the crime, assembles the circumstances of the mystery and sorts through all the facts which can be verified; from these, and from these alone, a hypothetical explanation *presents itself*. The moment between the final assembly of the evidence and the production of the solution is rather like the moment when an electric current arcs between terminals. The analyst, such a man as Dupin, rejoices in the ability to 'disentangle', yet, as Poe describes it, this power is at root the ability to assemble and then to conclude. The kind of person Poe presents is fond of enigmas, conundrums and hieroglyphics: 'exhibiting in his solutions of each a degree of *acumen* which appears to the ordinary apprehension preternatural. His results, have, in truth, the whole air of intuition.'

This admirable faculty possessed by Dupin is 'much invigorated' by the study of the highest branches of mathematics, yet Poe goes to a lot of trouble to assert difference between *calculation* and *analysis*:

> I will . . . take occasion to assert that the higher powers of the reflective intellect are more decidedly and usefully tasked by the unostentatious game of draughts than by all the elaborate frivolity of chess. In this latter, where the pieces have different and *bizarre* motions, with various and variable values, what is only complex is mistaken (a not unusual error) for what is profound. The *attention* is here called powerfully into play . . . in nine cases out of ten it is the more concentrative rather than the more acute player who conquers. In draughts, on the contrary, where the moves are *unique* and have but little variation, the probabilities of inadvertence are diminished, and the mere attention being left comparatively unemployed, what advantages are obtained by either party are obtained by superior *acumen*.[29]

Dupin has the mystic's or the seer's ability to perceive those things clearly and obviously which are obscured from normal viewers by the film of custom and familiarity. Dupin can see what would be obvious to all if only they would learn to look. He makes no astounding 'discoveries'. What he observes and what he reports would be visible to all those who would attempt to solve the mysteries on which he is engaged. This is brilliantly demonstrated in 'The Purloined Letter', although it is basic principle in all the Dupin stories, where the stolen letter has been hidden by being deposited 'beneath the nose of the whole world'.[30]

Wordsworth believed that the task of the poet was to take ordinary and familiar subjects and throw over them a certain colouring of the imagination, so that ordinary things 'should be presented to the mind in an unusual aspect'.[31] Dupin is, in fact, a true poet. He looks at the world in an unusual way. Poe establishes the link between poetry and mathematics in 'The Purloined Letter'. The Prefect believes that the guilty Minister

> is a fool, because he has acquired renown as a poet. All fools are poets; this the Prefect *feels*; and he is merely guilty of a *non distributio medii* in then inferring that all poets are fools.[32]

It is in this discussion that a very interesting aspect of the relationship between Dupin and Poe-as-narrator is put to the reader. Poe doubts that the Minister is a poet: 'The Minister I believe has written learnedly on the Differential Calculus. He is a mathematician, and no poet.'[33] Dupin disagrees; he says that the Minister is *both* a mathematician *and* a poet: 'As poet *and* mathematician, he would reason well; as mere mathematician, he could not have reasoned at all, and thus would have been at the mercy of the Prefect.'

Dupin's interlocutor answers:

> You surprise me . . . by these opinions, which have been contradicted by the voice of the world. You do not mean to set at naught the well-digested idea of centuries. The mathematical reason has long been regarded as *the* reason *par excellence*.

Dupin replies, quoting Nicolas Chamfort's comment: '*Il y a à parier . . . que toute idée publique, toute convention reçue, est une sottise, car elle a convenu au plus grand nombre.*'[34]

Dupin then deals with the common fallacy that mathematics, being in essence logic pure and simple, and poetry, the reckless flight of the imagination, are contradictory and irreconcilable aspects of human endeavour:

> The mathematicians . . . have done their best to promulgate the popular error to which you allude, and which is none the less an error for its promulgation as truth. With an art worthy of a better cause . . . they have insinuated the term 'analysis' into application to algebra. The French are the originators of this particular deception; but if a term is of any importance . . . then 'analysis' conveys 'algebra' about as much as, in Latin, '*ambitus*' implies 'ambition', '*religio*' religion, or '*homines honesti*' a set of *honorable* men. . . .
>
> . . . I dispute the availability, and thus the value, of that reason which is cultivated in any especial form other than the abstractly logical. I dispute, in particular, the reason educed by mathematical study. The mathematics are the science of form and quantity; mathematical reasoning is merely logic applied to observation upon form and quantity. The great error lies in supposing that even the truths of what is called *pure* algebra, are abstract or general truths. And this error is so egregious that I am confounded at the universality with which it has been received. Mathematical axioms are *not* axioms of general truth.[35]

It is Dupin's awareness of the relationship between poetry and mathematics, and that the combination of the two skills may produce that acumen which is the result of the exercise of the analytical powers of the mind, which causes him to respect the Minister D— so much *as an opponent*: '. . . if the Minister had been no more than a mathematician, the Prefect would have been under no necessity of giving me this check. I knew him . . . as both mathematician and poet, and my measures were adapted to his capacity.'[36] There are several concepts in this discussion to be noted. Above all there is the undeniable admiration called for in the contemplation of poetry when combined with logic; and equally striking, there is the acknowledgement that these qualities are rarely found in human kind. This is bound to be the case; the humdrum majority are mundane, men of genius are rare. But the opposition between orthodox opinions ('You surprise me by these opinions, which have been contradicted by the voice of the world. You do not mean to set at naught the well-digested idea of centuries . . .') and unorthodox ('*Il y a à parier . . . que toute idée publique, toute convention reçue, est une sottise, car elle a convenu au plus grand nombre . . .*') is very powerfully made.

5

The relationship between Dupin and the narrator of these tales is one which figures frequently in western literature from the late sixteenth century. It is one we seem to find satisfying and indeed revealing as to the nature of our humanity. Poe gives us a clue when he talks of the old philosophy of the Bi-Part soul in 'The Murders in the Rue Morgue'. Dupin is the intellectual genius of the partnership—the narrator is the admiring, regular guy. The narrator is 'astonished' at the 'vast extent' of Dupin's reading, and feels his 'soul enkindled' within him by 'the wild fervor, and the vivid freshness of his imagination'. He is soon convinced that 'the society of such a man' would be a treasure 'beyond price'. Typically in this type of relationship, the regular guy 'frankly confides' these feelings to the superior partner, and is happy to give himself up 'to his wild whims with a perfect abandon'.[37] There is a hint that Dupin's eccentric genius almost topples into madness, 'the result of an excited, or perhaps of a diseased intelligence'.[38]

The Dupin/Narrator relationship is one of the several reasons which makes the reading of these three so-called 'detective' stories so satisfying, for here Poe has delineated the classic Don Quixote/Sancho Panza partnership. Dupin is the detached genius, whose ice-cold racing intellect can solve crimes and unravel mysteries simply by basing his investigations on evidence brought to him by agents or which he garners by reading the newspapers; the rôle in which Poe seems to cast himself is that of the admiring, rather modest but carefully observing companion of the lofty genius. This is the relationship we find in Quixote/Panza, in Dr. Johnson/James Boswell, in Samuel Pickwick/Sam Weller, Sherlock Holmes/ Dr. Watson and in modern times that between P. D. James's Detective-Inspector Adam Dalgleish and Detective-Sergeant Martin. The theorizing genius in these relationships is often a poet, and the companion either a countryman or man of lowly occupation who has seen much of the world. Don Quixote has his head turned by reading romances; Sancho Panza is an earthy realist. Dr. Johnson was an eccentric intellectual who did strange things with orange peel, but was an outstanding scholar and poet; Boswell was a man of the senses and a worldly realist. Samuel Pickwick has all the unworldly perceptions of an innocent child; Sam Weller is worldly-wise and hard-boiled. Sherlock Holmes solves crimes which baffle Scotland Yard, plays the violin and takes drugs; Dr. Watson is an amiable old buffer who has seen much of the world. Adam Dalgleish is an intellectual and a published poet, but his Sergeant is 'a countryman by birth and inclination and was often heard to complain of the proclivity of murderers to commit their crimes in overcrowded cities and unsalubrious tenements'.[39] Very early in our lives we grow accustomed to this partnership, for it unquestionably established for us in that of Ratty and Mole. As well as being a master of the river and the skills of sailing and a master strategist, Rat is a poet and singer. After being treated to several verses of Rat's *Ducks' Ditty*, Mole says: 'I don't know that I think so *very* much of that little song, Rat.' He says this cautiously: 'He was no poet himself, and didn't care who knew it, and he had a candid nature.' Indeed, this is the very same relationship we find between the idealistic and ruminating Hamlet, and the down-to-earth Horatio. Hamlet asks him in the graveyard:

> To what base uses we may return, Horatio! Why may not imagination trace the noble dust of Alexander till 'a find it stopping a bung-hole? ... Alexander died, Alexander was buried, Alexander returneth to dust; the dust is earth; of earth we make loam; and why of that loam whereto he was converted might they not stop a beer-barrel?

Horatio's answer is as mundane as Mole's: ' 'Twer to consider too curiously to consider so.'[40] Its comic counterpart is to be found in the equally satisfying relationship between Arthur Daly and Terry McCann in *Minder*. It is the would-be tycoon and con-man with his head in the clouds, Arthur Daly, who talks poetically of being 'a small chip in the computer of life' and is given to philosophical musings on the state of the world; and it is the earthy Terry, ex-boxer and former resident of one of Her Majesty's prisons, who thinks of money, food and 'pulling the chicks'.[41]

These relationships seem to involve two opposing value systems, the intellectual and the worldly, the spiritual and the corporeal, mind and body; and they seem to become obsessive in western literature at approximately the time when Descartes put into circulation his cardinal point about the essential difference between spirit and matter and rejected scholastic tradition and theological dogma. Few things are as powerful as an idea which occurs at the right time, and western civilization seemed ready to accept Descartes' ideas, which led to the concepts of consciousness and existence and the mind/body dichotomy. Renaissance theology had placed great emphasis on the human mind as the seat of the rational soul which differentiated us from animals—in that brilliant phrase of Robert Henriques: 'a man was an animal with a mind added; the way that you added an auxiliary motor to a sailing boat.'[43] As Claudius says of Ophelia's insanity: '... poor Ophelia/ Divided from herself and her fair judgement/Without the which we are but pictures, or mere beasts. . . .'[44] Significantly our fascination with the contemplation of animals in zoological gardens dates from the same period.

We have bestowed these values on our hands. The right

hand is taken to stand for logic, virility, consciousness, rationality and harmony. The Latin *dexter*, which gives us dexterous, meant to the right-hand side, and dexterous originally meant right-handed. In heraldry the dexter applied to the right side of the shield of the person holding it (the left side of the one viewing it). It carried all the associations of order, stability, *right*. The left hand is taken to stand for the opposite qualities. Its Latin name, *sinister*, carries all the associations of disorder and disruption. It was considered unlucky to enter a room or a house with the left foot first. In ancient Rome wealthy citizens employed a boy to stand at doorways to remind guests to enter right foot foremost. In heraldry the bend-sinister (running across the shield from right to left) was an indication of bastardy. In augury the left side of anything was considered an unlucky sign. In politics the right stands for tradition, the left for radicalism and change. In the French National Assembly 1789 the reactionaries sat on the right, the democrats on the left. In many a social context today those who buck 'the system' and become labelled trouble-makers are said to be 'bolshie'.[45] The right-hand view of the world is the conservative and orderly one, personified in literature in the prosaic philosophy of Sancho Panza, worldly-wise and forever pulling his master back from the excesses of his own romantic imagination; Sancho finds his successors in Boswell, Weller, Watson, Sergeant Martin and Terry McCann. The left-hand view is bodied forth in the eccentric, wayward, ambitious figures who cause such a stir in the world, classically personified in Don Quixote and powerfully echoed in Samuel Johnson, Samuel Pickwick, Sherlock Holmes, Adam Dalgleish and Arthur Daly. These are the poets of politics; we should recall that Shelley called poets 'the unacknowledged legislators of the world'. Eccentric geniuses are frequently found to be left-handed.

The man of the left in these tales is the Chevalier C. Auguste Dupin, who looks at everything from an unusual point of view and refuses to take things on face value. We are several times given evidence of this, and he comments on it himself. In 'The Murders in the Rue Morgue' he compares the orthodox methods of police search with his own:

> The Parisian police, so much extolled for *acumen*, are cunning, but no more. There is no method in their proceedings, beyond

the method of the moment. . . . The results attained by them are not unfrequently surprising, but, for the most part, are brought about by simple diligence and activity. When these qualities are unavailing their schemes fail. Vidocq, for example, was a good guesser, and a persevering man. But, without educated throught, he erred continually by the very intensity of his investigations. He impaired his vision by holding the object too close. He might see, perhaps, one or two points with unusual clearness, but in so doing he, necessarily, lost sight of the matter as a whole. Thus there is such a thing as being too profound. Truth is not always in a well. In fact, as regards the more important knowledge, I do believe that she is invariably superficial. The depths lies in the valleys where we seek her, and not upon the mountain-tops where she is found. The modes and sources of this kind of error are well typified in the contemplation of the heavenly bodies. To look at a star by glances— to view it in a side-long way, by turning toward it the exterior portions of the *retina* (more susceptible of feeble impressions of light than the interior,) is to behold the star distinctly—is to have the best appreciation of its lustre—a lustre which grows dim in just proportion as we turn our vision fully upon it. A greater number of rays actually fall upon the eye in the latter case, but, in the former, there is the more refined capacity for comprehension. By undue profundity we perplex and enfeeble thought. . . .[46]

Dupin is able to solve the vexing case of the stolen letter by his ability clearly to see the obvious, not to seek truth in the infinitesimal. This is a technique acquired only after serving a long apprenticeship, not revealed by a sudden accidental glance. He explains this to the admiring narrator:

There is a game of puzzles . . . which is played upon a map. One party requires another party to find a given word—the name of town, river, state or empire—any word, in short, upon the motley and perplexed surface of the chart. A novice in the game generally seeks to embarrass his opponents by giving them the most minutely lettered names; but the adept selects such words as stretch, in large characters, from one end of the chart to the other. These, like the over-largely lettered signs and placards of the street, escape observation by dint of being excessively obvious.[47]

Dupin's penetration of the mystery of the case of Marie Roget similarly is the result of his trained ability to concentrate his attention on the wholeness and completeness of the situation:

> In that which I now propose, we will discard the interior points of this tragedy, and concentrate our attention upon its outskirts. Not the least usual error in investigations such as this is the limiting of enquiry to the immediate, with total disregard of the collateral or circumstantial events. It is the malpractice of the courts to confine evidence and discussion to the bounds of apparent relevancy. Yet experience has shown, and a true philosophy will always show, that a vast, perhaps the larger, portion of truth arises from the seemingly irrelevant. . . .[48]

This independence of Dupin's, this willingness to do things in a new way and thus to achieve practical results, is very American. He may be seen in some ways as a representative figure not so much of the French *ancien régime* as of a society the very founding of which was an attempt on a national scale to create something new, by applying human reason to the task of constructing a Great Society, applying theory to practice. Dupin does, in fact, frequently declare his independence from the traditional way of doing things.

The Dupin/Narrator stories exemplify the union of the left-hand/right-hand aspects of the human personality, which is a leading theme of Poe's *Eureka: A Prose Poem* (1848). Here Poe argues that the universe was a work of art, that there is no such thing as mathematical demonstration, that intuition alone is valid: 'All Things and All Thoughts of Things, with their ineffable Multiplicity of Relation, sprang at once into being from the primordial and irrelative One'—this is the opening thesis of *Eureka*. Poe dismissed all those who would place reason above intuition—such as Aristotle (Aries Tottle) among others, who are held in discredit because of their sluggish logic and their rejection of 'the Soul which loves nothing so well as to soar in . . . regions of illimitable intuition'.

Eureka proposes that a pre-existing Godhead created a 'primordial Particle' of absolute Unity combined with capacity to divide infinitely, irradiating spherically vast numbers of infinitely minute atoms. These atoms tend to unite, and this gives us the principle of gravity. They also have the power to repel, which is the quality scientists have termed heat, magnetism, electricity. In Poe's theory gravitation and electricity, attraction and repulsion, are the two principles of the created universe, the material and the spiritual. Attraction is the body, repulsion the soul.[49] The duality of personality is an obsessive theme in Poe's work. It is the basis of that deeply disturbing story 'William Wilson' (1839). In 'The Fall of the House of Usher' a logical and reasonable narrator collides with the bizarre world of the Usher household and is repelled by it— body and soul, consciousness and the unconscious, reality and dream come into direct conflict. In the right-hand/left-hand duality we get the partnership of attraction (right) and repulsion (left)—the body (earthy, realistic, mundane) and the soul (ineffable, flighty, other-worldly). It is classically embodied in the Narrator/Dupin. The narrator is the ordinary guy, Dupin the wayward genius. Significantly Dupin can only function at night, the time when the soul is freed from the prison of the body, when the censoring powers of reason relax and the subconscious is given free rein. But was Dupin left-handed?

NOTES

1. The lines Poe quotes at the opening of 'The Murders in the Rue Morgue' are from Chapter V of *Hydriotaphia, Urn-Burial* (1658) by Sir Thomas Browne (1605–82). Browne attended the University of Oxford and various continental medical schools at Montpellier, Padua and Leyden, preparatory to his career as a physician in Norfolk. He visited a site in this county where some workmen had discovered several burial-urns containing mortal remains possibly thousands of years old. He was moved to write *Hydriotaphia, Urn-Burial*, a resonant meditation on death and mortality and funeral habits. In the passage Poe quotes Browne asserts that there are some things which may seem deeply and mysteriously unknowable which may yet be revealed by conjecture, but there are some questions forever obscure: 'What time the persons of these ossuaries entered the famous nations of the dead, and slept with princes and counselors, might admit a wide solution. But who were the proprietaries of these bones, or what bodies these ashes made up, were a question above antiquarism: not to be resolved by man. . . .'

2. Suetonius, *The Twelve Caesars*, translated by Robert Graves (Harmondsworth: Penguin Books, 1957), p. 144.

3. Ibid., p. 143.

4. This is considered a sufficiently worthwhile comment on Edgar Allan

108

Poe to be quoted in Justin Wintle and Richard Kenin (eds.), *The Dictionary of Biographical Quotation* (London: Routledge and Kegan Paul, 1978), p. 602.

5. T. S. Eliot, 'Wilkie Collins and Dickens' in *Selected Essays* (London: Faber and Faber, 1953), p. 464.

6. See Alexander H. Krappe, *The Science of Folklore* (New York: W. W. Norton and Co., 1964), pp. 79, 201ff; Erich Fromm, *The Forgotten Language* (New York: Grove Press, 1957), pp. 198ff.

7. Ernest Jones, *The Life and Work of Sigmund Freud* (Harmondsworth: Penguin Books, 1961), pp. 39–40, 302–3, 367, 373–74 and 526.

8. Sophocles, *King Oedipus*, in *The Theban Plays*, translated by E. F. Watling (Harmondsworth: Penguin Books, 1947), pp. 73ff. See also Homer, *Odyssey*, II, 271–80 and Aeschylus, *Seven Against Thebes*, 742–1084. The Oedipus legend was also the subject of a tragedy by Seneca. See Richmond Y. Hathorn, *Tragedy, Myth and Mystery* (Bloomington: Indiana University Press, 1966), pp. 33ff.

9. Flavius Josephus, the great Jewish historian (A.D. 37–98), records in his *Jewish Antiquities* that Hiram, King of Tyre, and Solomon once had a contest in riddling, in which Solomon won a large fortune, later lost to Abdemon, one of Hiram's subjects. According to Plutarch, Homer died of chagrin because he was unable to answer a particular riddle.

10. *Hamlet*, V, 2, 208–17. Cf *Matthew* X. 29: 'Are not two sparrows sold for a farthing? And one of them shall not fall on the ground without your Father.'

11. George Steiner, *The Death of Tragedy* (London: Faber and Faber, 1961), pp. 5–6.

12. *Calendar of State Papers 1579–80*, edited A. J. Butler, Public Record Office (1904), pp. 227ff.

13. Cf. Erich Heller, *The Disinherited Mind* (Harmondsworth: Penguin, 1961), pp. 14–19.

14. Anthony Burgess, *Is America Falling Apart?* in *New York Times Magazine*, 7 November 1971, reprinted in Arthur M. Eastman *et al.* (eds.), *The Norton Reader: An Anthology of Expository Prose*, 3rd edition (New York: W. W. Norton), 1973 p. 427.

15. Cf. Max Weber: '. . . principally there are no mysterious incalculable forces that come into play. . . . one can, in principle, master all things by calculation. This means that the world is disenchanted. One need no longer have recourse to magical means in order to master or implore the spirits. . . . Technical means and calculations perform the service . . .', *Science as a Vocation* (1919), in *From Max Weber*, edited by H. H. Gerth and C. Wright Mills (London: Routledge and Kegan Paul, 1970), p. 139; see also Julien Freund, *The Sociology of Max Weber* (Harmondsworth: Penguin, 1972), pp. 24ff.

16. Lewis Mumford, *Literary Review*, 5 April 1924, 642.

17. Walter Ong, *Orality and Literacy: The Technologizing of the Word* (London: Methuen, 1982), p. 147, cf. ibid., 142ff.

18. See Marshall McLuhan, *The Gutenberg Galaxy* (University of Toronto Press, 1968), pp. 18ff and 24–8.

19. Walter Ong, op. cit., p. 144.
20. Berkley Peabody, *The Winged Word: A Study in the Technique of Ancient Greek Oral Composition as Seen Principally Through Hesiod's Works and Days* (State University of New York Press, 1975), pp. 172–79.
21. Latin *rhapsodia*, from the Greek *rhapsoidia*.
22. See Andrew Sinclair, *John Ford* (London: George Allen and Unwin, 1979), pp. 129–33 and Douglas Pye, 'Genre and the Movies: The Western' in Barry K. Grant (ed.), *Film Genre: Theory and Criticism* (New Jersey: Scarecrow Press, 1977), pp. 206ff., and Peter Wollen, *Signs and Meaning in the Cinema* (London: Secker and Warburg, 1972), pp. 94ff.
23. Walter Ong, op. cit., pp. 148–49.
24. See Killis Campbell, *The Mind of Poe and Other Studies* (New York: Russell and Russell, 1962), pp. 165–66. Poe got the basic idea of 'The Murders in the Rue Morgue' from the account of the murder of the Parisian prostitute, Rose Deacourt (see *Washington Post*, 3 October 1912); the rôle of the orang-outan probably came from Poe's reading in the *Shrewsbury Chronicle* of July 1834 the account of the apprehension of an orang-outan, trained by its owner to climb buildings and to rob apartments—see *Notes and Queries*, 17 May 1894. 'The Mystery of Marie Roget' was based on the murder of the New York cigar store assistant, Mary Rogers, which Poe read in the newspapers of the day—see Julian Symons, *The Tell-Tale Heart: The Life and Works of Edgar Allan Poe* (London: Faber and Faber, 1978), pp. 224–25; Alan Bold and Robert Giddings, *True Characters: Real People in Fiction* (London: Longman, 1984), p. 231; and John Walsh, *Poe the Detective: The Curious Circumstances Behind 'The Mystery of Marie Roget'* (New Brunswick: Rutgers University Press, 1968), pp. 5–21.
25. On the coin-operated hot-drinks machines at the college where I was once employed was the motto: 'If it's useful, it was invented by an American.'
26. *The Murders in the Rue Morgue*, in *Selected Writings of Edgar Allan Poe*, edited by David Galloway (Harmondsworth: Penguin, 1970), pp. 189–90.
27. See Marie Bonaparte, *The Life and Works of Edgar Allan Poe: A Psycho-Analytical Interpretation* (London: Imago, 1949), pp. 427–57.
28. 'The Murders in the Rue Morgue', op. cit., p. 189.
29. Ibid., 189–90.
30. 'The Purloined Letter', *Selected Writings of Edgar Allan Poe*, op. cit., p. 345.
31. Wordsworth, *Preface* to the *Lyrical Ballads* 1800; cf. Robert Giddings and Elizabeth Holland, *J. R. R. Tolkien: The Shores of Middle-earth* (Junction Books, 1981), pp. 254–55.
32. 'The Purloined Letter', op. cit., p. 342.
33. Ibid.
34. 'The odds are that all ideas held by the public at large, every received convention, are stupid, for the very reason that they suit the masses.' Nicolas Sébastian de Chamfort (1741–94), French *litterateur*, renowned wit and aphorist, committed suicide during the Jacobin terror.
35. 'The Purloined Letter', op. cit., pp. 342–43.

36. Ibid., p. 343.
37. 'The Murders in the Rue Morgue', op. cit., pp. 192–93.
38. Ibid., p. 194.
39. P. D. James, *Cover Her Face* (London: Faber and Faber, 1962), p. 48.
40. Kenneth Grahame, *The Wind in the Willows* (1908; London: Methuen, 1977), pp. 27–8.
41. *Hamlet*, V, 1, 197–206. This is the earliest recorded version I have been able to trace of that familiar plaint of those who nominate themselves the voice of the 'common-sense' view of the world, checking all tendency to question and examine the world's multifarious experiences with their restraining caution: 'But you are reading too much into it!' The relationship between Hamlet and Horatio is the collision between poetry and prose. Cf. Antonio Gramsci, *Selections From the Prison Notebooks* (London: Lawrence and Wishart, 1971), pp. 326ff.
42. *Minder*, a Thames Television drama series, had become a national institution by the early 1980s and gave several new phrases to the language, including 'her indoors' (a term of semi-endearment used by Arthur Daly to refer to Mrs. Daly). In May 1981 *Minder* was given the Ivor Novello Award for the Best T.V. Theme Music. Arthur is generally acknowledged one of George Cole's best creations, and the basis of the situation is invariably Arthur's setting up some shady deal involving stolen property or some racket, and then managing to disappear when the going gets tough, leaving his minder, Terry McCann, to fend for himself. The Arthur/Terry relationship is mirrored in the duo from the law who are set to bring them to justice, the righteous and clear-thinking Chisolm, and the bluff, jocular and easy-going Jones.
43. Robert Henriques, *No Arms, No Armour* (1939; London: Collins, 1951), p. 326.
44. *Hamlet*, IV, 5, 81–3.
45. Carl Gustav Jung, *The Psychology of the Transference*, in *The Practice of Psychotherapy*, translated by R. F. C. Hull, in *Collected Works of Carl Gustav Jung*, edited by Read, Fordham and Adler (London: Routledge and Kegan Paul, 1954), Vol. 16.
46. 'The Murders in the Rue Morgue', op. cit., pp. 204–5.
47. 'The Purloined Letter', op. cit., p. 345.
48. 'The Mystery of Marie Roget' in Edgar Allan Poe: *Tales of Mystery and Imagination* (New Jersey: Castle, Secaucus, 1983), p. 244.
49. I am greatly indebted to Julian Symons's elucidation of the complexities of *Eureka*—see *The Tell-Tale Heart*, op. cit., pp. 200–1.

6

'Impudent and ingenious fiction': Poe's *The Narrative of Arthur Gordon Pym of Nantucket*

by A. ROBERT LEE

1

The perception of *Pym* as an essential American literary landmark has come about only recently, and not without cavils and different shows of reluctance. Its latterday new lease of life, in fact, can be dated precisely—from W. H. Auden's inclusion of the full text in his Rinehart *Selected Prose and Poetry* of 1950.[1] Previous to that, and even in France where Baudelaire's *Aventures d'Arthur Gordon Pym* had been an admired translation since 1858, Poe's original cannot be said to have enjoyed much more than a fugitive existence, eclipsed by his better-known short stories and poetry and frequently out of print. Auden's intervention, therefore, was as unexpected as it was discerning and generous. He took it upon himself to proclaim *Pym* 'one of the finest adventure stories ever written', nothing less than 'an object lesson in the art'.[2] No doubt there was some over-pitching in this, a necessary insistence to win attention. Yet whatever his means, Auden deserves immense credit. Almost single-handedly he rescued

Pym from an obscurity which even the considerable anti-Poe lobby came to recognize had been unfair.

Not that so singular an act of reclamation has led to smooth sailing for *Pym*. Debate about its worth and meaning has been contentious, to the point on occasion of impatience and bad temper.[3] Poe has even been taken to task for having apparently flouted his own rules about 'objectionable' length in the novel as expressed in his celebrated 'Review of Nathaniel Hawthorne's *Twice-Told Tales*'.[4] As his only full-length work (with the exception of the unfinished *Journal of Julius Rodman*), did not Poe avail himself of a form which on his own appointed standard could not fail to be flawed? It was he, after all, who wrote:

> As [the novel] cannot be read at one sitting, it deprives itself, of course, of the immense benefit derivable from *totality*. Worldly interests, intervening during the pauses of perusal, modify, annul, or counteract, in a greater or lesser degree, the impressions of the book.[5]

To a later age more keenly exercised on reader-response theory and *Rezeptionästhetik*, this might signify a point of departure rather than of conclusion. But it remains a fact that Poe still gets called to account for his apparent inconsistency.

The point, however, does have some bearing on the ways and means of the text itself, and especially where the reaction has been antagonistic. Is not *Pym*, in fact, insufficiently a whole, merely a run of separate, or at least over-determined, episodes? Is it not, likewise, too evidently a victim of its own mixed means, at once purportedly verisimilar, a 'true' story, yet as often dream-like and fantastical? Does not all the surface high drama, the shipwrecks, imprisonments, mutinies, cannibalism and treachery eventually begin to pall? Similarly Poe's much-vaunted hoaxing. Does it in truth come off, or serve any better purpose than to be simply showy or mischievous, that of a precocious child rather than of a mature writer?[6] More specifically still, what of Poe's ending, or rather double-ending, first the gigantic white figure who bears down on Pym and his companions (an 'effect' which 'fails' according to Henry James because it aims simply 'at the horrific in itself'),[7] and then the report of Pym's own supposed death which puts the text on orphan status as it were, a body without a head? Here, as elsewhere, do not Poe's 'ideas', his 'mystery and imagination', outrun his text's ability to offer more than Gothic? One upshot, evidently, of *Pym*'s availability to modern interrogation has been the paradox of seeing it argued as essentially an oddity, another Poe enterprise gone awry.

But that has by no means been the whole account. *Pym* has won an array of latterday proponents, new and often dazzlingly ingenious, admirers of precisely its 'mystery and imagination'.[8] Not a few of these urge *Pym* as a text easily the equal of those which make up the canon of the American Renaissance, the likes of Emerson's Transcendentalist essays, Melville's *Moby-Dick*, Hawthorne's *The Scarlet Letter*, Thoreau's *Walden*, Whitman's *Leaves of Grass* and Emily Dickinson's poetry. Here the accent is made to fall upon *Pym*'s visionary interest, its 'prophetic glimpses'[9] into terrain far beyond historic nine-teenth-century South Seas time and place.

Poe's 'narrative', in brief, enacts an emblematic journey, a stunning cycle of metamorphoses which as much refers to our inward, psychic life as to any supposed literal exploration. *Pym*'s voyaging, first out to sea and then inexorably south-ward, thus signifies an endemic human need to decode each and every encyclopaedic world-sign as if we ourselves were figures of otherness marooned on some unchosen planet. *Pym*'s 'extraordinary series of adventures' (57), thereby, represent also a species of dream, fantasy happenings brilliantly masked as actuality. Pym, especially, is both 'real' and a figure of the psychic self, travelling uncertainly through disaster, reversals of circumstance and fortune, a whole complex of abrupt exits and entrances from one realm into another. The world he encounters, one displaced out of dream into fact, takes the form of entombments, narrow escapes, sensations of falling and transformation, as well as strangely enciphered signals and happenings. Only some final, 'polar' revelation at a degree-zero white Antarctic south will unlock the world's talismanic mystery, its pattern of hieroglyphs. In this *Pym* is also to be likened to Poe's own *Eureka*, equally a 'Book of Truths' and enquiry into 'First Principles' and equally, as he terms things, a projection of the will to 'Unity' over 'Diffusion'.

Pym, too, has attracted a related kind of interest, one to which this essay gives a fresh round of attention. Put at its most favouring, by its manifold tactics of textual double-play and hoax, its self-acknowledging inventedness, *Pym* amounts to a pre-Joycean tour-de-force. But not only is Joyce so indicated. Poe, runs the argument, points still further ahead to post-modern virtuosi like Nabokov and Borges. The impulse in their story-telling towards reflexivity, self-play, mimicry, equally marks out *Pym*, though by no means at the expense of a powerful story-line or a demonstrated familiarity with the facts of navigation and South Seas history. The matter, of course, can again be put unflatteringly. Is not *Pym* still too clever for its own imaginative good, too disposed to tease at the expense of all things else? Or put more neutrally, and in Poe's own phrase, in designating *Pym* an 'impudent and ingenious fiction' (43), was he speaking to its better or worse effects?

2

Impudence, or ingeniousness, or both, come engagingly into play in *Pym* even as the eye runs down the title-page. Poe's upper-case inventory of things to come does honest-seeming duty, the promise indeed of nothing less than 'true' if spectacular adventure. But as the list unfolds, one cannot but suspect the put-on, Poe the counterfeiter. THE NARRATIVE OF ARTHUR GORDON PYM is to comprise THE DETAILS OF A MUTINY AND ATROCIOUS BUTCHERY, a SHIPWRECK AND SUBSEQUENT HORRIBLE SUFFERINGS FROM FAMINE, and were that not enticement in plenty, INCREDIBLE ADVENTURES AND DISCOVERIES STILL FURTHER SOUTH. Mock-epic title-pages of the kind deployed by Fielding or Smollett may have gone out of fashion, unless as the overt pastiche of contemporaries like John Barth or Kurt Vonnegut. But Poe's for *Pym* plays matters all ways at once, as an authentic advertisement of coming attractions, as indeed mock-epic, and as mock-epic itself mocked. Poe's mode is thus one of multiple hype, companionable double-dealing. 'Incredible adventures' will refer not only to Pym's own Southwards pilgrimage, but to the entire manner of the story's unfolding, Poe's conceded imposture from start to finish.

Given that two instalments of *Pym* had first appeared under

Poe's name in the *Southern Literary Messenger* (for January and February 1837), how to make the transformation into a completed and book-length text appear to have been written by Pym himself? Poe's answer again depends upon subtly letting the reader in on the subterfuge, the true hoaxery behind '*this ruse*' (44), as he has Pym call it. The 'account' (43), one after all of 'facts' (44), we are enjoined to believe had been given by Pym to 'Mr. Poe' (43) to tell as if 'pretended fiction' (44), partly to meet Pym's own lack of vocation as a writer and partly to ensure his story's 'better chance of being received as truth' (44). '*Under the garb of fiction*' (44), thus, Pym's 'series of adventures' (43) have been told by 'Mr. Poe' in his rôle of amanuensis and collaborator, 'my adventures' (44) offered 'without altering or disturbing a single fact' (44) yet to be granted a certain understandable allowance for their 'air of fable' (44). Any 'difference in point of style' (45), a readership insinuatingly termed 'shrewd' (44) and 'full of common sense' (44) should have no difficulty in perceiving. This would-be '*exposé*' (44), mock-honest, plausible as need be, cannily shows its own fakery. The true 'ruse' at issue is not at all that of Pym or/and of 'Mr. Poe'; it is Poe's, manipulating at every turn the ostensible deceit practised a year before in the columns of the *Messenger*. Poe again so seizes the advantage on several counts. He manages to simulate an explanation of the pre-publication of parts of *Pym* in Thomas White's Richmond magazine, invent himself as a figure in his own fiction, anticipate a later age's controversies about 'fictions of fact' and, obliquely to a degree, indicate the larger tactics at work in *Pym* overall.

The juggling of terms of reference like 'truth', '*the garb of fiction*', '*ruse*', and 'the air of fable', especially helps in all these respects. Each, to be sure, plays its part in the mockery of what is already a mock-confession. Each, too, points forward to the artifice, the systematic hoaxery and falsifications, of *Pym* as a whole. But each, too, gives a clue to the text's more hidden—and more serious—purposes, the visionary journey which lies within or just out of sight of that on show. It is to this end, too, that Poe has his Arthur Gordon Pym appear to step free of his story to thank his collaborator and mentor, the Richmond 'late editor' of the *Messenger*, 'Mr. Poe' (43). For as 'Mr. Poe', Poe plays to the hilt his part as modest retainer, the reluctant ghost-writer of another's narrative. So that whether understood as having been written by 'A. G. PYM' (45), or 'Mr. Poe' (43), or some imagined mix of the two (44), or as indeed by Poe *in propria persona*, the Preface again is able to lay down its marker for *Pym* at large. The story-telling mask (or masks) are allowed to slip just enough. However plausible the '*exposé*' (and that it did its work is confirmed by contemporary response), it actually serves to underline Poe's own acknowledgement of the contrivance behind all of *Pym*. The Preface, in fact, offers exactly the self-same factitious kind of text as the 'narrative' which follows. And in this, too, it joins company with those two other equally surreptitious American Prefaces, Hawthorne's 'The Custom-House' in *The Scarlet Letter* and Melville's 'Etymology'—'Extracts'—'Loomings' sequence in *Moby-Dick*.[11]

3

Letting us in on the act, on Poe's own sleight-of-hand, applies in like manner to the *Ariel* episode. At a first level, Poe's opening chapter indeed offers the 'maddest freak' (47), a midnight caper and near-death aboard Augustus Barnard's sailboat as it heads into an October gale off the Nantucket shoreline. It also encapsulates the voyages aboard the *Grampus* and the *Jane Guy*, each a voyage into and through extremity, each a staging-ground for Poe's unriddling of a coded, cabalistic universe. First, Poe typically enciphers the surfaces of his text. The name Arthur Gordon Pym parallels his own in sound and syllable. 'Edgarton' (47), at whose bank his grandfather has made his cash, allows him another Hitchcock-like appearance. 'Old Mr. Ricketts' (47), one-armed and 'known to almost every person who has visited New Bedford' (47), blends the commonly shared childhood memory of a first teacher into rickets as an ailment. Even 'Augustus Barnard' (47) suggests Pym's 'Augustan' other self—though in fact he behaves as anything but an Augustan, being given to drunken, cataleptic urges to sail into an ocean storm. The name of the sailboat, *Ariel*, similarly hints of other realms, Shakespeare's mercurial spirit in *The Tempest* and Shelley's death-boat. Even Augustus's stories of 'the Island of Tinian' (47) track back on

Pym, one set of nocturnal stories to anticipate those of the 'blackskin warriors' (205) of Klock-Klock and Tsalal. All of these passing hints and touches play into, or comment upon, or hold up to scrutiny, the actual 'adventure' of the *Ariel* as it is run down by the *Penguin* under the command of the aptly named 'Captain E. V. T. Block' (52).

The *Ariel* adventure serves indeed as one of Augustus's 'maddest freaks' (47), but also 'by way of introduction to a longer and more momentous narrative' (48), that is, as indicated as our way into the voyaging of the *Grampus*, of the *Jane Guy* and of Pym in southernmost Antarctica. It is told as 'adventure' but also as dream-story, abrupt in its reversals and changes of fortune, typically shot through with references to 'ecstasy' (48), 'madness' (50), 'terror (50), imminent 'destruction' (51), and eventually, 'the mystery of our being in existence' (51). Storm, waves, a monster ship bearing down on Barnard's sailboat, call up stories like 'MS Found In A Bottle' in which Poe uses extreme states of 'agitation' (51) as a means of edging towards a condition of visionary clarity. The rescue is accordingly explained as total paradox: Pym survives by being seen upside down on 'the smooth and shining bottom' (53) of the *Penguin*, and Augustus (like Melville's Ishmael in his coffin), by having been tied umbilically to a timber of the *Ariel*'s deck and so found 'buoyed up' (54). The 'extraordinary' (53), the 'mad' (50), the 'terrible' (51), invert back into the explicable. Night-time 'ecstasy' (48) and 'intoxication' (50) give way to re-birth into the reasonable. Each transformation enacts Pym's double-voyage: one essentially oneiric and symbolic and pitched as a run of 'prophetic glimpses' (57), the other more assuring and adventurely, almost schoolboy high-jinks. No less, in a sense, will follow in the larger voyages which ensue, each, too, a species of dream-voyage and vision while remaining at the same time high adventure. Pym is even more to hint of his own begetter's tactics when he mentions the return home to the Barnard household the next morning. Both he and Augustus pretend to a surface of ordinariness, the cover-up of the every-day. 'Schoolboys . . . can accomplish wonders in the way of deception' (56) says Pym. As much, the text surely implies, might be said of Poe's own story-telling wiles, equally and at every turn 'wonders in the way of deception'.

118

4

With one 'wild adventure' (57) and 'miraculous deliverance' (57) in place, the text quickly advances to another, also 'sheer fabrication' (57) in the manner of one of Augustus's stories. Pym first sets out the 'visions' (57) which most compel him, the 'destiny' (57) he craves and which in fact the text of *Pym* will enact:

> My visions were of shipwreck and famine; of death and captivity among barbarian hordes; of a lifetime dragged out in sorrow and tears, upon some gray desolate rock, in an ocean unapproachable and unknown. Such visions or desires—for they amounted to desires—are common, I have since been assured, to the whole numerous race of the melancholy among men—at the time of which I speak I regarded them only as prophetic glimpses of a destiny which I felt myself in a measure bound to fulfill. (57)

Determined 'at all hazards' (58) to meet this 'destiny' (57), Pym falls back on 'intense hypocrisy' (58), as he calls it, 'an hypocrisy pervading every word and action of my life for so long a period of time' (58), as if to say that everyday life for him has become no more than secondary rôle-playing, a cheat, an outward shell. Only in 'my long cherished visions of travel' (58) can the true, essential drama of his life take shape.

To 'fulfill' this true 'destiny', he virtually shows himself the self-actualizing performer of his own script. He 'contrive[s] a hiding place' (59) by stowing away in the *Grampus* under Captain Barnard's captaincy. He relishes his imposture of a 'good-for-nothing salt water Tom' (60) before his baffled grandfather, 'old Mr. Peterson' (59). He buries himself deep inside the labyrinthine, coffin-like hold of the *Grampus* (itself a slightly preposterous, 'fishy' name), linked to escape only by a Cretan 'piece of dark whipchord' (62), the slenderest thread between sleep and wakefulness, 'vision' and fact. He remains there, biblically, 'three days and nights' (63), the as-yet unrisen self. Around him all is seeming decay, dissolution. Time runs down in the form of his stopped watch (64). His cold mutton turns to 'putrefaction' (64). He passes into catalepsy, highly animated trance. His 'dreams' belong with the canvases of a Dalí or Ernst, dreams of 'the most terrific description' (65). He repeatedly imagines his own immolation, by in turns smothering (65), 'immense serpents' (65), 'forlorn' deserts (65), humanoid trees (65), the 'burning sand plains of Zahara' (66), and finally, 'a fierce lion of the tropics' (66). Poe leaves very little doubt that in all these 'visions' (58), Pym serves as his own surrogate writer and voyager.

But, as ever, Pym's dreams oscillate at the very edge of reality. This 'lion' turns out to be none other than 'my Newfoundland dog Tiger' (66), a 'dream' inverted back into actuality. He so wakes to find fact re-enacting fiction. His lion-tiger-dog has aroused him to his situation of being literally 'entombed' (70), 'blocked' (70)—a sly echo no doubt of the name of Captain Block of the *Penguin*—and the possessor of a still to be deciphered half-message tied by string to the dog's body, '*blood—your life depends upon lying close*' (76). *Pym*, time and again, will use this and other half-messages, other similarly abstract engravings and signs and signals, to point to a cryptogrammatic universe, a world finally only to be deciphered through a form of visionary confrontation and reasoning. The beginning *Grampus* journey thus fuses one journey into another, one kind of actorly voyaging inside the other, in all the very pattern of *Pym* as a whole.

Locked amid 'innumerable narrow windings' (72) and in a 'tantalizing state of anxiety and suspense' (72), Pym attempts his first self-rescue, his first would-be decipherment of circumstance. He half-fathoms Augustus's message by the use of phosphorus (a 'momentary' message); witnesses his own dog indeed become a tiger as it maddens through want of water; drinks his 'single gill of liqueur' (78) out of 'perverseness' (78); and against all odds hears his name called by Augustus. Out of his 'incarceration' (80), both real and dreamlike, he has been called back, 'redeemed from the jaws of the tomb' (80). Once more, half in dream and half in 'fact', Pym has played out a script, enacted the voyager rôle in a world bound by imprisoning ciphers and contradiction.

'The brig put to sea' (57): so Poe launches Pym into his next phase, that of the insurrection aboard the *Grampus*. He awakens this time from 'slumber' (82) 'of the most tranquil nature' (82) to find, yet again, a world turned upside down. Captain Barnard has been usurped by the mate and is close to death. Punishment is administered by a gargoylish 'black cook' (83). 'Horrible butchery ensued' (84). And a new *alter ego*, soon to succeed the 'Augustan' Barnard Junior, emerges, namely Dirk Peters, the dwarfish 'son of an Indian squaw of the tribe of Upsarakokas' (84) and a one-time Lewis River and Missouri fur-trader. In *Moby-Dick*, Melville describes his Queequeg as 'a wondrous work in one volume', 'living parchment', and 'a riddle to unfold',[12] and the same might be said of Peters. 'One of the most ferocious-looking men I ever beheld' (84), stunted but with 'bowed and Herculean limbs' (84), he also wears a dog or grizzly-bear wig to cover his domed baldness, the phallic dwarf archetype *par excellence*. With his wide-gapped mouth and teeth 'exceedingly long and protruding' (85), he indeed amounts to a 'singular being' (85), the perfect outlandish witness, and participant, in all of Pym's subsequent doings. His exotic, amazing fictionality could hardly be apter, an almost insistently invented figure. And so Poe has his Pym aver when he observes:

> I shall have frequent occasion to mention (Peters) hereafter in the course of my narrative—a narrative, let me say, which will be found to include incidents of a nature so entirely out of the range of human experience, and for this reason so far beyond the limits of human credulity that I proceed in utter hopelessness of obtaining credence for all that I shall tell, yet confidently trusting in time and progressing science to verify some of the most important and most improbable of my statements. (85)

Following on the mutiny and with Pym and Augustus reunited (two selves in one) though utterly at risk from the mate, Poe again 'improbably' guys his own narrative: first through the reduction of numbers in the opposing parties; then through the crew names which contain a number of 'in' jokes about American types like William Gilmore Simms, Horace Greeley, and Poe's own Allan family; and finally, through the illusion of 'documentary' in the mock-meticulousness of dating events, as if the text were transcribing history not fantasy. Another digression puts in an appearance, on 'lying to' (108), not in itself inaccurate but (and again in the manner of Melville's *Moby-Dick*) a form of pastiche information. There follows a classic 'horror' death, that of Hartman Rogers, 'one of the most horrid and loathsome spectacles I ever remember to have seen' (111), Poe at his Grand Guignol campiest.

For it is this same Rogers that Pym brings back to life, a Ghost Scene played for all its worth 'in imitation of the horrible deformity of the swollen corpse' (112). Pym rubs white chalk over his face, equips himself with a bloated, false stomach, and streaks his eye with blood from a purposely cut finger, in all 'a most shocking appearance' (112) by which to haunt the mate and his fellow mutineers. What Poe again enacts through Pym is a script-within-a-script, a powerful actorly spectacle fashioned to his usual double-purpose. Pym's ghostly impersonation advances the plot surely enough. But it also provides still another pointer to the text's willingness to reveal its own artifice. For in insisting on all the scriptedness and histrionic, Poe again—as he does in stories like 'The Fall of the House of Usher', or 'Ligeia', or 'The Pit and the Pendulum'—shows the fabulatory, illusion-creating procedures of his text at large. *Pym*'s 'realism', if it be that, more than usually flatters to deceive.

In turn, too, even Pym's self-reflexive rôle half turns back on itself. When he looks in the 'fragment of a looking glass' (113), he experiences 'a sense of vague awe at my appearance' (113), and is 'seized with a violent tremor' (113) as he recalls 'the terrific reality which I was thus representing' (113). So kitted out, the perfect fake cadaver, or Pirate of Penzance, or actor-manager, he overhears the 'piratical plans' (113) of his adversaries and duly unleashes 'the terrific appearance of Rogers' corpse' (115). Livelier melodrama would be hard to find. The violent swinging of the cabin lantern causes a play of light and shadow. The mate falls 'stone dead' (117) and 'without uttering a syllable' (117). The other conspirators, 'pitiable objects of horror' (117), in turn are killed by Peters, Pym himself, Augustus and Tiger, and there remains but the unfortunate Parker—soon to be cannibalized with the break-up of the *Grampus*. At one level, Poe puts before us pure hokum, farce or preposterousness. Yet at another, he engages by giving away the game to perfection. He in fact offers a most shrewd *compte rendu* of his own effects. He speaks of Pym's imposture, and by implication the imposture of all art, as 'sudden apparition' (116), and also of 'the reality of the vision' (117) to the beholder. He even goes as far as to speculate upon the strange but familiar process of life imitating art and art life. Could it be that 'the apparition *might possibly* be real' (116)? Does not art, too, always tease in its appeal to credulity, its reference to some confirming and objective standard of truth? In 'acting out' his revenge drama, Poe as ever invites belief and the suspension of belief, the situating of ourselves both inside and at the margins of his text.

The ensuing events aboard the sinking *Grampus*—Augustus rotting into death through his gangrenous arm, Pym's delirious dreams of motion (124), the near-bisection of Peters by the rope about his waist, the ravages of hunger and thirst, and the repeated diving below only to encounter locked cabins and blocked corridors—takes this drama of illusions still further. Pym might again be both the subject and object of his own dream, the maker and the enacter of his own script. Perpetually, at least, he must serve as witness to things turned inside out apparently the one thing but in fact another, ever and always a charade.

Nowhere better is this the case than in the meeting with 'a large hermaphrodite brig' (130), a companion vessel to the *San Dominick* in Melville's 'Benito Cereno', and like Melville's vessel, the total opposite of what it appears. A death-ship rather than a ship of rescue, its crew are found to be 'smiling' (131) skullish death's-head smiles, grotesque imitations of benignity. Rather, too, than giving off the balmy scent of the South Seas dreamed up by Pym, the ship gives off 'a stench, such as the whole world has no name for' (132). All 'twenty-five or thirty human bodies' (132) represent not health but 'the last and most loathsome state of putrefaction' (132). To complete the horror a gull drops before them not real food but a half-eaten 'clotted and liverlike substance' (133) from a corpse aboard the ship. All the signs again have overwhelmingly cheated and Pym again has played an inadequate decipherer. 'Deliverance' (135), a word which recurs in the text, has yet to come about, and in nothing more than this 'most appalling and unfathomable mystery' (134) of death-in-life as projected in an apparitional, 'hermaphroditic', floating cemetery.

'Hunger' (135), 'thirst', 'our common deliverance' (135)

continue to contradict and perplex. Like T. S. Eliot's drowned Phoenician, Augustus deliriously asks for fish-scales to be combed out of his hair (138). All four, Pym, Peters, Parker and Augustus, verge 'on a species of second childhood' (139) regressing into 'simpering' (139) expressions, 'idiotic smiles' (139), and 'absurd platitudes' (139). A ship is spotted going cruelly in the wrong and opposite direction. In the midst of life, human or amphibian, Pym and Peters could not be closer to death. Yet to survive further they must kill, a reversion to the desperate but saving transgression of cannibalism. Parker it is who picks the short straw (and is promptly dispatched by Peters), but not before Pym—fearing chance might select him—experiences for the *Grampus* sailor 'the most intense, the most diabolical hatred' (145). Parker's flesh, however, keeps them going but temporarily, a mere staving-off of the inevitable end. But Poe again turns things about. Pym and Peters discover in 'the storeroom' (149) a Galápagos turtle, a living sea-larder of food and water taken paradoxically from the very ocean which has threatened them with storm, wave, shark and tempest.

None of which prevents the *Grampus* from heading into a last Coleridgean fate. Augustus rots and is given to the ravening sharks. Pym and Peters again endure 'great agony' (156), 'no prospect of relief' (156), and an impending end to their 'struggle for life' (157). But things, as ever in *Pym*, follow a zig-zag, turn-about pattern, confuting the predictable and denying the expected. As the boat keels over, Pym finds himself 'deceived' (157) in thinking this the end of his life. He is spun under, then up again, a whirling breach-birth which quite literally spins him out of disaster and back into life and consciousness—once again, too, anticipating Ishmael in his 'coffin life-buoy shot lengthwise from the sea' at the close of *Moby-Dick*.[13] The *Grampus*, likewise, transforms itself from a would-be coffin into a buoy of sorts, and also a supply-ship when '*excellent and highly nutritious*' (158) barnacles are found on its bottom, as well as crabs which afford 'several delicious meals' (159). The improbable survivors of an upside-down New England whaler water-logged in the Pacific, Pym and Peters are then improbably found by an equally improbable 'rakish-looking topsail schooner' (159), the *Jane Guy* (another 'hermaphroditic' craft?), which will take them still further down their contradictory passage into the polar south.

All of the *Grampus* journey, all the turn-abouts and connecting reversals, Poe has managed to tell both as literal and mock adventure, telling which folds back and in on itself. Ahead lies a still further circuitry of false fronts, snares, coded and eminently misreadable information, and all of it, under Poe's scripting, so narrated as again to implicate us in its own artifice and manoeuvre. From the safety of the *Jane Guy*, Pym glosses his *Grampus* experiences as follows: 'rather as a frightful dream from which we have happily awakened, than as events which had taken place in sober and naked reality' (163). Poe thus dissolves, as it were, his own text, 'dream' not 'reality', a story from start to finish emphatically the self-consuming artefact. Pym has all but drowned and then been saved against the odds in the *Ariel* caper. Aboard the *Grampus*, he has been entombed and resurrected, and then caught up in a revolt and counter-revolt, only in turn to end up saved by barnacles from an upside-down hull. Similarly, each disaster or storm or near-drowning can be seen as dream displaced into fact, Pym's 'glimpses' dramatically made over into seemingly literal events and a seemingly literal context. And Poe's 'impudent' and 'ingenious' story-telling throughout has been adapted to suit, neither quite fiction of fact nor quite factual fiction, and at once drawing us in while at the same time actually encouraging readerly circumspection and doubt.

5

With the entry of the *Jane Guy*, introduced by Poe mid-way through the text, the cycle begins again. Poe first surrounds the rescue and the ship in the most copious detail. He gives dates, latitudes and longitudes, a whole inventory of goods, crew, mate and captain, in all yet another instance of persuasive but nevertheless mock circumstantiality. Even Captain Guy, 'a gentleman of great urbanity of manner' (162), and a scion of the Guy family who own the ship, seems a mock three-dimensional presence. He is described as lacking 'energy' (162), 'that spirit of enterprise' (162), clearly the inner, visionary compulsion Pym himself embodies. The *Jane Guy's* trading voyage, thus, can be adapted by Pym to his own, a voyage less for goods than truths, less for 'any cargo' (162) than for Pym's encounter with his overwhelming 'destiny' (57). To presage this last phase of double voyaging, no sooner has the *Jane Guy* got under way with its two extra crew than conditions revert to extremities, 'one of the most tremendous seas I had then ever beheld' (164). The ship heaves and yawls until 'we were hurled on our beam-ends as if by magic, and a perfect wilderness of foam made a clear breach over us as we lay' (165), an escape Captain Guy construes as 'little less than miraculous' (165). Once more Poe pitches his story into a domain of the mock-real, an intermediate register between the verisimilar and the fantastical, which again entices while laying open its very fabrication.

Progress southwards aboard the *Jane Guy* Poe discloses through Pym as a succession of geographically descending references to Pacific islands. He mentions in turn the 'deceitful' Desolation Island (165), first discovered by Captain Cook, the Tristan d'Acunah group (171), and even the fabled, paradisial Auroras (173), replete with details of bird and plant life and still other discoveries and exploration. Pym also places himself among the ranks of prior South Pacific voyagers, Magellan and Cook foremost, the Russians Kretzenstern and Lisiausky, the Britishers Weddell and Briscoe, and the American Benjamin Morrell. To these, crucially, he adds the name of J. N. Reynolds, the great advocate of an expedition to test out the 'Hole at the Pole' or 'Hollow Earth' theories of John Cleves Symmes.[13] By the Reynolds-Symmes connection, Poe invokes not only an actual but a fantastical Antarctica, the white polar South as a then historical *terra incognita* but also his own imagined place of revelation, his own last synoptic version of things. In listing 'the principal attempts which have been made at penetrating to a high southern latitude' (180) and confessing to 'feelings of most intense interest' (181) at the news of Captain Guy's 'resolution of pushing boldly south-ward' (181), Pym also confirms the fiction of his own mag-netized condition, his individual polar 'destiny' (57).

To cross over into the Antarctic circle (182), accordingly, signifies not only a next phase in Pym's adventuring but a matching next phase in Poe's story-telling. For in descending to a point southward of all the known facts (or on Poe's terms mock- or pseudo-facts), Poe's text, also, becomes a perfect blank to be enscribed as for the first time *entirely* to his own invention and in which all story-telling and speculative bets are in play. So, legitimately, he may invent treacherous, fantasized 'blackskin warriors' (205), or new dramas of entombment and release, or Gulliverish aboriginal customs and cries, or wall-hieroglyphs which reach back to Genesis and Solomon and speak of a racially hierarchic world-order, or unprecedented animals and sights and colour-patterns each apparently at variance with but revelatory of the hemisphere left behind, or a warm South Pole, or, finally, a huge, white, God-like figure. Nowhere in *Pym* does either Poe's story or story-telling operate to more energetically 'impudent' or 'ingenious' effect.

Poe wastes little time getting under way. He gestures towards the circumstantial by again scrupulously dating Pym's ever more 'southerly' (182) course. Details pile up about climate, terrain, 'immense icebergs' and 'field ice' (183). A valued sailor becomes 'a man overboard' (183), an evident omen or death-warning. But 'real' as these matters seem, others of a more exotic, fantasized and imaginary, kind take over. 'A large bird of a brilliant blue plumage' (183) flies close, an almost painterly vision. The freezing air gives way to 'mild and pleasant' (184) temperature, a transposition of heat for cold. Peters kills a huge, bear-like creature, with 'blood red' (185) eyes, a 'bulldog' (185) snout, and a 'rank and fishy' (185) taste, a kind of misevolved and warning freak. On land, too, they discover 'a species of prickly pear' (185), no doubt another warning, then a mysterious canoe which Captain Guy thinks carved, emblem-like, with 'the figure of a tortoise' (186). Pym, throughout, exults in having now gone closer to the Antarctic pole 'than any previous navigators' (186). He presses Guy to go still further, and makes a reference to having met with 'one of the most intensely exciting secrets' (187) ever opened 'to the eye of science' (187). These different transitions from one realm to another could not be better sign-posted.

Yet more follows, especially 'the carcass of a singular-looking land animal' (188), with claws also 'of a brilliant scarlet' (188), its body covered in 'straight silky hair, perfectly white' (188), its tail long and 'peaked like that of a rat' (188), and its head essentially that of a cat but with 'flapped' (189) ears like those of a dog. Evolution seems to have gone yet further astray. This dead, white-bodied but mongrel beast, with teeth and claws blood-red as if it had fought some fatal last battle, makes the perfect forerunner to the 'jet black' (189) 'savages' (189) who now appear aboard four canoes. They, too, strike Pym as grotesque evolutionary parodies, with exaggeratedly negroid features, 'thick and woolly hair' (189) and clothes made from the 'skins of an unknown black animal' (189). They keep 'black stones' (190) in their boats. They 'jabber' (190), have 'never before seen any of the white race' (190), think the *Guy* 'a living creature' (190), and behave infantilely, worshipping the ship's tools as deities and consuming *biches de mer* like half-cannibal voluptuaries. Poe's story-telling positively thrives on the challenge of his literally unprecedented and enciphered world.

White on black, black on white: Poe's Southern, racially phobic, imagination also plays into this Antarctica, a displaced Deep South and fantasy Eden despoiled and hexed by brute, carbon tribesmen. Not only the temperature, but all assumed order, and especially racial order, has been put under transposition. Trees, for instance, resemble none previously witnessed. Rocks are 'novel in their mass, color and stratification' (193). Above all, the stream-water yields a warning against tampering with 'natural', decreed hierarchy. It is made up of 'distinct veins, each of a distinct hue' (194), none meant to 'commingle' (194). Pym observes, too, of this water that it provides 'the first link in that vast chain of apparent miracles with which I was destined to be encircled' (194). He has, at last, entered magic Antarctica, 'encircled' by 'apparent miracles', his anticipated 'destiny' (57) within reach. Poe, for his part, has so made one fiction generate another, the Antarctic circle as a species of 'text' or topographical scripture in which (and in black and white) the enciphered essence of the world-at-large is to be 'read'.

First 'the blackskin warriors' (205) provide the basis of a whole system of totem and taboo. They are projected with a Swiftian animus, sly, untrustworthy incarnations of total blackness. Their dwelling-places are covered with 'a large black skin' (195); their domestic hogs have 'black wool' (196); 'black albatross' (195) make the village of Klock-Klock their home; 'black gannets' (195) dwell among the bird population; the rest of the tribe appear in 'dresses of black skin' (197); and the Wampoo leadership dwell in 'black skin palaces' (197). They eat the innards of their hogs, pastiche sweetbread, out-landish 'black' food. Their black sexuality is carried in the further consumption of *biches de mer*, a source of renewal for 'the exhausted system of the immoderate voluptuary' (204). Behind all their seeming welcome, fawning even, lies truly a 'black' impersonation, the masking of 'the most barbarous, subtle, and bloodthirsty wretches that ever contaminated the face of the globe' (205). Swift's Lilliputian humankind re-appears in Poe as black devilry, fearsome insurrectionists who most surely personify slave-haunted Southern fears of a racial armageddon led by a Nat Turner, or Denmark Vesey, or Toussaint l'Ouverture. But in order to move Pym and Peters still further south, still deeper into this Antarctic 'region of novelty and wonder' (236), Poe again reverts to a series of 'ingenious' fades and dissolves. First the ship's party is buried alive by the perfidious Klock-Klock tribesmen. Then the remaining shipmates aboard the *Jane Guy* are overwhelmed and massacred by the natives, a thousand of whom in turn are blown up by dynamite. Meantime, having been saved by access to 'the mouth of [a] fissure' (207), once more 'entombed alive' (208), Pym and Peters survive, willed into continuance by Poe.

Another key dimension of this 'encircled' world is Poe's invented language. He develops a whole register of Klock-Klock idiom, echoic-mimetic words like *Anamoo-moo, Lama-Lama, Wampoo, TooWit,* and the warning cry *Tekel-li, Tekel-li*! To these is added the name *Tsalal*, to be pronounced in the manner of a hiss, a corruption of Solomon, and so the augury of a fallen, black counter-world. For all of this 'language', Poe's own neologized blend of Hebrew, Coptic, and Hamitic (there have been guesses, too, of some Maori), telegraphs a dire Solomonic message: white over black represents a first of all laws and has been fatally transgressed. All the words mean darkness in one way or another, a language which confirms that God-sanctioned hierarchy has been inverted and that His curse is upon the land. The same, too, applies to the series of 'alphabetical characters' (225) engraved in the 'very black and shining granite' (222) of the 'vast pit' (221) into which Pym and Peters take flight. These 'figures', or logos, add further hieroglyphic warning. Tsalal represents the black, other half of the world's 'polar' order, its infernal language yet another of Poe's fictions-within-a-fiction.

Again, too, one world yields violently to another, as Pym enacts a classic falling dream, his 'rushing and headlong descent into the abyss' (229), in fact a descent down the pit face in which he falls into the arms of Peters—momentarily transformed into 'a dusky, fiendish, and filmy figure' (229). Given time for recovery, Pym feels 'a new being' (229), re-born once more. And so it is, with their own captive Man Friday, Nu-Nu, Peters and he sail a yet further 'vast distance to southward' (235), three mythy, emblematic world figures, a black-bodied, black-toothed Tsalal islander, an American Indian half-breed, and a white New Englander.

Poe's polar seascape grows even more dream-like, more fictive. It is full of 'continual light' (235), iceless, smooth, marked by 'unusual phenomena' (236) and 'streaked' (236) by the Aurora Borealis (236). The surrounding water turns hot and milky. Pym speaks of his *'numbness* of body and mind—a dreaminess of sensation' (237). Nu-Nu expires, having revealed something of his people's history—their governance by King Tsalemon, their warrior dress ('from an animal of a huge size', 236), and their cultism about black and white. 'One of the white animals' (238) which has caused a 'wild' 'commotion' (238) in Klock-Klock floats by. 'White ashy material falls' (238), and the vapour begins to form into a 'gigantic curtain' (238), as if indeed this ending were dream, one vast theatrical imagining.

Interpretation of the 'figure . . . of the whiteness of snow' (239), the 'shrouded' (239) form which appears from within 'the embraces of the cataract' (239), has to remain open. It may assuredly be some whited guardian of a Symmsian hole, or the personification of Unity over Diffusion, or Pym's projected image of self-perfection, or some emissary God-figure. But in all of these is it not also yet another massive blank to be given signification as much by the reader as by Pym? For in a way, Poe is handing over to the reader his story and story-telling, the imagining of the hitherto unimagined. *Pym* moves towards closure as openly and speculatively as possible, its protagonist's consciousness slowly eviscerated and put up for transfer. The reader is so enjoined, even defied, into taking on the next stage of imagining, the text (as yet) not written.

6

Poe's concluding Note, accordingly, provides all the more of a jolt when it refers us back to the actual, historic world, a last dissolve told in the put-on style of the Preface. Pym's 'late sudden and distressing death' (240) is reported as being 'well known through the medium of the daily press' (240). The very notion of a 'daily press' after such polar, oneiric voyaging, carries its own irony. Poe himself, presumably as 'Mr. Poe', 'declines' to believe 'the latter portions of the narration' (240). Even Peters, whose fate has not in fact been given, 'cannot be met with at present' (240), though 'alive, and resident in Illinois' (240). All these past narrators, so to speak, have stepped down, ceded authority. Any suggestions, therefore, that the text's 'statements in relation to these regions' (240) may soon be 'verified or contradicted' (240) by a forthcoming 'governmental expedition now preparing for the Southern Ocean' (240), can only be parodic. *Pym* ends as it began, a *ficcion* or artifice, not to mention a seemingly posthumous and disowned piece of writing.

These adroit gestures of abdication again throw the burden of bringing off the text as a whole even more than usually upon the reader, and especially its 'prophetic glimpses' (57). As it stands, the Note purportedly adds a further mock-scholarly gloss on the language of Tsalal together with an epitaph from the Book of Job as evidence of God's warning curse upon the realm. But in fact it cannily says still more about Pym's textual status. If ambiguously authored, *Pym* is also ambiguously incomplete, a text whose last two or three chapters have been 'lost' (240) and therefore looks to us to supply, or like Jules Verne even write, its ending.[14] Then, too, whoever can be assumed to have written the Note makes reference to Tsalal's language and iconic wall-markings as 'a

131

wild field for speculation and exciting conjecture' (242). So much, and more, might all have been Poe's remit in *Pym*. For few narratives, nineteenth-century American or otherwise, can quite so resourcefully have shown the setting out, the enfabulation, of their author's will to 'speculation and exciting conjecture'. However unlikely to win over all tastes, in this respect if no other Poe's only full-length fiction represents him as much as any of his stories at his most 'impudently' and 'ingeniously' inspired.

NOTES

1. W. H. Auden (ed.), Edgar Allan Poe: *Selected Prose and Poetry* (New York: Rinehart, 1950).
2. Auden (op. cit.), Introduction, p. vii.
3. For a most useful summary of the state of criticism on *Pym*, see J. V. Ridgely, 'Tragical-Mythical-Satirical-Hoaxical: Problems of Genre in *Pym*', *American Transcendental Quarterly* (Fall 1974), Vol. 24, Part 1, 4–9.
4. The review, in fact, appeared twice, first in *Graham's Magazine* (April–May 1842), and then with slight changes in *Godey's Lady's Book* (November 1847). For the two versions, see James A. Harrison (ed.), *The Complete Works of Edgar Allan Poe* (New York, 1902; reproduced, New York: A.M.S. Press, 1965), Vol. XI, pp. 102–13, and Vol. XIII, pp. 141–55.
5. 'Review of Nathaniel Hawthorne's *Twice-Told Tales*' (op. cit.).
6. The classic formulation of this view is that of T. S. Eliot in 'From Poe to Valéry', *Hudson Review*, 11 (1949), 327–43: 'That Poe had a powerful intellect is undeniable: but it seems to me the intellect of a highly gifted young person before puberty. The forms which his lively curiosity takes are those in which a pre-adolescent mentality delights: wonders of nature and of mechanics and of the supernatural, cryptograms and cyphers, puzzles and labyrinths, mechanical chess-players and wild flights of speculation. The variety and ardour of his curiosity delight and dazzle; yet in the end the eccentricity and lack of coherence of his interests tire. There is just that lacking which gives dignity to the mature man: a consistent view of life. . . . What is lacking is not brain power, but that maturity of intellect which comes only with the maturing of the man as a whole, the development and coordination of his various emotions.'
7. Henry James, Preface to *The Altar of the Dead, The Beast in the Jungle, The Birthplace and Other Tales* (*Novels and Tales*, New York: Scribner's, 1910–17), Vol. XVII. James, to be sure, was using Poe as a touchstone for his own kind of suspense narrative. His comments contrast interestingly

with those spoken by Prince Amerigo in *The Golden Bowl* where Pym is described as 'a wonderful tale by Allan Poe . . . a thing to show, by the way, what imagination Americans *could* have'. The observations in the New York Edition Preface run as follows: 'the safest arena for the play of moving accidents and mighty mutations and strange encounters, or whatever odd matters, is the field, as I may call it, rather of their second than of their first exhibition. By which, to avoid obscurity, I mean nothing more than I feel myself show them best by showing almost exclusively the way they are felt, by recognizing as their main interest some impression strongly made by them and intensely received. We but too probably break down, I have ever reasoned, when we attempt the prodigy, the appeal to mystification, in itself; with its "objective" side too emphasized the report (it is ten to one) will practically run thin. We want it clear, goodness knows, but we also want it thick, and we get the thickness in the human consciousness that entertains and records, that amplifies and interprets it. That indeed, when the question is (to repeat) of the "supernatural," constitutes the only thickness we do get; here prodigies, when they come straight, come with an effect imperilled; they keep all their character, on the other hand, by looming through some other history—the indispensable history of somebody's *normal* relation to something. It's in such connexions as these they they most interest, for what we are then mainly concerned with is their imputed and borrowed dignity. Intrinsic values they have none—as we feel for instance in such a matter as the would-be portentous climax of Edgar Poe's "Arthur Gordon Pym," where the indispensable history is absent, where the phenomena evoked, the moving accidents, coming straight, as I say, are immediate and flat, and the attempt is all at the horrific in itself. The result is that, to my sense, the climax fails—fails because it stops short, and stops short for want of connexions. There are no connexions; not only, I mean, in the sense of further statement, but of our own further relation to the elements, which hang in the void: whereby we see the effect lost, the imaginative effort wasted.'

8. I particularly want to acknowledge the following: Patrick F. Quinn: 'Poe's Imaginary Voyage', *Hudson Review*, 4 (1952), pp. 562–85; Edward H. Davidson: *Poe: A Critical Study* (Cambridge: Harvard University Press, 1957), pp. 156–80; Sydney Kaplan: 'Introduction' to *The Narrative of Arthur Gordon Pym* (New York: Hill and Wang, 1960), pp. vii–xxv; Walter E. Bezanson: 'The Troubled Sleep of Arthur Gordon Pym', Rudolf Kirk and C. F. Main (eds.): *Essays in Literary History, Presented to Milton French* (The Rutgers University Press, 1960), pp. 149–75; L. Moffitt Cecil: 'The Two Narratives of Arthur Gordon Pym', *Texas Studies in Literature and Language*, Vol. V, No. 2, Summer 1963, pp. 232–41; J. V. Ridgely and Iola S. Haverstick: 'Chartless Voyage: The Many Narratives of Arthur Gordon Pym', *Texas Studies in Literature and Language*, Vol. VII, 1966, pp. 63–80; Joseph J. Moldenhauer: 'Imagination and Perversity in *The Narrative of Arthur Gordon Pym*', *Texas Studies in Literature and Language*, Vol. XIII, No. 2, Summer 1971, pp. 267–80; Joseph V. Ridgely: 'The End of Pym and the ending of *Pym*', Richard P. Veler

(ed.): *Papers on Poe: Essays in Honor of John Ward Ostram* (Springfield, Ohio: Chantry Music Press), pp. 104–12; Robert L. Carringer: 'Circumscription of Space and the Form of Poe's *Arthur Gordon Pym*', *P.M.L.A*, May 1974, Vol. 89, No. 3, pp. 506–16; Eric Mottram: Poe's *Pym* and the American Social Imagination', Robert J. DeMott and Sanford E. Marovitz (eds.): *Artful Thunder: Versions of The Romantic Tradition in American Literature In Honor of Howard P. Vincent* (Kent State University Press, 1975), pp. 25–53; Harold Beaver: 'Introduction', *The Narrative of Arthur Gordon Pym of Nantucket* (Harmondsworth: Penguin Books, 1975), pp. 7–39; John T. Irwin: *American Hieroglyphics: The Symbol of The Egyptian Hieroglyphics in the American Renaissance* (New Haven and London: Yale University Press, 1980), pp. 42–235.

9. Harold Beaver (ed.): *The Narrative of Arthur Gordon Pym of Nantucket* (Harmondsworth: Penguin Books, 1975), p. 57. For ease of access all subsequent page references are to this edition.

10. Poe can also be said to point backwards in *Pym*, most notably to Laurence Sterne's *Tristram Shandy* and behind that to the *Lazarillo de Tormes*. As a direct forward influence *Pym* can probably claim no greater descendant than *Moby-Dick*.

11. There I have tried to analyse in the following: A. Robert Lee: ' "Like a Dream Behind Me": Hawthorne's "The Custom-House" and *The Scarlet Letter*', pp. 48–67, in A. Robert Lee (ed.): *Nathaniel Hawthorne: New Critical Essays* (London: Vision Press, 1982) and A. Robert Lee: '*Moby-Dick*: The Tale and the Telling', pp. 86–127, in Faith Pullin (ed.): *New Perspectives on Melville* (Edinburgh University Press, 1978).

12. *Moby-Dick*, Chapter 110.

13. For the Symmes-Reynolds-Poe connection, see Beaver (op. cit.), pp. 10–14, and Davidson (op. cit.), pp. 156–58.

14. Jules Verne: *Le Sphinx des Glaces* (1897).

7

'A Strange Sound, as of a Harp-string Broken': The Poetry of Edgar Allan Poe

by DAVID MURRAY

Poe's poetry has usually been an embarrassment to all but his most uncritical admirers, and Harold Bloom's recent dismissal of his use of language[1] ('Translation even into his own language always benefits Poe') and his relegation of him to 'twelfth place with Sidney Lanier' is only the latest in a long line of comprehensive denunciations.[2] His poetry is often seen as the logical and unfortunate result of a theory of poetry which sits uneasily as the heir to English and German Romanticism and the precursor of French Symbolism, but the *precise* nature of Poe's poety can only be found by locating the contradictions in Romantic theories of poetry out of which changes and developments in the direction of Symbolism develop, since it is at the point of these contradictions that Poe's poetry most characteristically operates.

Rather, then, than another by-rote evaluation of Poe's poetry, this essay offers an approach to it through a re-examination of the basic terms in which Romantic poetry has, until recently, been discussed. According to Richard M. Fletcher, 'the one critical statement most contemporary critics would not object to about Poe is that he was a symbolist',[3] and yet it is precisely this description which needs to be challenged.

135

To do so will also involve challenging the cluster of terms in relation to which symbolism is usually defined—unity, organicism, imagination and, particularly, allegory, and I shall draw upon the quite separate but curiously parallel insights of Walter Benjamin and Paul de Man into the workings of allegory in particular.

A late occasional poem 'To ——' can be used to open up the area of concern and to exemplify many of Poe's themes. It presents, conventionally enough, the poet, 'the writer of these lines', disclaiming his ability to express the depth of his feelings for his loved one. It begins with him admitting that earlier 'in the mad pride of intellectuality' he had been encouraged to think that there was nothing that could not be expressed in language. By the end of the poem, though, he is presented as being without words—almost without faculties—in entranced contemplation of 'the gorgeous vista' of 'thee only'. A conventional enough compliment, this, which would seem to be asserting a reality prior to language—the poem can only be inadequately *about* the lady. What happens in the middle of the poem, though, forces us to re-think it completely, and leads into a characteristic Poe concern. What has opened up the 'gate of dreams' and the vista of the lady is 'two words', her name, which have stirred 'unthought like thoughts that are the souls of thought'. These words are presented as provoking his imagination, but words in general are seen as preventing his *expression* of it. As the title of the poem indicates, though, the two words themselves are never given to us, so we are at an infinite remove from an actual person. Even at the end, when Poe describes being led to the prospect of the lady by the two words, her actual presence turns out to be a virtual and dispersed one. 'With thy dear name as text' he is led to

> the golden
> Threshold of the wide-open gate of dreams,
> Gazing entranced, adown the gorgeous vista,
> And thrilling as I see, upon the right,
> Upon the left, and all the way along,
> Amid empurpled vapors, far away
> To where the prospect terminates—*thee only*.[4]

This is not so much seeing the lady as seeing her *in* everything, seeing a visionary landscape as expression of her, and so our game of 'find the lady' continues in a circle, since the poem presents two situations which are inversions of each other. *He* has the words which lead him to the landscape in which he sees the lady embodied, but not the power to express it. We have the absence of the words but the actual expression, which he denies his ability to produce, in the poem. What neither of us has is the lady. It is important to stress this, since it is precisely with the *separations* of language and the real world, and of the real world and the ideal world, in Poe's poetry that this essay will be concerned.

'To —— —' is a poem which seems to be rejecting the 'power of words' but which in fact *demonstrates* the power of words not to describe the actual but to lead or inspire the imagination to create the ideal, and the idea of creation by words is clearly for Poe not simply a metaphor for literary inventions, as is shown in one of his colloquies written a few years earlier. In 'The Power of Words' Agathos is instructing the newcomer Oinos in the ways of Aidenn, a place, or state of being, to which they have come as immortals after the recent destruction of earth. In explaining the nature of infinity, and the consequent endless efforts and ramifications of any physical change in any part of the universe, Agathos refers to the physical aspect of words, since every spoken word is 'an impulse on the air'.[5] Coming, in their journey through space, upon a star which is particularly green and beautiful yet turbulent, Agathos then reveals, to prove his point, that this star is literally the product of his love when on earth, 'I spoke it—with a few passionate sentences—into birth.'[6] Here, as in *Eureka* and elsewhere, Poe posits a unity of the material and the spiritual, the implications of which will need to be explored later, but important for the present argument is the way that it is the very *materiality* of language which creates the ideal. That is, it is not what the words *refer* to but the *sound* of them which is crucial. Language has a dual aspect, therefore, in Poe. It is both the mark of absence—a word is not a thing in this world, and words cannot capture the things they refer to—and, in another aspect, a mark of a presence which is *not* in this world. It would be wrong, though, to over-emphasize this second aspect in Poe as it would not only turn him into an early Symbolist with a belief in correspondences, but would also deflect attention from the way language in Poe occupies a *dual* rôle, as divider and connector of discontinuous realms. This is exemplified in one of his earliest and most ambitious poems, 'Al Aaraaf'.

Like the dialogue 'The Power of Words' the poem takes place after the destruction of Earth on a star inhabited by angelic creatures. The ruler, Nesace, has been charged by God to take his message to other realms, and there is a hint that as part of her rôle she may have destroyed Earth for its sinfulness. Poe's epigraph, referring to the star discovered by Tycho Brahe which 'attained, in a few days, a brilliancy surpassing that of Jupiter—then as suddenly disappeared, and has never been seen since', is meant not so much to identify Al Aaraaf as to present an analogue, a reminder, typical of Poe, that such brilliant suns *do* exist in infinite space, and to juxtapose and interrelate, as in all his science-fiction, the physical and the mental or spiritual. The poem's origins are clearly enough in Milton and Thomas Moore's 'Lalla Rookh', and its moral argument, carried in exchanges between Nesace and God and the lovers Angelo and Ianthe, is unremarkable—a celebration of Harmony and Beauty in their pure and eternal aspects. What is more interesting is the extent to which Poe uses language not to write *about* this Platonic conception of absolute beauty, but to attempt to embody it, or rather, to find a verbal *equivalent* to it, which is different from a description.

The name Poe chooses for his planet is, he tells us, 'from the Al Aaraaf of the Arabians, a medium between Heaven and Hell',[7] but as well as describing its limbo-like qualities, Poe's likely sources also described it as a veil between the blessed and the damned and a 'wall or partition', finding the derivation in 'the verb *arafa*, which signifies to *distinguish* between things or to *part* them'.[8] As Stovall points out, Poe's vision of Al Aaraaf rather than being a barrier to separate Hell and Heaven is a place of beauty and peculiar happiness in its own right, and if we accept his carefully substantiated case for 'Al Aaraaf' as an expression of Poe's ideas about poetry, we can say that instead of being the barrier between discontinuous realms, between material and spiritual, language when used in poetry opens up an area which is neither, but gains its special existence from its *relation* to both.

To do this, though, language must subvert its normal

functions and must, as in the case of 'To — —', lead *away* from the referent. It is important to stress, here, that this special state can only be reached in the *absence* of the thing to which the word normally refers *and* the inevitable absence of the absolute to which this special use of language aspires. God is not present in Al Aaraaf, nor is human life. Language cannot embody both worlds, and this is a crucial distinction between Poe's use of language and the generally accepted Romantic view of the symbol, which is seen as unifying, healing the breach rather than operating *in* the breach—of which, more later.

When Poe comes to describe the voice of God in Al Aaraaf the referential qualities of language are explicitly dismissed, and even thrown into reverse, so that 'Silence' comes to be the best way to describe this voice and presence:

> 'a voice was there
> How solemnly pervading the calm air!
> A sound of silence on the startled ear
> Which dreamy poets name 'the music of the sphere'.
> Ours is a world of words: Quiet we call
> 'Silence'—which is the merest word of all.
> All Nature speaks, and ev'n ideal things
> Flap shadowy sounds from visionary wings—
> But oh! not so when, thus, in realms on high
> The eternal voice of God is passing by,
> And the red winds are withering in the sky![9]

The use of synaesthetic effects to create those 'indefinite sensations' which are the province of poetry is part of the evidence used to relate Poe to the French Symbolists, but distinctions have to be made. As Patrick Quinn has demonstrated, Baudelaire attributes a significance to some of Poe's ideas that was not there for Poe. He saw Poe as substituting the world of spirit for the world of dull materiality; 'From the midst of a world gluttonous for only material things, Poe soared out into dreams.'[10] Certainly, Poe stresses the ideal quality of Beauty but his more characteristic view is that poetry is 'the Human *Aspiration* for Supernal Beauty' (my italics).[11] It is not the realm of dreams or of the infinite but, like Al Aaraaf, the realm in between, and it creates its effects precisely out of that in-betweenness. The materials used by the poet must be reproduced, said Poe, 'through the veil of the soul',[12] but the veil does not lift. The imagination is supremely important for Poe because for the possessor it

> brings his soul often to a glimpse of things supernal and eternal—to the very verge of the *great secrets*. There are moments, indeed, in which he perceives the faint perfumes and hears the melodies of a happier world.[13]

If these hints and glimpses are attained, though, it is by that indirection and indefiniteness which Poe professed to admire in Tennyson, and certainly aimed at himself, a 'suggestive indefinitiveness of meaning, with the view of bringing about a definitiveness of vague and therefore spiritual *effect*'.[14]

John T. Irwin's important and far-reaching discussion of the rôle of language in Poe is mostly confined to his prose, and to the theme of hieroglyphics as 'the symbol of self-evidential visual presence in writing', but he decodes indefinitiveness of meaning, ranging all the way to the point at which language stops and music begins, as in a reciprocal if antithetic relation to the hieroglyph, and sees music as 'the symbol of immediate intuitive conviction'.[14] The connecting idea which links indefiniteness to an intuition of the absolute or inexpressible is that of the sublime, and Irwin also makes the connection a way of distinguishing Poe's prose from his poetry:

> Inasmuch as the experience of the sublime involves an intuition of undifferentiated Being, it is necessarily an indefinite experience, an experience beyond words and images that can only be approximated by that sense of the indefinite that *can* be conveyed in words and images. But the question is whether the indefinite is to be evoked by a figure/ground opposition between the clearly defined verbal image and the indefinite verbal music, the sharp limits of one outlining the vague realm of the other, or by a fusion of the two in which the indefiniteness of the verbal music blurs the verbal imagery. The latter method is that of Poe's poetry, while the former influences the structure of many of the tales[15]

In Irwin's terms, therefore, when Poe claims that 'indefinitiveness is an element of the true music',[16] he is seeing music as the antithesis of the normal uses of language, in the name of 'the creation of supernal Beauty', and Poe even suggests that the transcendence of human limitations, if possible at all, may be possible here: 'It *may* be, indeed, that here this sublime end is, now and then, attained *in fact*.'[17] Rather than just accepting the epistemological claims for indefiniteness and intuition, and seeing them almost as outside language, we need to see them, and their relation to the sublime, as linguistic devices, creating psychological effects. The origin of the sublime has long been located not just in the perception of something incommensurable but in the breakdown of possibilities of *representation* that this implies. Building on Kant's definition, Thomas Weiskel eventually arrives at the formulation that

> we call an object sublime if the attempt to represent it determines the mind to regard its inability to grasp wholly the object as a symbol of the mind's relation to a transcendent order.[18]

The effect, then, is created by the breakdown of representation *and* the consequent use of that breakdown as a signifier of a larger state of affairs, the inability of the finite mind to grasp the infinite: 'In the sublime a *relation* to the object—the negative relation of unattainability—becomes the signifier in the aesthetic order of meaning.'[19]

In different ways both of the examples from Poe's poetry I have used so far do this, in that both are premised upon an absence but *present* themselves as aspiring to reach towards a creation of presence by means of language, but the crucial perspective added by Weiskel's definition allows us to see this as a structure designed to create a psychological effect *not* of transcendence but of the sublime which is generated out of the *failure* of language to transcend the finite. The setting of 'Al Aaraaf' after the destruction of Earth is parallelled on a more localized and personal level in many of Poe's poems which are constructed around death, but Poe is not a 'post mortem poet' in the sense that Lawrence described Whitman. Rather than celebrating a merging with the infinite, Poe's poetry uses death as evidence of separation—the discontinuity of this world and the ideal—and builds its psychological structures on the contemplation of this. The sense of separation, loss, discontinuity, then, is often the *basis* for the poetic impulse. In

'Stanzas', for instance, an early and rather confused poem in a Wordsworthian mode, Poe describes the visionary power of his youthful communings with nature. The exact provenance and operation of this power is obscure, but Poe's way of describing its awakening is very striking. The power, he says, is all around us, but

> . . . only bid
> With a strange sound, as of a harp-string broken
> T'awaken us—'Tis a symbol and a token
> . . . .
> of what in other worlds shall be[20]

Not harmony and proportion, then, but the end of it, gives us a momentary inkling of the transcendent. Poe has a classical source for this particular sound, in that the statue of Memnon was supposed to produce it when struck by the rays of the morning sun, and his other reference to it in his poetry is similarly interesting. In 'The Coliseum', a set-piece meditation on the ruins of classical antiquity, originally meant as part of 'Politian', Poe suggests that these ruins can speak to us as Memnon's statue did:

> Prophetic sounds and loud, arise forever
> From us, and from all Ruin, unto the wise
> As melody from Memnon to the Sun[21]

It is from brokenness, ruins, then, that we receive the prophetic sounds, not from the actual experience of harmony. Interesting psychoanalytic avenues may be opened up by the fact that the sound was also reputed to be that of Memnon saluting his mother,[22] but on a more obvious level the use of ruins to evoke a state of mind relates to that aspect of the sublime exemplified by Poe's gothic landscapes elsewhere. There is another link between 'Stanzas' and 'The Coliseum' to be found in another early piece, 'Spirits of The Dead', a meditation which echoes the passage quoted from 'Stanzas'. In describing a state of solitude in which the spirits of the dead seem to blot out all light and hope, Poe creates a landscape in which the stars from Heaven offer 'a burning and a fever' rather than any benevolence and God appears to be absent:

> The breeze—the breath of God—is still—
> And the mist upon the hill
> Shadowy—shadowy—yet unbroken
> Is a symbol and a token—
> How it hangs upon the trees
> A mystery of mysteries.[23]

In the absence of (the breath of) God, the presence of the dead remains, here signified by the mist, uncleansed by the wind. Once again, then, what is signified is an absence, and the *insistence* on its signifying power ('a symbol and a token') is much more noticeable than any clear indications of *what* it signifies. Irwin discusses at length the use of the figure in the mist at the end of *The Narrative of Arthur Gordon Pym* in terms directly applicable to my argument here:

> The mist's indefiniteness and its quality of simultaneously revealing and veiling make it a particularly appropriate representation of that undifferentiated sublime which, as Poe claims in another context is experienced in 'brief and indeterminate glimpses'.[24]

In different ways, then, all of the poems cited have used a scenario in which a sort of beauty or sublimity is achieved by recognition of its absence, or the inexpressibility of it in its absolute forms. Probably the most complex development of this scenario is in 'Ulalume', where the climax of the poem is the arrival at the tomb of Ulalume, which forces the recognition of absence and separation. Typically, though, it is a word, a name, which is crucial

> And we passed to the end of the vista—
> But were stopped by the door of a tomb—
> By the door of a legended tomb:—
> And I said—'What is written, sweet sister,
> On the door of this legended tomb?'
> She replied—'Ulalume—Ulalume!'[25]

Halliburton makes the connection with other poems very clear: 'Ulalume never assumes bodily form. The speaker confronts her as a name, much as the mourner of "The Raven" and other protagonists, confront some baffling, overpowering word: *discovery, silence, nevermore.*'[26]

The complexity—or confusion—of the poem, and in

particular the relation of sound to sense in it, has attracted extensive critical discussion, and it is worth looking briefly at the characteristic critical terms used and trying to clarify them before developing any further my own argument about Poe's use of language. Yvor Winters complains that 'the subject of grief is employed as a very general excuse for a great deal of obscure and only vaguely related emotion.' In other words, he objects to the failure of the 'indefiniteness' to add to, or be orchestrated towards, a final meaning. His strictures against 'The City in The Sea' are, he makes clear, as appropriate to 'Ulalume'. As well as 'an intense feeling of meaning withheld', we have 'all of the paraphernalia of allegory except the significance'.[27] Brooks and Warren, too, see it as a hamfisted allegory of love, or something like it, leading the poet to the door of death, dressed up with easy supernatural effects.[28] Eric Carlson's careful attempt to reconstruct a psychological reading which avoids using large-scale and reductive Freudian categories offers an alternative to these dismissive accounts. In particular, Carlson subjects what is usually seen as allegory in Poe to more careful scrutiny and concludes that 'If classical in its allegorical symbolism, "Ulalume" employs a modern (non-rationalistic) psychology in its development and resolution of the conflict.'[29] Carlson nowhere explains how he is defining symbol and allegory, but any further examination of the exact nature of Poe's relation to Romantic theories of poetry as well as his own practice requires a more careful look at these terms.

My discussion of these critical terms needs to be clearly distinguished from the outset from Poe's own usage, which is fragmentary and misleading. His strong attack on allegory in his review of Hawthorne's tales seems to be based on his dislike of didacticism and the reduction of a work of art to a single moral lesson. Allegory, in these terms, is acceptable only when kept out of sight, 'judiciously subdued, seen only as a shadow or by suggestive glimpses, and making its nearest approach to truth in a not obtrusive and therefore not unpleasant *appositeness*.'[30] 'Symbol' is likewise a word seldom used by Poe—in fact, his use of it in the phrase in the two early poems cited above ('a symbol and a token') is totally untypical—and Fletcher detects a deliberate avoidance of the term.[31] The weight of meaning which the two terms bear, then, is mainly a critical codifying and systematizing of Romantic theory, but since the issues are so close to my argument about Poe's language, they can best be dealt with in these established critical terms. Both Walter Benjamin and Paul de Man, from their different perspectives, have subjected the romantic privileging of symbol over allegory to close and critical examination, with the intention of re-making the case for allegory, which had come to provide 'the dark background against which the bright world of the symbol might stand out'.[32] Benjamin rejects the Romantic view, which has continued in circulation and become dogma, that allegorical representation merely signifies a general concept or idea, whereas symbolic representation is the actual embodiment of it. According to this view, allegory is *in place* of what it represents but symbol partakes of a totality which is recognized through it. Thus symbol is supposed to deny or overcome the split, not only between sign and thing, but also potentially between finite and infinite, in the manner of a religious symbol. When this idea is carried over to aesthetics, 'As a symbolic construct, the beautiful is supposed to merge with the divine in an unbroken whole.'[33]

Poe's debt to Romantic theories of poetry, via Coleridge and ultimately Schlegel, is clear enough, and it is easy to find statements which seem to have him subscribing to the view of the rôle of symbol (even if he does not use the word) in Coleridge's descriptions of imagination as

> that reconciling and mediatory power, which incorporating the reason in images of the sense . . . gives birth to a system of symbols, harmonious in themselves and consubstantial with the truth of which they are conductors.[34]

Poe's ideas of the unity of a work of art clearly stem from this, as does his idea here of the poem achieving a unity which aims to make it part of what it represents:

> Inspired by an ecstatic prescience of the glories beyond the grave, we struggle, by multiform combinations among the things and thoughts of Time, to attain a portion of that Loveliness whose very elements, perhaps, appertain to eternity alone.[35]

Poe's borrowings from Coleridge are so evident and pervasive that Floyd Stovall, in charting the influence, tends to dismiss those places where Poe openly *disagrees* with him:

> I feel confident that he agreed with Coleridge in every respect; but, impelled by the desire to be original and painfully conscious of his obligation to Coleridge, he sought to avoid the obligation by opposing him.[36]

Even if Stovall is right here, such a clear case of Bloomian anxiety of influence needs to be looked at more closely. Coleridge's stress, in the passage quoted above, on the consubstantiality of the symbol with what it represented is a crucial part of the distinction between symbol, and the organicist conception of totality implied, and allegory. It is parallelled by Coleridge's celebrated distinction between fancy and imagination, whereby fancy combines while the imagination creates. The imagination has the power to create symbols which not only re-combine old elements, but bring new entities into being, on the model not only of natural, organic creation, but of divine creation. Poe flatly rejects this, and his rejection has far-reaching implications. He refers to Coleridge's distinction between fancy and imagination in terms of creativity as a distinction

> without a difference; without even a difference of degree. The fancy as nearly creates as the imagination; and neither creates in any respect. All novel conceptions are merely unusual combinations. The mind of man can imagine nothing which has not really existed. . . . It will be said, perhaps, that we can imagine a *griffin* and that a griffin does not exist. Not the griffin certainly, but its component parts. It is a mere compendium of known limbs and features—of known qualities[37]

The griffin, then, is not organic, it is a combination rather than a fusion, and it is interesting to note that even when he seems to be arguing for the fusing and creative powers of the imagination, he uses a mechanical rather than an organic metaphor.

> The pure Imagination chooses *from either beauty or deformity*, only the most combinable things hitherto uncombined. . . . But as often analogously happens in physical chemistry, so not unfrequently does it occur in this chemistry of the intellect, that

the admixture of two elements will result in a something that shall have nothing of the qualities of one of them—or even nothing of the qualities of either.[38]

Here we have the rationale for what I believe to be an important distinction in Poe between totality and unity of *effect*, and a totality or unity created in the poem and existing as an entity consubstantial with the ideal, and also, of course, the rationale for the painstaking and mechanical *assembling* of elements to create these effects, rather than their mystical embodiment in symbols. The poem does not *grow out* of an experience or set of subject-matter, to which it refers. It is *assembled towards* an end, namely a totality of effect which is different in kind from that given by prose.

Here, it could be argued, is a crucial distinction between Poe and his Romantic predecessors, but in the light of Paul de Man's analysis of the Romantic view of symbol, which follows a remarkably similar course to Benjamin's much earlier work, we can also see Poe's own paradoxical position as a particularly clear case of a general contradiction involved in the privileging of symbol. De Man's careful deconstruction of the notion of symbol reveals the contradictions both in the Romantic poets and in later critics which suggest that the claims for totality involved in this view of a symbol can only ever be part of a dialectical movement. Whenever subject and object are merged, or language as signifier is identified with language as embodiment, there is always, de Man insists, a sleight of hand involved, which, when discovered, reveals the impossibility of separating out symbol from allegory straightforwardly. De Man describes the different claims very clearly:

> Whereas the symbol postulates the possibility of an identity or identification, allegory designates primarily a distance in relation to its own origin, and, renouncing the nostalgia and the desire to coincide, it establishes its language in the void of this temporal difference. In so doing, it prevents the self from an illusory identification with the non-self, which is now fully, though painfully, recognised as the non-self.[39]

The introduction here of the element of temporality is central to de Man's argument and to his distinction, since it is the desire to heal the breach caused by time itself that

147

generates the rhetorical strategies and claims of the symbol. A unity is asserted in which 'the intervention of time is merely a matter of contingency', whereas in allegory time is 'the original constitutive category'. Since any attempt to deny temporality can only ever be a temporary stratagem it is misleading to see the symbol as the exclusive and definitive mode. Even within Romantic writing itself it is constantly giving way to, and being infiltrated by, temporality and, therefore, by all those allegorical elements which have apparently been rejected. De Man's account of Romantic poetry, then, is of 'a conflict between a conception of the self seen in its authentically temporal predicament and a defensive strategy that tries to hide from this negative self-knowledge'. Mankind's temporal predicament is characterized by death and loss, and it is on this that Poe's most characteristic poetry dwells. The last quotation from de Man, above, could in fact be a description of 'Ulalume' or any number of Poe's poems, and it is worth looking again at 'Ulalume' and at 'The Sleeper' in relation to it.

The circularity of the time-sequence in 'Ulalume' is prefigured in the phrase in the first verse—'my most immemorial year'—which immediately presents a curious block to understanding. 'Immemorial', blending and almost disappearing into the words around it through echoes and repetitions of sound, suggests both memorable and unrememberable, and the poem acts out in its compulsive circularity the irreconcilability of the two—that is of remembering and coming to terms with death, or of forgetting it. It would be wrong, though, to see this as a poem *about* coming to terms with mortality, or *about* the inextricability of love and death, and therefore an ironic expression of human limitations. This is because in Poe there is really no experienced *tension* between the joys of love and the pain of loss. The former state is always short-circuited, the time of plenitude has always already passed, and the process of temporality is already closed, in Death which is both its denial and its ultimate end.[41] Poe uses death not as an expression of limits but as the most important of the elements to be combined to create the effect of beauty— which is, as he insists, an effect and not a quality. Death is only ever, then, a sign, the name on the legended tomb, to be combined with other signs to create, by novel combinations, the distortions of our senses which give the effect of supernal beauty, and the death of a beautiful woman is the most poetic subject, for Poe, precisely because it creates the greatest effects of incongruity, the greatest 'strangeness'. This strangeness works upon the imagination, which 'is exalted by the moral sentiment of beauty heightened in dissolution'.[42]

'The Sleeper' is a good example of this, in its contemplation of the sleeping lady who will never wake. She is presented as an object to be contemplated, twisted and turned so that all possible angles of aesthetic 'strangeness' can be produced. As such, her past, or her relation to the poet, is irrelevant, and like Berenice she is seen 'not as a thing to admire but to analyse; not as an object of love, but as the theme of the most abstruse, although desultory speculation'.[43] In developing this scenario, though, Poe creates a characteristic time-shift. He speculates upon her being buried in a remote family vault, but adds to this a further imaginary tableau in which, as a child, she used to throw stones at the door of the vault:

> Some sepulchre, remote, alone,
> Against whose portals she has thrown,
> In childhood, many an idle stone—
> Some tomb from out whose sounding door
> She ne'er shall force an echo more,
> Thrilling to think, poor child of sin!
> It was the dead who groaned within.[44]

Clearly here we have an arranging and combining of elements for the peculiar aesthetic effect which Poe identifies as Beauty— the contrast of the young child and the dead woman, but also of the child and the grim echoing vault. Less obvious, but I think equally characteristic, is the use of the door as *separation* of spheres which can itself be used to create effects. The girl creates echoes of *this* world (the stone bangs the door, and that noise echoes back from the vault) which, because of the circumstances, she imagines are from the dead. Now—in the poem's present—she is dead, beyond the divide, but Poe is, metaphorically, throwing stones at the door to create echoes. This could almost serve as a microcosm of Poe's use of images of death and ruin, not for any moral significance which could be culled from them, but for the aesthetic effects to be achieved. It is possible, for instance, to see the use of effects like the refrain of 'nevermore' as very close to creating echoes on the door of the tomb. The word reverberates back into this world in response to the narrator's questions (i.e. he gives it significance), but there is a suggestion that its resonance comes from the other side (the sinister power that he gives to the Raven). As so often, it is a word or sound, rather than any real object, which constitutes the divide and from which the frissant comes, and the same argument can be applied to 'The Bells', where the cheerful associations of wedding bells quickly give way to the nightmarish insistence of the tolling of funeral bells.

In 'Ulalume' and 'The Sleeper' and elsewhere, Death is neither transcended by a merging of finite and infinite nor made into a moral lesson, a reminder of mortality, but is used to create a frame of mind which leads us to what Poe calls Beauty and what we would call the sublime. Davidson identifies a parallel strategy in 'Dream-land' in which he says 'what began as an apocalypse ended in the picturesque', and he terms poems of this sort 'picturesque of consciousness'.[45] Poe's use of landscape fits this description, and reflects an attitude to time in his poetry which corresponds to his use of Death. It is neither a natural landscape, which would imply a cyclic passage of time independent of man, nor is it quite a man-made landscape, which would imply historical time. Instead, we have various forms of frozen time, with people absent. In his use of ruins and silent cities, as in 'The City in the Sea', Poe substitutes a general eschatological framework for the death of the beloved but the effect is similar.

Here Poe presents the Kingdom of Death, but the stillness here is like a frozen moment, always about to break, rather than eternity. We have the *moment* of Death hypostatized. Time *has* been—we have the 'time-eaten towers'—but eternity has not yet closed around that transitional moment between it and life. There is a tremulous stillness before

> The wave—there is a movement there!
> As if the towers had thrust aside,
> In slightly sinking, the dull tide—
> As if their tops had feebly given
> A void within the filmy Heaven[46]

150

As Halliburton notes, the poem is full of negative constructions and these serve, characteristically, not so much to describe something as to deny us access to it, thereby creating a state of mind in which we look, and wonder, at the barrier rather than pass through it. Language serves, then, to generate sensations concomitant with recognition of our relation to the infinite rather than to redeem us from our limitations and our mortality. Walter Benjamin's description of allegory's operation in eighteenth-century German baroque drama is remarkably appropriate:

> Whereas in the symbol destruction is idealised and the trans-figured face of nature is fleetingly revealed in the light of redemption, in allegory the observer is confronted with the *facies hippocratica* of history as a petrified, primordial landscape . . . This is the heart of the allegorical way of seeing, of the baroque, secular explanation of history as the Passion of the world; its importance resides solely in the stations of its decline. The greater the significance, the greater the subjection to death, because death digs most deeply the jagged line of demarcation between physical nature and significance[47]

It would be wrong, though, as I have tried to show, to see Poe's use of allegory as an action totally against the grain of Romanticism. My argument, following de Man, is that allegory is a constant feature in Romantic poetry, and one direction which could be usefully pursued to show the connections between Poe and the major Romantic poets is certainly the rôle of melancholy in the period. Melancholy was seen as the enemy of Imagination and the poet's power to see the world whole and vitally alive with energy, but Keats certainly saw the close relation between it and Beauty in his 'Ode on Melancholy':

> She dwells with Beauty—Beauty that must die;
> And Joy, whose hand is ever at his lips
> Bidding adieu; and aching Pleasure nigh,
> Turning to poison while the bee-mouth sips:
> Ay, in the very temple of Delight
> Veil'd Melancholy has her sovran shrine

Where for Keats there is the poignancy of joy and beauty recognized in their frailty and temporariness, Poe starts at the point when melancholy has *done* its work, and again Benjamin is relevant:

> If the object becomes allegorical under the gaze of melancholy, if melancholy causes life to flow out of it and it remains behind dead, but eternally secure, then it is exposed to the allegorist, it is unconditionally in his power.[48]

Rather than write poems dramatizing the inability of the imagination to unify and vivify in the face of the deadness created by melancholy, Poe uses precisely that deadness in combinations for psychological and aesthetic effects. If these combinations and effects too often bear all the marks of being unacceptably contrived and mechanical, they do provide us with a particularly clear view of elements within Romanticism which have been unduly obscured.

NOTES

1. Harold Bloom, 'Inescapable Poe', in *New York Review of Books*, Vol. XXXI, No. 15, October 11, 1984, pp. 23–37.
2. See in particular Yvor Winters, 'Edgar Allan Poe: A Crisis in the History of American Obscurantism' rept. in Eric W. Carlson (ed.), *The Recognition of Edgar Allan Poe* (Ann Arbor: Michigan University Press, 1966).
3. Richard M. Fletcher, *The Stylistic Development of Edgar Allan Poe*, Janua Linguarum: Series Practice, No. 55 (The Hague: Mouton, 1973), p. 9.
4. Floyd Stovall (ed.), *The Poems of Edgar Allan Poe* (Charlottesville: Virginia University Press, 1965), p. 108. From now on referred to as Stovall, *Poems*.
5. *Complete Works of Edgar Allan Poe*, ed. James A. Harrison (New York: A.M.S. Press, Inc., 1965), VI, p. 143.
6. Ibid., VI, p. 144.
7. Thomas O Mabbott (ed.), *Collected Works of Edgar Allan Poe*, Vol. 1, Poems, (Cambridge, Mass.: Harvard University Press, 1969), p. 96.
8. Floyd Stovall, *Edgar Poe the Poet* (Charlottesville: Virginia University Press, 1969), p. 112.
9. Stovall, *Poems*, p. 140.
10. Quoted in Patrick F. Quinn, *The French Face of Edgar Poe* (Carbondale: Southern Illinois University Press, 1957), p. 153.
11. *Complete Works*, ed. James A. Harrison, ibid., XIV, p. 290.
12. Ibid., XVI, p. 164.

13. Ibid., XIV, p. 187.
14. John T. Irwin, *American Hieroglyphics* (New Haven & London: Yale University Press, 1980), p. 115.
15. Ibid., p. 117.
16. Ibid., p. 212.
17. Ibid., p. 116.
18. Thomas Weiskel, *The Romantic Sublime: Studies in the Structure and Psychology of Transcendence* (Baltimore & London: Johns Hopkins University Press, 1976), p. 23.
19. Ibid., p. 23.
20. Stovall, *Poems*, p. 20.
21. Ibid., p. 58.
22. Mabbott, op. cit., p. 231.
23. Stovall, *Poems*, p. 16.
24. Irwin, op. cit., pp. 224–25.
25. Stovall, *Poems*, p. 105.
26. David Halliburton, *Edgar Allan Poe: A Phenomenological View* (Princeton, N.J.: Princeton University Press, 1973), p. 146.
27. Yvor Winters, in Carlson, op. cit., p. 192.
28. C. Brooks & R. P. Warren, *Understanding Poetry* (New York: Holt, Rinehart & Winston, 1960).
29. Eric W. Carlson, 'Symbol and Sense in Poe's "Ulalume" ', in *American Literature* 35, 1963–64, p. 37.
30. *Complete Works*, ed. James A. Harrison, ibid., XIII, p. 154.
31. Fletcher, op. cit., pp. 13–14.
32. Walter Benjamin, *The Origin of German Tragic Drama* (London: New Left Books, 1977), p. 161.
33. Ibid., p. 160.
34. Quoted in Stovall, *Edgar Poe the Poet*, p. 160.
35. *Complete Works*, ed. James A. Harrison, XIV, p. 274.
36. Floyd Stovall, *Edgar Poe the Poet*, p. 161.
37. *Complete Works*, X, p. 61.
38. Ibid., XII, p. 38.
39. Paul de Man, *Blindness and Insight: Essays in the Rhetoric of Contemporary Criticism*, 2nd edn. (London: Methuen, 1983), p. 207.
40. Ibid., p. 208.
41. Cf. Georges Poulet, 'Whether it moves in the limitless eternity of dream or in the limited temporality of awakening, the work of Poe thus always presents a time that is *closed*', in Eric W. Carlson (ed.), *The Recognition of Edgar Allan Poe* (Ann Arbor, Michigan University Press, 1966).
42. *Complete Works*, ed. James A. Harrison, ibid., XIV, p. 279.
43. Ibid., II, p. 22.
44. Stovall, *Poems*, pp. 53–4.
45. Edward H. Davidson, *Poe: A Critical Study* (Cambridge, Mass.: Harvard University Press, 1957), p. 83.
46. Stovall, *Poems*, p. 51.
47. Benjamin, op. cit., p. 166.
48. Ibid., pp. 183–84.

8

Law, Lawlessness and Philosophy in Edgar Allan Poe

by ERIC MOTTRAM

1

In Poe's domain that atmosphere of obedience and disobedience that informed Puritan America became rarified and
a main part of the early stages of that anarchism of power that
pressured the plots of Hawthorne and Melville. The arbitrary
manichean belief that needed the soul to be the battleground
for Jehovah and Satan, and which stabilized social conflicts
within theocracy, had decayed. Disobedience had become 'the
perverse', and society and the soul the spaces of its operations.
The plot of *The Narrative of Arthur Gordon Pym* (1838), for
instance, is that reversals of traditional security patterns must
be expected. Once embarked on the Ocean, yielding to urges
to go South, the desire for polar experience, for knowledge out
of curiosity, you will be absorbed into a maze whose interpretation is occulted and may be interpreted only by a
specialist. The last stage of your voyage will polarize you into a
form of perfection which totally envelops—'the perfect whiteness of snow', as Poe gives it at the end of *Pym*.[1]

Or you may be mesmerized in a room, a cell, a tomb by a
singular and superior control, unless your intelligence and
imagination have the 'mental balance' of unified perception,

the ability of Monos in 'The Colloquy of Monos and Una' (1841), and of Poe's amateur aristocratic detective, Auguste Dupin. Poe informs Americans of the early and optimistic republic that they would have to encounter dominance and submission situations in the form of new aristocrats, the *Doppelgänger*, criminal intelligences, barely controllable apes, barbarians and lunatics. Subterranean 'psychal' forces, a holed Earth, madness and disease would undermine easy optimism. Law, or the system of social obedience, could vanish within the anarchy of individual freedoms struggling for survival against other egos and against pressures from the state. What protection could the magazine-reading American expect against chaos, arbitrary controls and the competitiveness of the success ethic? In a counter-logic of security, could he retreat to a paradisal domain, a secluded anti-entropic garden and cottage? What might be the limits of the social contract's supposed laws of non-interference?

Poe appears, then, as a kind of Dryden, the sceptical writer of texts for a sceptical post-revolutionary society. In a culture trained to believe in the expanding frontier as the main figure of free democratic rights, what laws could sustain the individual? Is there a basis for local law in global nature or natural or universal law? Poe dramatizes such questions which were suspended between eighteenth-century Enlightenment beliefs in Newtonian or Leibnitzian order and a Romantic revolutionary belief in the necessity of a law-breaking definition of the Rights of Man. The overwhelming gist in Poe's work is that disorder underlies and undermines the artifices of social and psychic order. Goya's *Los Desastres de la Guerra* (1820) signals a similar breakdown. As James Thurber would put it many years later, there is no safety in numbers, or in anything else. In *Hermes V* (1980), Michel Serres brings us up to date: 'We have to change laws. Henceforth the global does not necessarily produce a local equivalence, and the local itself contains a law—that does not always and everywhere reproduce the global.'[2]

'Premature Burial' and its related stories expose fears that the limits of life may enclose too early from some grim artifice— an Inquisitorial torture, a ship's hold, a wine-cellar niche, a hole in the Ocean, cannibalization, interment, immuration, hypnotic suspension between old age or sickness and death—unable to be reborn; in fact, any interference with normal assumptions. Law may not rescue either immediate or existential oppression. What is an unavoidable event?

> The unendurable oppression of the lungs—the stifling fumes of the damp earth—the clinging to the death garments—the rigid embrace of the narrow house—the blackness of absolute Night—the silence like a sea that overwhelms.

Immediately after Virginia Clemm's death, Charles F. Briggs ended his serial *roman à clef, The Trippings of Tom Pepper*, with his Poe character, Wicks, writing advertisements for quack medicines and falling 'victim to his own arts, . . . buried alive at the expense of the public'.[3] Nasty, but containing sly minimal truth. Certainly, Poe wrote entertainments about law-breaking, pleasure in aroused anxiety and feelings of abjection, often enough the enormous staples of popular fiction. But Virginia Clemm exemplified in Poe's daily life that melting of death into life within beauty which he used as plots for a number of his stories, the sexuality of death which so horribly breaks his wife in January 1842 and for which Poe had been drinking to alleviate torment and for which he had no money for treatment. That constant need for a basic energy—money—penetrates his fiction and is as socially real as everything else in his work. On 10 May 1837, all New York banks suspended payment; on 4 May the president of the Mechanics Bank had committed suicide; Poe's living ended when the *Review* had to suspend publication.[4] Horror may be to love the sick and deathly ('Berenice', 1835). Death is repeatedly enclosed in a pale female form; the conditions can be narrative but not alleviated. Assume a protective rôle and your duplicity may be discovered and break you down. Poe often concealed his name and age. Alternatively, horror may be a withdrawal of the very means of survival.

Competitive society may produce premature burial. The unbalanced and unbalancing social life is continuous with the existential individual life. Poe senses that the boundaries between waking and dream, consciousness and trance, sanity and madness are unstable. Poe's drinking under tension is a commonplace, and his readers paid well to consume the tensions they recognized in his stories. He had a popular following in a nation obsessed with belief in rights to the pursuit of happiness in this life as the prime basis of democracy. But the pursuit is confused between sources within the self and within society, together with the belief that an inheritance of some kind governs both conditions. America is founded within this triangulation. It predicates, for instance, the bulky motivational alternatives of Theodore Dreiser's *An American Tragedy* in 1925. If happiness is an internal condition based on property and labour in a class society, what hope for an end to anxiety for the majority? Poe dramatizes the chances of destruction within imbalanced social and personal conditions. Animals and 'the Negro' haunt him because he, like most of his public, assumed these were the threat to human distinctiveness. Therefore they must be reduced to the control of property, and the process must be believed as part of laws. For example: 'in continuing to command the services of slaves, [our people] violate no law divine or human.'

Baudelaire grasped the core of 'The Imp of the Perverse' (1845–46)—the release of perverseness from 'instigation of the arch-fiend', the secularization of irrational intervention into assumed laws of relationship, conventions of behaviour, reliabilities, decisions between human beings. It remains perverse, and no Marie Bonaparte Freudian hunt for security in psychological 'origins'[5] or Wayne C. Booth academic panic as a preface to the dismissal of Poe—his 'special kind of morbid horror'—can conceal it.[6] Baudelaire and Valéry, and Michel Butor later,[7] had the intelligence to grasp Poe's system, just as Marshall McLuhan understood some of the Blakean implications of 'A Descent into the Maelstrom' and Auguste Dupin.[8] In 'The Imp of the Perverse', Poe writes: 'We perpetuate them merely because we feel that we should *not*. Beyond or behind this, there is no intelligible principle.' And then he adds the ambivalent passage Baudelaire used: 'and we might, indeed, deem this perverseness a direct instigation of the arch-fiend, were it not occasionally known to operate in furtherance of good.' Poe's protagonist is a murderer self-convicted by irresistible confession—a major secular motivation in modern fiction. He feels the 'burst' of his secret but his language remains rational, the Poe relationship between the irrational and composition, between compulsion and form or law: 'They say that I spoke with a distinct enunciation, but with little marked emphasis and passionate hurry, as in dread of interruption before concluding.' In 1853 Baudelaire believed that reading this material in Poe had damned him (*Le Peintre de la vie*) and his immediate example corroborates the 'perverse' with 'curiosity', still secularized, even if the scene's archetype is the Eden myth. Poe prefaced 'The Man of the Crowd' (1840–45) with an epigraph from La Bruyère: '*Ce grand malheur, de ne pouvoir être seul.*' His narrator is released from *ennui* by an ecstasy of clarity, 'inquisitive' and 'enchained' in attention, which climaxes in his London hunt after an old man who looks like an 'incarnation of the fiend': 'extreme despair' as the traditional condition of the satanic. In a night 'brilliant with gas', the man reaches a gin 'temple' just as it closes, returning to the crowd at dawn. Poe ends by modifying La Bruyère into a diagnostic principle: 'the type and genius of deep crime. He refuses to be alone.' The tight brevity of the story opens up into unanalysed belief, reflecting back into the narrator's decision to leave his isolation for the crowd and the street, his involuntary choice of the criminal scene. Crime is the necessary subject because it concentrates crucial issues of obedience and disobedience. The Miltonic despairs of Satan, carried over from 'the romantic agony', become an instrument with which to examine a post-revolutionary culture, unstable in its sense of law and order. The frontier was New York and Baltimore. The poverty, crime and gin intemperance of 'London' and its 'crowd' comprise an analogue of despair which the bourgeois revolution in America had not withstood.

Poe needed and devised a method of composition which exposed by narrative example what he had already concluded:

> Poe was one of the greatest technicians of modern literature. As Valéry pointed out, he was the first to attempt the scientific story, a modern cosmogony, the description of pathological phenomena. . . . and in Poe's spirit [Baudelaire] wrote: 'The time is not distant when it will be understood that a literature which refuses to make its way in brotherly accord with science and philosophy is a murderous and suicidal literature.'[9]

The literary engineer required his method to have a 'philosophy'; his consciousness of being posited, as it were, between the Enlightenment and the Romantic, the Whig and the revolutionary elements, in America shaping history, had to be to that degree self-conscious. 'The Philosophy of Composition' (1846) opens with Poe placing himself in the line from the anarchist philosopher William Godwin, writing a novel based on 'a very powerful interest' (preface to *Caleb Williams*, 1794) by inventing the narrative container of ideas from the end to the beginning. He also mentions Dickens's note on it in response to Poe's examination of 'the mechanism of *Barnaby Rudge*'. By 'the consideration of *effect*' Poe means the production of a 'very powerful interest'. Harold Rosenberg takes this into his account of some of the beginnings of modernism:

> Poetry and criticism from Poe through the present day is filled with diagnoses and outcries on the profession. . . . a poet must understand the means whereby the work is produced, that is, he must be aware of its *laws*, he therefore has the 'makings of a critic'. . . . The direction of Baudelaire is that the poet can no longer wait for inspiration to provide the poem; he must consciously, experimentally, set it in motion.[10]

Poe is the type of the writer who does not await the Coleridgian 'wedding garment' process of consciousness and Nature (the anxiety source in 'Dejection: A Ode', 1802), and refuses the futile attempt to bridge the gap between them; in Paul DeMan's terms, he counters 'a nostalgia for unmediated contact with the natural object'.[11] For 'originality' the writer must engineer 'effect' rather than from 'ecstatic intuition', construct 'design' from 'intention'. But this is not simply an aesthetic programme. Poe's 'interest' lies deep in the necessities of his materials and in the cultural determinacies of his position in the 1830s and 1840s in the United States. He is highly conscious, not only in his essays and reviews, but in his fiction, of the inadequacy of wasteful anarchic intuition and the breakdown of both law and individualism in tradition.

The new republic embodied, through some of its dominant founders, especially Thomas Jefferson and Benjamin Franklin, principles of order out of Locke and Newton. By the end of the eighteenth century, Romantic individualism and its transcendental poses set up encounters with both Enlightenment and

Puritan definition of self and society. *Eureka* (1848) is published only two years before *The Scarlet Letter*, another fiction whose energies derive from acute awareness of the polarities of individual transgression and social order, of private life and state pressure, and the need for a radical vision which destroyed neither the active self nor the law. Poe's youthful memories of a crumbling Old World and of the Ocean between Old and New Worlds encountered the Jeffersonian classicist programme at the University of Virginia. By 1844 he could write to James Russell Lowell, 'I have no faith in human perfectibility. I think that human exertion will have no appreciable effect on humanity.' Four years later he writes to George W. Eveleth, during the composition of *Eureka*, on 'the perfect totality, or *absolute* unity' of the universe of Gravitation, perceived, if at all, only through a language of intellect apprehending law. But Poe's obsessive gambling, while at Virginia, suggests not only his chronic need for money, but, as it does in Dostoevsky's life, an obsession with chance active within totality, a manic philosophy of luck, the need to act with the irrational. The West Point period likewise combines needs for order: for a livelihood, reconciliation with John Allan and publication of his poems. During his relationship with the lawyer William Wirt, he was encouraged to read Blackstone and Marshall for both style and knowledge of order. Then, through *Biographia Literaria* he worked at the idea of a total poetic order—his review of Joseph Rodman Drake's *The Culprit Fay* (1836) indicates his concern for 'effect' as *affect* on the reader's sensibility as a combination of reason and imagination by design, the logic of 'exciting the powers of Causality'.[12] Poe's 'test for poetry' is precisely the achievement of this process. He does not confuse, as Wordsworth does in the *Preface* (1800) cause (text) and effect: 'For a poem is not the poetic faculty, but *the means* of exciting it in mankind.'

But his tales tell how order as design harmony is continually threatened by desire for authority over nature and human nature. If the analytic imagination is primary, it can operate malignantly as well as in the mind of Dupin or the poet or a sailor in a maelstrom. The deity in *Eureka* imagined perfect order, and universal laws show it. But 'The Cask of Amontillado' (1846) narrates a perfect crime. The avenging narrator plans 'definitive' punishment, one of the ways men and women attempt to define themselves as gods: 'I must not only punish but punish with impunity.' Carnival is the occasion for a murderous pun on the order of masonry. The punishment for personal 'injuries' is personal. No state court is even mentioned. Revenge requires personally 'felt' commitment without 'retribution'. The victim is to be made into a hidden object, literally immured, as a fool in 'tight-fitting' motley with bells. Fortunato's fortune is to be reversed; he is to be totally abject; his moan becomes silence, broken by fool's bells as he moves to his end in a niche underground. Poe's story incorporates the history of incarceration and its future, and challenges all assumed permissions to enclose for life. Or does not, since the implicity of Montresor's operation may appeal to the believer in personal punishment. Sadism and masochism occupy a permanent joint throne in the realm of justice. The theory is:

> The offender may justly be subjugated to certain deprivations because he deserves it; and he deserves it because he has engaged in wrongful conduct—conduct that does or threatens injury and that is prohibited by law. The penalty is thus not just a means of crime prevention but a merited response to the actor's deed, 'rectifying the balance' in the Kantian sense. . . .[13]

'Landor's Cottage' (date unknown) offers the obverse: an uncompromising man-made New York paradise—an enclosure but delectable, a watershed domain between classic and romantic which affords a garden sense,[14] and, further, a sense of nature and garden as theatre for human compositional perceptions. The grass is 'like green Genoese velvet', the roadside stones are 'carefully *placed*' and the roads are 'works of art'. Poe refers to the 'natural capabilities' in books on landscape gardening and 'composition'. The sun 'slid into the position described' as in 'theatrical spectacle or melodrama'. The theatrical nature painter, Salvator Rosa; a reflecting pool of objects 'perfectly reflected' as 'heaven'; a French quotation from *Vathek* applied to the house—'*d'une architecture inconnue dans les annales de la terre*'; the effect of '*tout ensemble*' and 'poetry'; the guardian mastiff resisted by a hand 'in token of amity'; a young woman exemplifies 'the perfection of natural in contradistinction from artificial *grace* and suggests both 'enthusiasm' and 'romance'—

she defines 'womanhood'—in fact, the narrative ends with the interior of the house, with only a passing statement on Mr. Landor, the owner and presumably the designer. The artist has done his work and now resembles Flaubert's or Joyce's artist retired and impersonal beside his artifice.[15]

The laws of enclosure are in themselves neutral. By the 1840s, Control itself stood under radical discussion in the United States, and 'law' under constant debate. In the early decades of the republic, lawyers were confused between municipal law in a sovereign state, Common Law precedent (from colonial years), absence of decisional records, ignorance of federal law and its relations to state law, and 'a deep hostility among the people to the whole conception of the Common Law, which patriots now identified with British tyranny and with Tory endeavours to hoodwink them out of their hard-won gains'. 'Ignorant judges' could not control 'the emotions of democratic juries' and 'chauvinistic passions'.[16] The dominant Protestant conviction remained: lawyers were immoral hypocrites since they defended both good and bad causes for money. Law appeared as corruption, despite Americans' notorious litigiousness.

But what were the 'natural' principles of law, responding to the 'natural' emotions of obedience and disobedience, and the social necessities through which individual and society sustained each other? After the Reformation, the Enlightenment and the Age of Revolutions what universals of law could there be? Thousands of new Americans had immigrated specifically for permission to make a vertical thrust of individualism, if necessary to the point of lawlessness. Independence meant release from European systems of obedience and disobedience domination and submission, in class structures with restricted ownership of the means of production, distribution, education and religion. The newly placed individual must be the focus of law; ownership of property must be preserved even if its chronic results might make Hobbes's State of Nature appear to be a peaceable kingdom. Poe's fictions and the attached nonfictions move precisely in this domain: the enclosure can be hell or heaven, and in both cases it is human artifice. That 'nature' may cause the reversal of assumed order is the very plot of *Arthur Gordon Pym*.[17] Poe's tales dramatize the

162

instabilities of permission and prohibition in the first decades of the nineteenth century which were to confuse Americans for the following one hundred years. Conscience could be collapsed into an arbitrary if not absurd unreliability, the anarchism of democratic, capitalist and frontier definitions of behavioural programmes. In 1846, the Georgia justice and classical scholar, James Jackson, declared, in *The Knickerbocker Magazine*:

> It is one of the dicta of the infallible mob, that the legal profession necessarily involves many practices inconsistent with elevated integrity, or even common honesty. A successful lawyer is a sort of licensed knave, refined perhaps in his mode of cheating, but really little better than a prime minister of Satan, or at least a member of His Majesty's cabinet.[18]

He then places his discourse in a fictional domain similar to the stories of Poe and Hawthorne, emphasizing that law, too, is mythical. His irony and sarcasm reinforce his legal aristocraticism, but he does understand central issues of democracy and the professions, especially exemplified in the United States, and in its literature, and certainly in Poe:

> Excellence of any kind has a tendency to produce envy in the minds of some men; and intellectual superiority and eminence in a learned profession are sufficient causes to arouse the bitter feelings of an ignorant rabble. . . . The profession of the advocate is eminently one of confidence, and there is no method of gaining an ascendancy over the minds of others so direct and complete as that of becoming master of their secrets.

The 'liberal professions' in general have ample opportunities to 'steal the livery of Heaven to serve the devil in'. If Poe participated in the undermining of the already unstable myth of the New Adam of American promise, Jackson places the professional—the physician is his immediate instance here—as 'the serpent in the garden of Eden', the very figure of false confidence, a centre of evil. Hawthorne's fictions—*The Scarlet Letter* in particular—mythicize fact: 'evils all flow', writes Jackson, from false legal and medical confidence; professionals 'seduce the mass' and 'corrupt the fountain of the happiness of the whole people', even if there is nothing in 'the science or practice of law which necessarily involves a stifling of conscience . . .'—which is Poe's fictional speciality. Certainly,

Melville's masters-at-arms, surgeon-captain Cuticle Cad-
wallader, and many others, take part in these seductions.[19] The
issue in Jackson is 'degrees of guilt' in those who control
democracy. Poe is adept at the advocate lawyer's game,
'standing in the place of the accused'. The edging of conscience
and law into crime and lawlessness is a main site, whether the
Inquisition in 'The Pit and the Pendulum' (1843–45) or the
revenges of Montresor and Hop-Frog.

But the latter's story (1849) moves revenge justice not only
out of state laws and the laws of 'will and idea' but through the
thresholds of the man of reason into the naturalist world of man
as residual animal (a paradox which lurked in 'The Murders in
the Rue Morgue' eight years earlier). The crippled dwarf jester
is compelled to behave the 'fool' to 'power' (and so relates to
Fortunato), but his nickname shifts him towards naturalist fears
for the human rational. With his strong compensatory arms, he
'much more resembled a squirrel, or a small monkey, than a
frog'. He is a 'barbarian' slave, a gift captive from a victorious
general to the king.

The king is an analogue of Poe's magazine fiction clientele,
demanding 'something novel—out of the way' to alleviate 'this
everlasting saneness'. The story will therefore move, as so often
in Poe, towards the madness of art, towards madness itself and
to the breakdown of social-legal order. Hop-Frog is forced by
the king to drink—and again the issue is deeply in Poe's life:
'the effect of wine on his excitable brain'. The tyrant's joke
becomes the fool's 'half-insane stare'. The jester at court
provides the analogue of the artist within the republic. The
tyrant and his seven ministers become a naturalist masquerade
of 'eight chained ourang-outangs', a game of beasts escaped
from human enclosure, inside the court enclosure. Their tarred
shirts and drawers are very nearly feathered but in fact are
stuck with flax—but the relationship to 'The System of Doctor
Tarr and Professor Fether' and to Hawthorne's 'My Kinsman
Major Molineux' is keen, and the ape uniform moves the event
towards the rue Morgue. The transformation of costume and
saloon into death enclosure brings the tale into the site of all
Poe's cell and burial stories. The judge is not the Roman
Catholic priesthood but a Caliban barbarian who holds the
keys to a locked enclosure. The chandelier descends, as the

heated walls move in and the pendulum comes down and swings in the Inquisitional Christian chamber of dogma enforcement. The 'monkey' confronts the apes, the maniac executes government. Poe's theme is major to the modern state: terrorism, when power confers obsolescence on justice by law. As Jean Baudrillard has recently reminded the late twentieth century,. terror is one element in the lethal dominant triad which marks 'the end of the social': 'In their triangular affinity, the masses, the media and terrorism describe the presently prevailing process of implosion.'[20] The terrorist situation reveals who the terrorists are; tyrant and opponent inhabit the same performance. As the eight men reach premature execution by fire, Hop-Frog says 'I now see *distinctly* what manner of people these maskers are', and vanishes with his beautiful dwarf girl. (Poe published this story in 1849 in the *Flag of Our Union*.)

Major elements in popular fiction—as in film and television today—predicate the return of the repressed and the repressors in barbarian and proletarian invasion of the social. Bondage is released by terror. The black uniform invites fire. The assumed sanity of professional Control is radically challenged in the very hall and rooms of power, the centre of social system, as well as in its basements—this is Baudrillard's 'breakdown of the social simulacrum'.[21] Social violence begins and ends in individual violation. 'Delirium' not only activates revenge but the laws themselves. The tale of incineration ends in silence. It is nearly the end of the mutual delirium of tyrant and victim, as in 'The Pit and the Pendulum', but in the latter the political prisoner is released by a victorious general.

'The laws of GOD and man', in Jackson's phrase, have vanished in that silence. This is the end of assumptive harmony and hierarchy taken for granted by the 1840s American lawyer:

> Of LAW, the world's collected wisdom, the good man's defence, the bad man's dread, founded as it is on moral rectitude and the principles of eternal truth, 'no less can be said, than that its seat is the bosom of GOD, its voice the harmony of the world. . . .'[22]

By 1846 the definition of system—law, principles, harmony—was changing again. The reversible Newtonian and Christian model code of energies distributed in a space governed by universal law is displaced, during the first Industrial Revolution, towards a model based on the theory of heat in enclosure, and machines, equilibrium within which 'energy dissipates and entropy increases'. Time is, therefore, 'endowed with direction', is irreversible. Most philosophical systems wished the universal machine would never stop, remain the same within enclosure patterns of eternal return.[23] Poe's stories dramatize disruptions of reversible system and belief by perverse actions. The imprisoning wall will never release Fortunato. The bottled message on the ocean, an enclosure recording human descent into a global enclosure—the south pole hole—will be sucked into the geographical void. Poe is careful to provide a little contemporary philosophy for 'MS. Found in a Bottle' (1833). The narrator's uncommon education, paid for by 'hereditary wealth', has developed his Pyrrhonism, or scepticism for perceptual knowledge, and his 'restlessness'. He becomes a tourist, the modern figure of mobility for curiosity under dissatisfaction. He experiences shipwreck, a standard nineteenth-century image of resistance to human law and confidence, a dream reality of helplessness and threat, which stretches at least as far as Conrad, *the* early twentieth-century novelist of sailing-ship space and time. Technology is overwhelmed by 'the unfathomable ocean'; an unrising sun reduces the globe to a hot 'ebony' desert. Time cannot be calculated. The ship swings between albatross and kraken. 'Analysis' fails. Descent is irreversible. ('A Descent into the Maelstrom' will attempt the recovery of this fate by a hoax of ratiocination or analytical powers.)

The second ship is called *Discovery* and related to the previous paragraph's claim: 'the people *will not* see.' It is undefinable, possibly growing. Its senile crew are surrounded by archaic scattered instruments. The hurtling current is the very embodiment of the irreversible. Useless charts, folios and scientific instruments litter the captain's cabin; he pores over his commission from a monarch. The narrator's soul is a ruin but he clings to that absurd belief in progress which obsesses the modern, and absorbs especially those who identify science and technology with progress: 'It is evident that we are hurrying onwards to some exciting knowledge—some never-to-be-imparted secret, whose attainment is destruction.' Poe formulates in 1833 the very futility of such excitements, and necessarily ends his tale at its climax, in a roar of absurdity, the urge to apocalypse. Needs for law and harmony based on universal principle give way to schizophrenic desire for an ultimate power-conferring secret at the very moment of irreversibility. 'The madman's voyage is at once a rigorous division and an absolute Passage'; he is imprisoned in passage. The ocean in Poe's story is the strongest example of Control, and not the Romantic image of free passage possibilities. The narrator is 'the prisoner of the passage' without homeland.[24]

The 'private Mad-House' which encloses 'The System of Doctor Tarr and Professor Fether' offers a further approach to insanity. Tourist curiosity again brings the narrator to a place where private 'regulations' are 'more rigid than the public hospital laws'. The place of mad passage now includes doctors:

> *Homo medicus* was not called into the world of confinement as an *arbiter*, to divide what was crime from what was madness, what was evil from what was illness, but rather as a *guardian*, to protect others from the vague danger that exuded through the walls of confinement.[25]

The château of *One Hundred and Twenty Days of Sodom* (1785) is not far away, as Foucault reminds those foolish enough to be ignorant of it: 'There, the most infamous excesses are committed upon the very person of the prisoner. . . .'[26] Poe's *Maison de Santé* is a 'fantastic château' in a gloomy forest at the base of a mountain—a place of 'dread', that metaphysical condition which penetrates the Romantic from Kierkegaard through to Kafka and Mailer. 'The metaphysics of *mania*' may be masked as sanity. 'The soothing system' has been found dangerous to 'rational humanity' or the guardians. It excluded punishment, since 'to repose confidence in the understanding or discretion of a mad man, is to gain him body and soul'—and also dispenses with 'an expensive body of keepers'. The 'raging maniac' is placed in 'a secret cell' and then 'removed to the public hospitals'. Dinner in the château becomes 'Pandemonium *in petto*', reminding a reader of the ancient identification of madness with devil possession. The conversation turns to sanity, insanity, liberty and 'practical reason'. Government and 'lunatic government', revolution and 'counter-revolution' are exchanged. The sedate orchestra breaks into 'Yankee Doodle' and, as in 'Hop-Frog', the 'perfect army of . . . Chimpanzees, Ourang-Outangs, or big black baboons of the Cape of Good Hope' are in fact the rulers, but in this case in counter-revolt. The superintendent has become a 'patient', and under his crazed 'system', the guardians have been 'tarred, then carefully feathered, and then shut up in underground cells'. One escaped through a sewer to free the rest. The beaten-up narrator sees both systems as good of their kind—as they certainly are, as systems.

Poe's story analyses the semantics of 'system' as a term without stability, a characteristic anxiety in a society whose chief poet was to declare a decade later that he was a barbarian with 'all to make'. System constructors forcibly impose, or are allowed to impose, totality on society and language, and then speak of murder, law and stability. After civil war, the ensuing culture—America in the early nineteenth century, for example—has to be particularly concerned with bases in 'natural law' to justify victorious revolt. And as Michel Serres observes:

> In whose interests is it to lay down a law of history if not in the interest of whoever wishes to stop time? . . . whoever pursues power in economics, politics, or philosophy . . . The law is a theft.[27]

So the reversals in *Pym*, 'the Cask of Amontillado', 'Hop-Frog', 'The System of Doctor Tarr and Professor Fether', and many other Poe tales, dramatize the destabilization of assumed systems of order and analyse what 'law' might mean. The detective Dupin emerges as the ratiocinator who stands in the space rather than the time of information (knowledge) in order to bring the culprit to death. Death appears in some form at the end of many Poe stories since,

> to know is to put to death . . . knowledge now becomes military, a martial art. It is then more than a game; it is, literally, a strategy. These epistemologies are not innocent: at the critical tribunal they are calling for executions. They are policies promulgated by military strategists. To know is to kill, to rely on death, as in the case of the master and the slave.[28]

The interchange of image meanings in Magritte, who admired Poe and drew titles from his work—'The Imp of the Perverse', for example—presents desire pushed 'towards instability when we aspire to safety'.[29] Both artists are Pyrrhonists, sceptical gamesters inside whose works the masks of perception lead to the death of confidence, an engineered dissolution of patterns of meaning and identity, of all rigidities. Poe signals part of the early nineteenth-century re-orientation of art away from Romantic transcendental and religious towards conceptual art—hence Valéry's recognition of his engineering. His stories present mad urges to limit-breaking, part nostalgic and part fascinated, a reflection of his need to fuse transcendence and engineering, to create a law system and impose it as logically natural. This is part of the duplicity Lawrence noticed in 1918, between freedom and constraint, in American writing: 'pull the democratic and idealistic clothes off American utterance, and see what you can of the dusky body of it underneath.' D. H. Lawrence also noticed the key doubleness in Poe: he is 'rather a scientist than an artist, [with] an almost chemical analysis of the soul and consciousness'. Like Serres later, he notes the relations between knowledge and destruction as he moves out from Wilde, and perhaps Blake's 'Never seek to tell thy love . . .', towards Poe:

> It is easy to see why each man kills the thing he loves. To *know* a living thing is to kill it. You have to kill a thing to know it satisfactorily. For this reason, the desirous consciousness, the SPIRIT, is a vampire. . . . It is the temptation of a vampire fiend, is this knowledge. . . . Poe was an adventurer into vaults and cellars and horrible underground passages of the human soul.

The Prospero court incarcerates itself against the Red Death (1842–45), an analogue for the early nineteenth-century epidemics which ravaged eastern seaboard towns. 'The wall had gates of iron'; inside, magnificent pleasures in 'a voluptuous scene' are enacted as a Pascalian *divertissement* against Nature—disease—and time—'a gigantic clock of ebony' in the 'blood-tinted' light of the 'western or black' chamber—a loud pendulum of death, perpetually marking irreversibility. ('The Pit and the Pendulum' is contemporaneous.) Prospero's fête—'bizarre', 'delirious with fancies such as the madman fashions', 'writhing dreams'—is penetrated by a masker enacting the Red Death who is the disease itself. The duke's strategy of resistant enclosure fails. The first law of thermodynamics is not relevant.

In 'The Tell-Tale Heart' (again 1843–45), disease 'sharpens' the narrator's senses to the point of madness. Hysteric anxiety again follows. With 'cunning' he murders in defence against a beloved old man's Evil Eye, 'a pale blue eye with a film over it'. He very slowly penetrates the black room at midnight: 'a watch's minute hand moves more quickly than did mine.' Silence is broken by the old man's amplified heart which sounds out beyond death from under the floorboards, like a time measure, breaking 'the wild audacity of my perfect triumph'. The law (the police) cannot hear it, but the murderer can, and he hears it as irreversible time: 'a watch . . . enveloped in cotton'. He betrays himself in his own terror; sight terror becomes sound terror; law and conscience are irrelevant. Undermined confidence has instigated crime; mad anxiety has caused it; failed confidence has undermined security in it. The walled corpse sounds out its own time, as it does in 'The Masque of the Red Death', and 'The Black Cat' (1843–45). In the latter, fondness for animals becomes a 'principal source of pleasure'. That a dog's fidelity is more secure than human fidelity becomes the narrator's paranoid belief. His wife 'procures' a variety of pets, including a black cat. The witch's traditional disguise is mentioned but the beast is named Pluto. The Fiend Intemperance causes the narrator to attack his wife and the other pets, but not the hellishly named cat—until he cuts one of its eyes out. In a 'final and irrevocable' act of 'PERVERSENESS'—'a perpetual inclination . . . to violate that which is *Law*, merely because we understand it to be such'—he hangs the creature. The crime is given as a sin—'a deed without a name'—beyond 'the reach of the infinite mercy of the Most Merciful and Most Terrible God'.

Cat-murder becomes an example of violation of a universal law, intense enough to move into transgression of a taboo. The house immediately catches fire, as if part of a 'chain' of perfect facts. The second cat, one-eyed, causes 'dread' in its caresses and clawings; the white fur on its breast shapes a gallows (the tale here moves into the area of signs occupied five years later by the A in *The Scarlet Letter*). The narrator immures his furiously axed wife in the cellar, in the Fortunato manner, sleeps soundly and lives guiltlessly. Again, the law discovers nothing—until the incarcerated cat turns informer—found inside in a Stephen King condition: 'with red extended mouth and solitary eye'. Again Poe ends his tale at the climax: silence follows the destruction of law and disobedience assumptions, the onset of anxiety and dread, and the ambiguous renewal of superstitious belief in retribution and a possible 'chain' of universal connections.

2

Strategies of discovery and engineering, discoursing on connective irreversibles and reversibles, control Poe's work, placed as it is within Law's uncertain bases and those essential questions of permission and restraint which extend from De Sade in the Bastille, through Brockden Brown's sense of deception and uncertainty at the roots of religion and social security, Natty Bumppo's ambivalences on law in *The Prairie* (1827), and on into the discussions of Romantic self-reliance and World Soul among the Transcendentalists of the 1840s.[31] Ahead lies Mailer's masterly documentation of the irrational within Law, *The Executioner's Song*. Government is impregnated with lawyers—'nearly half of the signers of the Declaration of Independence and of the drafters of the Constitution had been "lawyers" '.[32] In those texts the device of 'Nature' is itself insecure, quite apart from popular suspicion of law as mystery and conspiracy. Perry Miller offers a trenchant statement of this condition:

> When the General [Andrew Jackson] entered the field, ran a characteristic blast in 1835, all power was centred in his person: 'the law of nations, the civil law, nay, the law of nature, were at once annihilated, and the bayonet, the prison or exile, rendered the legislator, the judge and the citizen, obedient to his will, or removed them from his path'. The ludicrous hyperbole of such a passage shows that the hysteria was excited not merely by the spectre of 'King Andrew'. Instead, as the effectiveness of Cooper and [David] Crockett demonstrated, the mood was something more pervasive than either of the parties [Whig or Jacksonian] could control, something deep, atavistic, persistent in the community.

Cooper's Leatherstocking kept alive 'the concept of a man who knows justice not by law but by instinct', maintaining 'the dignity of sublime Nature against the constricting efforts of the intellect and of the intellect's vice-regent, the law'. Poe's fictions register the death of this concept. Nature includes the perverse. Order is invented and destroyed. *Eureka* is less a discovery than a necessary artifice of security against dread (Kierkegaard's analyses of dread were composed in the 1840s). As Daniel Chipman, Chief Justice of Vermont, declared in 1793, Blackstone's *Commentaries'* principles and reasonings were not 'universal'; the American student of law should recognize American need: 'He should be led through a system of laws applicable to our governments, and a train of reasoning congenial to their principles. Such a system we yet want. Surely genius is not wanting in America.'

The French aristocratic amateur detective, the Chevalier Auguste Dupin, steps into a field of connections to discover their law by the deliberate operation of his own genius where the police have failed. He is Poe's artist 'freed from dependence on religious systems, and from legal and philosophical systems'; and since he is not a trained professional, he can 'rediscover the creative energies of the whole community'.[33] Self-reliance could reach no further. The preface to *Poems* (1831), the 'Letter to B ——',[34] criticizes inspiration as preparation for composition, since it is dependent on impulse which in turn is dependent on metaphysics and justified by alleged moral utility. He misquotes Dryden (but not radically) to expose the romantic inclination to seek for truth below surface fact (Dupin gazes before he connects and makes his elucidatory mosaic):

> 'Trifles, like straws, upon the surface flow,/ He who would search for pearls must dive below', are lines which have done much mischief. As regards the greater truths, men oftener err by seeking them at the bottom than at the top; the depth lies in the huge abysses where wisdom is sought—not in the palpable palaces where she is found.

In his *Marginalia* for 1846,[35] Poe criticizes those who speak of 'thought . . . beyond the compass of words': 'I do not believe that any thought, properly so called, is out of the reach of language.' Writing is 'deliberateness' and 'method'. But it is difficult to verbalize certain 'fancies' which are 'rather psychal than intellectual'. These are, like Hawthorne's various definitions of romance territory ('a poetic or fairy precinct', 'where the Actual and the Imaginary may meet'), 'points of time where the confines of the waking world blend with those of the world of dreams'. So by this clinamen is the new achieved, 'a synthesis of inspiration and conscious method'.[36] In Godwin's words in his *Caleb Williams* preface, 'We were all of us engaged in exploring the entrails of mind and motive, and in tracing the various rencontres and clashes that may occur between man and man in the diversified scene of human life.'

The function of language, therefore, is to control the psychal and the entrails; and beyond that, to invent or discover order, as in 'Murders in the Rue Morgue', or the semblance of order, as in 'The Gold Bug' (1843), the most popular of Poe's tales—300,000 copies circulated by 28 May 1844, according to him. Mesmerism is to afford access to unknown territory, and thereby pass it into knowledge through language (the process of psychoanalysis by 1900), to give the word 'immortality' a meaning. In 'Ligeia' (1838–45) death is to be challenged by 'will'—irreversibility at least halted for information (as the maelstrom is conquered by information). The language set reads: 'the tumultuous vultures of passion', 'gigantic volition', 'fierce energy', 'immense learning'. The narrator gives himself to a woman's guidance with 'child-like confidence', and later, in the English abbey, to luxury and opium 'with child-like perversity'. Marriage to Rowena is 'a moment of mental alienation' (the term would be read close to 'madness' in the 1840s). The medievalism and orientalism of the bridal chamber fuses sex to 'an endless succession of ghostly forms', an entombment paralleling Ligeia's. Rowena, like Valdemar and Vankirk, moves out of time and known place, between life and death, inhabited by Ligeia. Either the narrator killed her or, in view of the Glanville epigraph, is confronted with Ligeia's will to live requiring vampiric entry. The story belongs to the group including possession and *Doppelgänger* ideas—'A Tale of the Ragged Mountains' and 'William Wilson' (1839–45).[37] The space and time of the self is destroyed or used or mutated.

The Dupin stories present speculation as ratiocination rather than a play with the psychal, the mesmeric and the vampiric-schizophrenic possessive. Poe is again highly contemporary in his use of Franz Mesmer's assertions and opportunities. Robert Darnton begins his study of mesmerism:

> If the greatest political treatise of the age [Rousseau's *Social Contract*] failed to interest many literate Frenchmen, what form of radical ideas *did* suit their tastes?. . . . Mesmerism aroused enormous interest during the pre-revolutionary decade; and although it originally had no relevance to politics, it became . . . a camouflaged political theory very much like Rousseau's.[38]

Mesmer demonstrated that a man could totally control another person irrespective of rank, education, religion and profession. The totalitarian system at last had its nucleus. But in Dupin Poe invented another opposition to law in the post-revolutionary decades, the figure of 'analytic ability' opposed to 'ingenuity', imagination differentiated from fancy. Dupin's 'wild fervour' and the vivid freshness of his imagination are ideal. He and the narrator incarcerate themselves by day in a 'time-eaten and grotesque mansion' and emerge to another darkness at night. Dupin's quality may be 'the result of an excited or perhaps of a diseased intelligence', but he can analyse and lacks faith in the police as law agents: major qualities in the modern. The perceptive reader is given a carefully placed clue to the criminal, but the moral issue is elsewhere, defence of an innocent man mistakenly charged by law, and Dupin's satisfaction in defeating the law's agency. Dupin's 'Calculus of Probabilities' surfaces again in 'The Mystery of the Marie Roget' through mathematics applied to 'intangible . . . speculation'. As in 'Ligeia', the issue is a matter of 'will' not 'power', and, characteristic of the interim condition of the terms 'God' and 'Nature' in the 1840s, the story centres on a particularly dated logic: 'That nature and its God are two, no man who thinks will deny. That the latter, creating the former, can, at will, control or modify it, is also unquestionable.' Contrary to Einstein's later hope, God may well be a joker, and Poe supports this with an evidence system of statistical analyses—what is usually called chance—as well as the Dupin method. Reason is defeated because it seeks 'truth *in detail*' (against the advice of Aristotle in the *Nicomachean Ethics*).

But mystery remains. Poe resists totalizing. In 'The Purloined

Letter' police investigation is again posed against mental ratiocination. Dupin's process—for a large sum of money—is 'an identification of the reasoner's intellect with that of his opponent', suitable since the latter is a poet and a mathematician. Dupin's aristocratic intellectualism is victorious, and reinforced from Chamfort's *'toute idée publique, toute convention reçue, est une sottise, car elle a convenue au plus grand nombre'*. How like James Jackson that sounds! But ratiocinative imagination, the very type of the modern creative, may be diseased—or neurotic, even psychopathic, to use twentieth-century terms— and played out against madness induced by crazed religious politics, the Inquisition, with its engineered torture and its Sadean pleasure on watching a man committed to delirium for Christian dogma. These Christians line up for identity with all Poe's transgressors of humanity, all his law-breakers who replace justice with legal or illegal power. His anxiety situations dramatize major situations of stress in western societies, against which little redress or defence is possible:

> The now almost instantaneous dissemination of disquieting news and revolutionary new ideas permeates every part of society so that a reliable code of behaviour and an unchanging ideal to lean upon for support become more and more difficult to formulate.[39]

No Dupin can solve a society. 'The Gold Bug' is a cryptogram puzzle whose secret is not totally revealed, and the detector of the treasure is peculiar enough to be suspected of madness. His assistant, Jupiter, a black slave, is independent to the point of reversal, threatening his master with flogging him into sanity. In any case, the treasure is guarded by unsolved skeletons—death and money are linked in some undetectable origin (both Marx and Dickens would have appreciated the point). But William Legrand, the 'perfect reasoner', needs the Negro slave to wrest gold from the deadly past; the tale rehearses both capitalist opportunism and the ambivalences of slavery (those kinds of revision associated today with the fictions of Ishmael Reed). Information needs decoding, but Dupin is 'diseased', and Poe's epigram to the tale ridicules Legrand: 'This fellow is dancing mad!/ He hath been bitten by the Tarantula.' Spider venom is poisonous need for unearned wealth; corrupt desire is imaged as an event in nature rather than history. Legrand's depressive alternative of 'enthusiasm and melancholy' is his foundation. He is bitten by the gold bug, a scarabeus and instrument of divination, a treasure tracer, the geiger-counter's predecessor. His fate parodies Emerson's optimistic American individualism—'Nothing is at last sacred but the integrity of your own mind'—and exemplifies that condition offered by Matthiessen in 1941, in an otherwise very limited understanding of Poe's work:

> To such a degree did the provincial American mind, driven in upon itself, point the way through its intense self-consciousness, to the kind of material which the French symbolists were to explore, and even to something of the method by which modern psychology was to investigate this material further.[40]

3

In *Eureka* Poe believes that 'science should leap ahead by means of intuition. . . . poetry, however, must produce scientifically.' In 1925 Whitehead will write 'the greatest invention of the nineteenth century was the invention of the method of invention . . . the technique of beginning at the end of any operation whatever, and of working backwards from that point to the beginning.'[41] Poe's composition between science and imagination he calls 'arabesque', a plotted design, and his detective story is arabesque; 'The Gold Bug' is a puzzle design. Solutions plan the tale. The House of Usher (1839–45) entombs 'excessive antiquity', absence of 'external air'; the rooms are a 'web' without vitality, 'cataleptic' resistance to change, the 'hysteria' of retention, the threat of system entropically become 'incoherent' with in-turned efforts to sustain itself. Enslavement to any narcissistic dogma or obsession is entombment. One way through is the opening of 'The Murders in the Rue Morgue': 'As the strong man exults in his physical ability, so glories the analyst in that moral activity which disentangles.'

But suppose the processes of retracing are not to be compared to the processes of composition—that, for example, psycho-analysis leads back to the social system itself, within which the subject is controlled even before birth? As Dupin says, 'truth is not always in a well.' The 'surfaces' where truth is found may be social, therefore—out there. *Eureka* has to include both 'well' and 'surfaces' in 'universe' in order nostalgically to re-establish confidence his stories often demonstrate to be impossible. Poe needs a vision of Control against individualist permissions:

> The *Universe* . . . in the supremeness of its symmetry, is but the most sublime of poems. Now symmetry and consistency are controllable terms:—thus Poetry and Truth are one. . . . *A perfect consistency*, I repeat, can be nothing but an absolute truth.

Roderick Usher exemplified 'an incoherence—an inconsistency'. The 'laws of mesmerism' led to an enslavement quite as deadly as Vankirk's phthisis. Now the self is entered into the symmetry of *Eureka*. When Poe writes 'the plots of God are perfect. The Universe is a plot of God', he tries for both the unity of metaphysical artifice and the suggestion of multiplicity, reluctant to close space into a single reversible time plot. The creativity of the 'Heart Divine' is to be a sort of pre-Hoyle structure of continuous creation, a human-divine reciprocity. Poe, in common with many nineteenth-century thinkers, needed an analogue of machinery as safety, and his system is akin to that of Laplace, a model which would never stop, would be reversible, and would never be invaded by the perverse, or betrayed by a trickster God. Entropy and negentropy would be simultaneous.[42]

The hole in symmetry had been murder, the perverse, Symmes' Hole (the origin of 'MS Found in a Bottle' and the maelstrom), madness, dogmatically insane reason, animals, barbarians, the invasion of any force that threatens the mobile,[43] and the pressure of black on white. Harry Levin asks the arising question:

> Tar-and-feathering was an American system, the next thing to lynch-law, the roughest and readiest way of disciplining coloured persons and Northern abolitionists. It is as if Poe were asking the persistent question: What would happen if the slaves tired of slavery and dispossessed their masters?[44]

Blackness must never be universe for Poe. 'The Pit and the Pendulum' postulates an enclosure quite as evil as the South Pole with its blacks and its white controlling mist, as tar-and-feathering in an asylum, and as all his chambers, houses, cells, premature burials and holes: 'Then silence, and stillness, and night were the universe.' 'Premature Burial' is total oppression, 'the blackness of absolute night', the imagination's result of working on Young's *Night-Thoughts* and the Black Hole of Calcutta. 'Al Araaf' (written while Poe was in the army and under an assumed name, 1827–29) uses the Muslim image of the narrow wall between heaven and hell, a limbo for the dead who are neither good nor bad (religions are prototypical science fiction). The poem concludes with the self-obsessed lovers annihilated in endless night, the scene that would obsess Twain in 'The Great Dark' (op. post., 1962). Poe recognized that death might no longer be considered only 'natural' as a new sense of vulnerability invades the West. *Eureka* is really an intellectually comforting game:

> It is in that perception of death that the individual finds him-self, escaping from a monotonous average life; in the slow, half-subterranean, but already visible approach of death, the dull, common life becomes an individuality at last; a black border isolates it and gives it the style of its own truth. Hence the importance of the Morbid. The *macabre* implied a homogenous perception of death, once its threshold has been crossed. The *morbid* authorizes a subtle perception of the way in which life finds in death its most differentiated figure. The morbid is the *rarified* form of life, exhausted, working itself into the void of death; but also in another sense, that in death it takes on its peculiar volume, irreducible to conformities and customs, to received necessities. . . . Death left its old tragic heaven and became the lyrical core of man: his invisible truth, his visible secret.[45]

But the social context in America which contains Poe's regis-tration of the end of the tragic sense of death must be given also. The Romantic image of the isolated individual, homeless and dependent for vitality on self-expression and communion with 'nature', is countered by the anti-vitality of the will to power and the invasion of disease. H. B. Parkes has shown the end of belief in 'a kind of organic whole to which the individual belongs and has his appointed place' in the United States, without 'corresponding metaphysical conception of the natural universe as an ordered unity which harmonizes with human ideals'. Parkes traces out a line from Jonathan Edwards to the 'drive of the will', conspicuous in the 'American Renaissance'. This 'intoxication with the idea of omnipotence, the cruelty that it implied, and the overweening pride of logic with which it set out to explain the entire universe, represented tendencies that pervaded the writings of Poe and Melville. . . . Each individual must find his own way of dealing with chaos.'[46] In a theoretically equitable society the individual continually clashes with laissez-faire behaviour. This is Poe's theatre of realization for the popular readership. 'The Colloquy of Monos and Una' (1841) is, as the title suggests, a statement on unity; and it is based in a note Poe added on music as an ideal unified field in the *Republic*. Monos reports his rebirth to Una—an emergence from death and from systematic abstraction, 'enwrapped . . . in generalities', in defiance of 'the laws of *gradation* so visibly pervading all things in Earth and Heaven'—with God at the top. 'Wild attempts at an omni-prevalent Democracy were made', but this is an 'evil' out of 'the leading evil Knowledge', manifest in, for example, the industrial city. Monos survives entombment through 'a mental pendulous pulsation . . . the moral embodiment of man's abstract idea of *Time*'. So Poe's dream of resistance to decay and duration reaches another form of discourse. But as Alterton and Craig show, Poe is once again using ideas common in America and exemplified in 'American Social Elevation', published in the *Southern Literary Messenger*, and recommended in his review of Frederick von Raumer's *England in 1835* in 1836, and widely praised in the South since it opposed 'a love of gain' and aspiration to aristocracy and political power. The remedy is to be 'universal mental elevation', mental balance produced by the development of all human powers. But Poe retreated from the essay's democratic beliefs. The 'Colloquy' prefers hierarchy. Poe understood that capitalist democracy is a term barely concealing social gradations. The American social contract did not afford legal correctives to victimization.[47] Poe understood that no modern system could be governed by the old general equations.

NOTES

1. Eric Mottram, 'Poe's *Pym* and the American Social Imagination' in *Artful Thunder: Versions of the Romantic Tradition in American Literature*, ed. R. J. DeMott and S. E. Marovitz (Kent: Kent State University Press, 1975).
2. Michel Serres, *Hermes*, ed. J. V. Harari and D. F. Bell (Baltimore and London: Johns Hopkins University Press, 1982), p. xiv.
3. William Bittner, *Poe* (London: Elek Books, 1963), p. 224.
4. Bittner, p. 129.
5. Marie Bonaparte, *The Life and Works of Edgar Allan Poe: A Psycho-Analytic Interpretation* (London: Imago Publishing Company, 1949).
6. Wayne C. Booth, *The Rhetoric of Fiction* (Chicago: University of Chicago Press, 1963), p. 203.
7. Michel Butor, *Histoire Extraordinaire* (London: Cape, 1969).
8. Marshall McLuhan, *The Mechanical Bride* (London: Routledge and Kegan Paul, 1967), pp. 75, 109.
9. Walter Benjamin, *Charles Baudelaire* (London: NLB, 1973), pp. 42–3.
10. Harold Rosenberg, *The Tradition of the New* (New York: Horizon Press, 1959), pp. 108–9.
11. Paul DeMan, 'Intentional Structure of the Romantic Image' in *Romanticism and Consciousness*, ed. Harold Bloom (New York: Norton, 1970), p. 69.
12. Edgar Allan Poe, *Essays and Reviews* (New York: Library of America, 1984), pp. 505–30.
13. Andrew von Hirsch, *Doing Justice: The Choice of Punishments* (New York: Hill and Wang, 1976), p. 51.
14. A. O. Lovejoy, 'On the Discrimination of Romanticisms' in his *Essays in the History of Ideas* (Baltimore: Johns Hopkins, 1948), pp. 228–53.
15. Francis Steegmuller (ed.), *Selected Letters of Gustave Flaubert* (London: Hamish Hamilton, 1954), p. 186; James Joyce, *Portrait of the Artist as a Young Man* (London: Cape, 1944), p. 245.
16. Perry Miller (ed.), *The Legal Mind in America* (New York: Doubleday, 1962), p. 17.
17. Mottram, pp. 25–53.
18. Miller, pp. 275–79.
19. Eric Mottram, 'Orpheus and Measured Forms: Law, Madness and Reticence in Melville' in *New Perspectives on Melville*, ed. Faith Pullin (Edinburgh: University Press, 1978), pp. 229–54.
20. Jean Baudrillard, *In the Shadow of the Silent Majorities . . . or The End of the Social* (New York: Semiotext (e), 1983), p. 58.
21. Baudrillard, p. 71.
22. Miller, p. 283.
23. Serres, pp. 71–2.
24. Michel Foucault, *Madness and Civilization: A History of Insanity in the Age of Reason* (London: Tavistock Press, 1967), p. 11.
25. Foucault, p. 205.

26. Foucault, p. 208.
27. Serres, pp. xvi–xvii.
28. Serres, p. 28.
29. Renée Riese Hubert, 'The Other Wordly Landscapes of Edgar Allan Poe and René Magritte' in *SubStance*, No. 21, 1978.
30. D. H. Lawrence, *Studies in Classic American Literature* (1923) (New York: Doubleday, 1953), pp. 92, 14–18, 74, 79–92.
31. E.g. Emerson, 'Aristocracy' (1848) and 'On Student Rebellions at Harvard' (1842); Thoreau, 'Resistance to Civil Government' (1849).
32. Perry Miller, *The Life of the Mind in America* (New York: Harcourt, Brace and World, 1965), pp. 101–6.
33. Rosenberg, pp. 103–8.
34. *Essays and Reviews*, pp. 5–12.
35. *Essays and Reviews*, p. 1383.
36. Rosenberg, p. 110.
37. Ralph Tymms, *Doubles in Literary Psychology* (Cambridge: Bowes and Bowes, 1949), pp. 88–9.
38. Robert Darnton, *Mesmerism and the End of the Enlightenment in France* (Cambridge, Mass.: Harvard University Press, 1968), p. 3; see also Maria M. Tator, *Spellbound: Studies on Mesmerism* (New Jersey: Princeton University Press, 1979).
39. Hans Seelye, *Stress Without Distress* (London: Hodder and Stoughton, 1977), p. 7.
40. F. O. Matthiessen, *American Renaissance* (London: Oxford University Press, 1941), p. 233.
41. A. N. Whitehead, *Science and the Modern World* (New York: New American Library, 1948), pp. 98ff.
42. Ilya Prigogine and Isabella Stengers, *Order Out of Chaos* (London: Heinemann, 1984), Book One.
43. Eric Mottram, 'Fears of Invasion in American Culture' in the *New Hungarian Quarterly*, No. 8, Budapest, 1980.
44. Harry Levin, *The Power of Blackness* (London: Faber, 1958), p. 99.
45. Michel Foucault, *The Birth of the Clinic* (London: Tavistock Press, 1973), pp. 171–72.
46. H. B. Parkes, 'Poe, Hawthorne, Melville: An Essay in Sociological Criticism' in *Partisan Review* 16 February 1949, p. 159.
47. M. Alterton and H. Craig (eds.), *Edgar Allan Poe: Representative Selections* (New York: Hill and Wang, rev. edn., 1962), pp. lxxii–lxxvii.

9

'I am a Virginian': Edgar Allan Poe and the South

by RICHARD GRAY

'I am a Virginian', wrote Poe in 1841, 'at least I call myself one, for I have resided all my life, until within the last few years, in Richmond.'[1] Poe describes his relation to the South in a characteristically slippery way, here and elsewhere; and critics have been divided ever since over the question of his 'Southernness'. Two recent commentators, for instance, dismiss any suggestions of a significant attachment to the Old South. Poe, they point out, hardly ever used a Southern landscape; he usually avoided direct comment on social and political issues; and there are, at most, two or three references in his work to the 'peculiar institution' of slavery.[2]

Yet other accounts of Poe or of Southern writing in general offer arguments and evidence to the contrary. Harry Levin, for example, talks at some length about Poe's 'Southern self-consciousness'. Jay Hubbell, in his definitive *The South in American Literature* (1954) insists that, while Poe had little interest in describing the Southern scene, his imagination was essentially Southern; that in his attitudes to women and blacks, his distrust of the idea of progress, his belief in hierarchy and the indelible nature of evil, he thought and felt like a Southerner. While Marshall McLuhan, in two pioneering essays on the subject, argues that Poe is best understood in terms of a tradition derived from the South of his day. This tradition, McLuhan suggests, went back as far as the Greek sophists and can most conveniently be described as 'Ciceronian humanism'; it was 'perfectly adapted to agrarian estate-life' and had as its ideal 'the rational man reaching his noblest attainment in the expression of eloquent wisdom'.[3]

So what are the facts in the case of Edgar Allan Poe and the South? What was his relationship to the place where he spent most, but by no means all, of his life? Any attempt to answer such questions has to begin by acknowledging that—as my title quotation indicates—Poe often thought of himself as a Southerner. Believing, evidently, that he had to invent his life as well as his art, Poe played many parts in the course of just over forty years; but the part to which he was most fiercely and consistently attached was that of Southern gentleman.[4] There was some basis in personal experience for the pursuit of this particular rôle. He had been raised in considerable comfort in Richmond, Virginia, in a household with slaves; he had been educated there, for a while, and then briefly at the University of Virginia. And this at least partly Southern education had been supplemented by a period of attendance at West Point: in the sense that, as many historians have noted, the military tradition has always been strong in the South—not least because it tends to reinforce Southerners' obsession with the concept of honour.[5] Admittedly, the dubious privilege of being waited on by black slaves was something Poe was to grow unfamiliar with in his adult years, when his connections with the Southern ruling class became (to say the least) tenuous; and his Southern education was scrappy and incomplete. But like Twain, Poe seems to have been profoundly affected by those early years spent amidst a conservative, slaveholding community; and, unlike Twain, he clung to its conservatism, and many of its prejudices, even after he had become, to all intents and purposes, an exile, an outsider. This is perhaps most poignantly illustrated in his letters: where Poe tries to play the part of Southern aristocrat while soliciting financial assistance, or complaining about his treatment at the hands of those with wealth and power. In 1827, for instance, he wrote this to his foster-father John Allan:

> You suffer me to be subjected to the whims and caprice, not only of your white family, but the complete authority of the blacks— these grievances I could not submit to; and I am gone.[6]

The touchy pride, the angry sense of offences to personal honour, the racial bigotry (it is clearly the submission to 'the complete authority of the blacks' that rankles most): all these are part of a *persona* that Poe constructs for himself in his correspondence—as a face-saving device, it may be, a way of preserving self-respect, and even as a prop to identity, a way of convincing himself and others that he is somebody and does have a substantial presence.

This attempt to construct a Southern identity for himself takes many forms in Poe's correspondence. There is, for instance, his insistent adoption of the kind of philosophical conservatism, and resistance to the idea of Progress, that found little widespread support in nineteenth-century America outside of the Southern patriarchal tradition. 'I have no faith in human perfectibility', he wrote to James Russell Lowell in 1844, 'I think that human exertion will have no appreciable effect upon humanity. Man is now only more active—not more happy—nor more wise, than he was 6000 years ago'.[7] On a more practical level, there are his unremitting but, in the end, unsuccessful attempts to establish a Southern magazine that might rival the products of Boston and New York: to be published in the South, written largely by Southerners, and enjoyed by Southern gentlemen. This was one way, as he saw it, of challenging the hegemony of the North. Another was to give a public dimension to his rôle of aristocrat, to offer it to his readers as an alternative version of the American character: a rival possibility to the rôles of democratic Yankee, ruminative New Englander, or Boston Brahmin. This he did, most noticeably, in his essays and reviews, where again and again we find him playing the part of indolent but intelligent aristocrat, the dandy who— in conspicuous contrast to the earnest theocrats and frantic scribblers to the North—wears his learning easily, like an expensive suit of clothes. 'During a rainy afternoon, not long ago', begins one contribution to the *Democratic Review*,

> being in a mood too listless for continuous study, I sought relief from *ennui* in dipping here and there, at random, among the volumes of my library—no very large one, certainly, but sufficiently miscellaneous; and, I flatter myself, not a little *recherché*.[8]

A library just like that of Poe's aristocratic heroes, in fact; and as if to prove just how *recherché* it is, Poe scatters his writing with (frequently inaccurate) references to obscure or difficult texts. Not only that, like his disciple Baudelaire, he seems sometimes only too eager to shock his more bourgeois readers or, at least, to dislodge their complacency, their innate American belief in the unchallengeable nature of democracy. 'The sense of high birth is a moral force', he declares in one piece, 'whose value the democrats, albeit compact of mathematics, are never in condition to calculate. *"Pour savoir ce qu'est Dieu"*, says the Baron de Bielfeld, *"il faut être Dieu même"*.'[9]

Of course, it could be argued that the rôle of Southern dandy sat uneasily on a man who was not born in the South, never really belonged to the Southern patriarchy, and attempted to earn his living as an editor and writer. There is some truth to this. Quite apart from anything else, the part of professional writer that Poe either chose or was forced to adopt ran directly contrary to the Southern belief that literature was the prerogative of the gifted amateur; like William Gilmore` Simms, he discovered that there was an inherent and sad contradiction in his desire to become a Southern aristocratic man of letters. It needs to be pointed out, however, that if Poe simply *played the part* of gentleman, then so do most (and perhaps all) of those commonly described as gentlemen; for, as J. M. Huizinga has argued, an aristocratic culture is one in which people *imitate* some idea of aristocracy, some 'illusion of heroic being, full of dignity and humour, of wisdom and, at all events, of courtesy'.[10] And to this it needs to be added that if Poe's Southern patriarchal status was primarily a product of his imagination, a matter of knowing rather more than being, then so was that of, say, the so-called First Families of Virginia or that of the supreme fictional embodiment of Southern aristocratic ambition, the protagonist of Faulkner's *Absalom, Absalom!* Thomas Sutpen. The point is not an idle or perverse one. The fact is that the Old South invented itself, in the way that perhaps all patriarchal cultures do, by trying to interpret and regulate life according to some idealised version of the past. This is why so much recent historiography has concerned itself with the *idea* of the South: because the 'Old South', or to be more accurate 'the aristocratic Old South', was and is primarily a concept, a convenient but by no means always appropriate mythology, a device for mediating and structuring experience.[11] The South, observed one Southern writer John Donald Wade, is 'one of the really great abstractions of our race'.[12] And Poe was perhaps never more of a Southerner than when he was imitating one: applying himself assiduously to the rôle of Virginia dandy, even when much of the historical evidence was against him.

So far, most of the discussion of Poe's 'Southernness' has been concerned with the particular *persona* he tried to construct for himself in his private and public writings. But just as important, in this context, was the position he chose to adopt in the literary battles of his day. As an earlier reference to Poe's abortive attempts to found a magazine suggest, he chose much of the time to act as intellectual flag-bearer for the region. 'It is high time that the literary South took its own interests into its own charge', he insisted while editing the *Southern Literary Messenger*, and then followed this up a few months later by announcing boldly, 'we are embarking in the cause of *Southern* Literature and (with perfect amity to all sections) wish to claim especially as a friend and co-operator, every *Southern* Journal.'[13] There were certain specific reasons why Poe adopted this stance: fear of 'being ridden to death by New-England', resentment of what he saw as some New Englanders' attempts to persuade the world that 'there is *no such thing* as Southern literature', and perhaps the rather more calculated belief that controversy would help him make a name for himself—just as it had helped make a name for those Scottish reviewers who had attacked Leigh Hunt and his circle. But whatever the particular reasons, there is little doubt that this stance made him a formative influence as far as the ideas of a recognisably 'Southern' literature and 'Southern' culture are concerned. He lost no opportunity of pouring vitriol on New England—and Boston in particular, which he labelled 'Frogpondium'. 'We like Boston', he insisted with heavy irony,

> We were born there—and perhaps it is just as well not to mention that we are heartily ashamed of the fact. The Bostonians are very well in their way. Their hotels are bad. Their pumpkin pies are delicious. Their poetry is not so

good. . . . But with all these good qualities the Bostonians have no soul. . . . The Bostonians are well-bred—as *very* dull persons very generally are.[14]

And along with these aristocratic sneers at bourgeois notions of correct behaviour went a not entirely unself-interested defence of Southern writers: who, Poe felt, had never received their just deserts largely because they *were* Southerners. 'Had he been even a Yankee', he declared of William Gilmore Simms,

> His genius would have been rendered *immediately* manifest to his countrymen, but unhappily (*perhaps*) he was a southerner, and united the southern pride—the southern dislike to the making of bargains—with the southern supineness and general want of tact in all matters relating to the making of money.[15]

It does not take a great deal of ingenuity to see that Poe's championing of the Southern cause was getting him into difficulties here. It was all very well to adopt the pose of indolent dandy; but this sat uneasily with his insistence that the South could only establish its intellectual independence if it shook off its 'long-indulged literary supineness'[16] and acted with vigour, thoroughness and enthusiasm. Aristocratic carelessness was something that he could simultaneously praise and criticize, admire and lament, as the rather ambiguous tone of the passage just quoted indicates. In this, he was not alone: the very same blend of affection and irritation is to be found in the work of many Southern writers of the period—including John Pendleton Kennedy and William Gilmore Simms. In novels like Kennedy's *Swallow Barn* (1832) and Simms's *The Sword and the Distaff* (1853), the Southerner and, in particular, the Southern planter, was simultaneously cherished for his easy habits, his generosity and candour, and challenged for his want of energy, calculation, and ambition; the aristocratic idea was celebrated and then, in the very next moment, treated with profound misgivings. The Old South's own uneasy relationship with the rest of the nation largely accounts for this. Placed in the position of an aberrant minority, forced to recognize that theirs was an old and shrinking economy set amidst a young and growing nation, challenged on every front—morally, intellectually, racially, and politically—Southerners felt themselves compelled to defend their position and yet at the same time explain why they were in decline, to stick by the choices they had apparently made while trying to work out why those choices had not enabled them to prosper. Even those committed most fiercely to the pose of feudal aristocrat could not entirely suppress the hope that the Southern economy and Southern society might be revitalized. Even those who, like Poe, insisted that they had, quite simply, been born out of their due time into a contemptibly bourgeois culture could not wholly resist the idea of cultural renewal. Hence the contradictions at the heart of so much Southern writing of the time, its strange mix of defiance and depression; and hence the uneasy, ambivalent tone that characterizes so much of Poe's own flag-waving for the South.

A qualification or two needs to be entered about this flag-waving. Most of Poe's propaganda for the South coincided with the earlier part of his career; and, even then, he often claimed that he was attacking 'Frogpondium' in the name of places other than the South, simply challenging the cultural hegemony of New England rather than speaking in the voice of the regionalist. After he moved to New York, he even presented himself as a literary nationalist, concerned to promote the idea of a genuinely American literature. However, these qualifications need themselves to be qualified. His claims, in some of his earlier essays, to be speaking for the West as well as the South ring decidedly hollow, when set beside his insistence elsewhere that he was embracing the cause of a specifically Southern literature. And they ring even more hollowly still when it is remembered how very little interest Poe took in, not only the landscapes, but the imagery of the frontier; in his poetry, there is only the exotic allegory of 'Eldorado', and in his prose, little more than the abortive, unpublished *Journal of Julius Rodman*. Even his claim that he was an Americanist, made after he had arrived in New York, is, as Perry Miller indicates,[17] highly suspect. It seems likely, in fact, that he only made this claim in order to guarantee the support of Evert Duyckinck: an important consideration for any young man trying to establish himself in one of the few cities in nineteenth-century America where it was possible to earn a living as a writer. This is not to discount such claims entirely; after all, it could be argued that 'Poe the nationalist' and 'Poe the friend of the West' were no more the products of artifice, personal invention, than 'Poe the Southern gentleman' was. But it is to suggest that they were less central to Poe's life, less symptomatic of his deepest impulses. His rôles of spokesman for the South, and Southern dandy, were adopted early and then held fast to through most of his career; his desire to speak from and for the region clearly issued from the pressures of his own background, the urgencies of his own being. This surely makes such rôles and desires rather more crucial, as a key to the mystery of Poe, than attachments or allegiances that, whatever their interest, were initially the result of calculation, a wish to flatter others and so help him make his way in the world.

But Poe is best known, of course, not for his editorial work or reviewing but for his poetry and, even more, his fiction. A number of critics have tried to suggest that there is something peculiarly Southern, too, about his verse. Killis Campbell, for example, argues that Poe's 'scrupulous avoidance of the didactic'[18] is a mark of his regionalism, setting him at odds with the moralists of New England; while Stedman traces the sometimes excessive musicality of his poems back to the Southern love of rhetoric, words chosen for their melody rather than their meaning. This seems, to say the least of it, a little strained. Poe did not have to look very far in the Romantic tradition for examples of anit-didacticism or preoccupation with verbal music; and such inherently Romantic tendencies were probably reinforced, not by any lingering Southern influence, but by his hatred of what he saw as the utilitarianism of American culture. Certainly, dislike of utilitarianism, of functionalism of form and content, is something that distinguishes a good deal of Southern thinking; but it marks a great deal of non-Southern thinking too, and in particular a great deal of American poetry. The circumscribed Eden that Poe conjures up in his verse is, in this sense, not very different from the misty other-worlds that are the site of so many decidedly commonplace nineteenth-century poems; and it seems safe to assume that he would have written in the gently sentimental 'musical', vaguely mystical fashion he favoured even if he had never set foot in Virginia.

Things are rather different with the fiction. Admittedly, a case could be made, and frequently has been made, for Poe's total reliance on sources outside the South—on the exotic, sensational stories of the Gothic tradition, for instance, the narratives of Scott and Bulwer, and on the tales of adventure and escape so popular at the time. There is no doubt that, whatever else may be said about him, Poe belongs to a great tradition of aberrant literature—Romantic, Gothic, and subsequently Symbolist and Surrealist; and many commentators would prefer to leave things there, to confine him to this particular company. To say, however, that Poe is a part of (or, to be more accurate, a key figure in) American and European writing of the past two hundred years is, in this case, not to deny the Southern dimension. On the general level, there is the rather obvious point that all good Southern writers have managed to anchor their work in their region while at the same time utilizing what was to hand in other regions or countries; and there is the even more obvious point that the imagination of any writer can operate on several levels, exploiting resources that may sometimes complement and may, at other times, contradict one another but that, in any event, help to enrich and enliven his texts. That is the general level. On the particular, personal level of Poe's own writing, there is the simple fact that, while he was sublimely indifferent to the Southern landscape, and made very few references to its social and political institutions, he tapped many of the secret fears and guilts of his region. Unlike his poetry, his fiction is soaked in the imagery and frequently shaped by the obsessions of the place where he spent most of the formative years of infancy and childhood. The South appears in his tales, not as a convenient setting nor as the object of direct, critical analysis, but as a formative influence—an ancestral voice so deeply submerged in the text that only its distant echo can be heard, and the author himself often hardly seems to realize that it is there.

One way in which this ancestral voice makes itself heard, at least to the attentive reader, is through the structure of feeling, the frame of values that lies behind nearly every tale and that, just occasionally, Poe makes explicit. Not surprisingly, those

190

values are profoundly conservative ones: a sense of evil, a distrust of 'meddling' and change, a preoccupation with the past, a rejection of the ideas of perfectibility and progress, a hatred of abstractions and a belief in hierarchy. 'Some Words with a Mummy' illustrates the way in which Poe sometimes brings those ideas into the foreground of his stories. In it, he uses the pretext and *persona* of an Egyptian mummy, reawakened after several thousand years, as a way of using the example of the past to act as a corrective to the present. Here is a typical passage:

> We sent for a copy of a book called the 'Dial', and read out of it a chapter or two about something which is not very clear, but which the Bostonians call the Great Movement or Progress.
> The Count [the mummy] said that Great Movements were awfully common things in his day, and as for Progress, it was at one time quite a nuisance, but it never progressed.[19]

As this brief passage suggests, Poe's approach at such times is not especially subtle. And the ideas he expresses in stories like 'Some Words with a Mummy'—or similar tales, like 'The Colloquy of Monos and Una' and 'Mellonta Tauta'—are not particularly striking or profound; they are, in fact, little more than a rehearsal of the standard Southern argument of the time, used in defence of the region's economic and political position and, more specifically, in support of slavery. But it was precisely these 'political' ideas that provided the cornerstones of his writing, in the sense that Poe's 'philosophy', as expressed in *Eureka* and enacted in his tales, is merely his 'political' argument raised to a higher level. The sense of human imperfection, for instance, that Southern apologists, and Poe, invoked in defence of the *status quo* (things should be left alone, the argument went, because nothing is perfect and meddling would only make them worse) is central to *Eureka*: where it is transformed into the vaguely metaphysical belief that all created life is evil, because it involves fragmentation— the emanation of the imperfect Many from the perfect One.

Similarly, the distrust of 'rectangular abstractions' like 'equality' and 'progress' that was central to the pro-slavery argument ('I do not like to deal in abstractions', declared one apologist, '. . . There are few universal truths'[20]—and those few clearly did not include, for him, the ones invoked by the

Abolitionists): this, in Poe's hands, was transmogrified into an almost fetishistic attitude towards intuition and memory, a virulent hatred of rationalism or 'physical philosophy', and a firm conviction that all existence would eventually return upon itself. This is not, of course, to say that Poe ever worked out a systematic relationship between his 'political' and 'philosophical' thought, or that he relied entirely on the South for his conceptual framework. But it is to suggest that the Southern argument was indispensable, in that it helped him to build that framework—or, if that implies too conscious a process, helped shape the means whereby Poe saw the world.

'We see and hear and otherwise experience very largely as we do', insisted the linguist Edward Sapir, 'because the language habits of our community predispose certain choices of interpretation.'[21] And Poe's 'language' was at least in part a Southern one. This comes out clearly, not only in his conceptual framework, but in his imagery and the obsessions that haunt so many of his tales. As several critics have observed, he makes few overt references to slavery and Southern blacks. When he does so, however, he reproduces the familiar racist stereotype. A character called 'Toby', for example, in *The Journal of Julius Rodman* is said to have 'all the peculiar features of his race: the swollen lips, large white protruding eyes, flat nose, long ears, double head, pot-belly, and bow legs'.[22] More to the point, when Poe tries to describe his vision of evil, the darkness at the heart of things, as in *The Narrative of Arthur Gordon Pym*, it is noticeable that he sometimes adopts the familiar Southern strategy of associating that vision with black people. Southerners, and Southern writers in particular, have always tended to associate feelings of fear and guilt, the sense of Nemesis or Original Sin, with the black race, for obvious historical reasons; William Faulkner is only the most famous example. And in his portrait of the island of Tsalal, and the Tsalalians, at the end of *Arthur Gordon Pym*, Poe simply pushes that tendency to extremes: so that the Tsalalians become blatantly racist caricatures, grotesque exaggerations of an already exaggerated image. The Tsalalians are, in fact, an absurdist extension, or rather reversal, of the 'nigger minstrel' figure: with all the features that pro-slavery writers invented to reassure themselves become somehow threatening and sinister, so that the familiar dream is translated into nightmare. They are, we are told, utterly black (they even have black teeth!), with 'thick and long woolly hair' and 'thick and clumsy' lips.[23] Like the 'darky' of plantation romance, they clap their hands and slap their sides when they are amused; they keep hogs and their favourite food is a species of fowl. However, they are also deceitful and thieving, cruel and yet cowardly; they inspire, in the white protagonist, feelings of distrust, misgiving, and even paranoia. And these feelings are proved accurate when, finally, they turn on Pym, attempting to kill him. Like 'Hop-Frog' the dwarf in the story of that name, and like Nat Turner, they rebel against their alleged superiors, thus confirming that they were smiling villains whose affability was merely a disguise for pure hatred. In this way, Poe not only turns the comforting stereotype on its head; he supplies a—necessarily indirect and, perhaps, quite unconscious—expression of that greatest of all Southern fears: the fear that the slaves would one day rise and destroy a people who (all rationalizations and comforting stereotypes notwithstanding) had exploited, victimized, and oppressed them.

But when Southern imagery and obsessions are the issue, the key test is not so much *Arthur Gordon Pym*, for all its haunting use of black stereotypes and the colour of darkness, but a story like 'The Fall of the House of Usher'—one, that is, in which the controlling metaphors, and the dominant structure of feeling, can all be traced back to the author's childhood home. Admittedly, the literal setting of 'Usher' is not the South; it is a vaguely anonymous territory of the kind familiar to readers of Gothic narratives. Imaginatively, however, it *is* the South: a glamorous yet disastrous place that is indistinguishable in its figurative details from the world conjured up in the work of William Faulkner, Allen Tate, Robert Penn Warren and, more recently, in the fiction of Eudora Welty and William Styron. At the centre of the tale, of course, is Roderick Usher. To say that he is an idealized portrait of Poe himself—with his thin lips, enormous brow, nose 'of delicate, Hebrew model', and so on—is only to make the first and most obvious point. Beyond that, he is a blueprint for the central protagonist of Southern fiction: a figure whom W. R.

Taylor christened 'the Southern Hamlet' and whose avatars include Quentin Compson, Horace Benbow and, in that most popular of all Southern books *Gone with the Wind*, Ashley Wilkes.[24] Neurotic, imaginative, introverted, obsessed with the past, he is a supreme embodiment of aristocratic alienation, the young noble or dandy born out of his due time. More to the point, he is an incisive because utterly personal and particular figure for the South's sense of its own distinctiveness: its separation, as it saw and to some extent still sees it, from the bourgeois, utilitarian norms of the nation, its impotence and apparently irreversible decline. Like so many Southern heroes, in fact, the reasons for his superiority are also the source of his weakness; he can achieve, at best, a moral or imaginative victory—literally, historically he must experience defeat.

The other surviving representative of the 'very ancient family' of Usher is, of course, Madeline Usher who seems to belong to this world even less than her brother does. She is an ethereal creature, a fleeting presence of a kind familiar to readers of Poe, more like a spirit or a statue than a woman, with pale skin, large eyes, and dressed in white. There are, no doubt, personal reasons why she is portrayed in this way (to do with Poe's loss of his mother) and broader, 'philosophical' reasons (to do with Madeline's rôle as an arbiter between this world and the next); but there is no denying that there are also historical ones. For, as W. J. Cash was neither the first nor the last to observe, Southerners, particularly in the nineteenth and early twentieth centuries, have tended to identify the sanctity of their society with the purity of white womanhood: an ethereal, female figure, set apart, hardly belonging to the earth. The white woman, as Cash puts it, was

> the South's Palladium. . . . Athena gleaming whitely in the clouds . . . the mystic symbol of its nationality in the face of the foe. She was the lily-pure maid of Astolat. . . . And—she was the pitiful Mother of God. . . . There was hardly a sermon that did not begin and end with tributes to her honour.[25]

Any threat to the fabric of Southern society, real or assumed, was consequently interpreted as an indecent assault upon her: hence what Cash christened 'the rape complex', the paranoid belief that any black man who did not demonstrate complete subservience was after white women. The purity of white womanhood became a rallying call; and the idealized figure of Woman became a totem—which, in an odd way, is just what it is for Roderick Usher. Madeline Usher becomes the site of Roderick's obsessions. He identifies her with everything that he feels he once possessed but has now lost: a sense of wholeness and identity, feelings of being and meaning. She is the mirror in which, so he believes, he can see what he is or might be; she enacts for him his sense of self—just as the more generalized figure of white womanhood came, eventually, to dramatize Southern self-consciousness.

But Madeline is not just any white woman. She is Roderick's sister. Not only that, she is a strangely absent presence, like so many female characters in Southern fiction: Caddy Compson, say, in *The Sound and the Fury*, or Peyton Loftis in William Styron's first novel, *Lie Down in Darkness*. As far as absence is concerned, there are several probable reasons for this; and it would be wrong to pretend that all the reasons are the same for all Southern tales. However, there is a certain dimension they all share: absence, disinheritance, loss are common to every one of them, at least in part, because they issue from the same region—and from a similar sense of the region's history. The point is not really a difficult one to grasp; the absence of the object of affection and/or desire in so many Southern stories can be said, on one level, to correspond to those feelings of decline, dispossession, and nostalgia that have always characterized the Southern self-image. In the colonial period, men like William Byrd of Westover looked back with longing to the 'polite pleasures' of the old country from what Byrd termed the 'great wilderness' of the New World. In the early nineteenth century, people such as John Randolph of Roanoke gazed, with an equally fierce sense of deprivation, at the imagined land of colonial Virginia: a land, so Randolph averred, studded with 'spacious and costly' mansions furnished with 'taste and elegance' and inhabited by 'lively and hospitable' patriarchs. And in the later nineteenth century, on into the twentieth, writers such as John Esten Cooke, Thomas Nelson Page, and later Margaret Mitchell turned *their* eyes towards the 'high times' before the Civil War when 'peace and plenty reigned over a smiling land'.[26] The object of affection varied, the impulse remained the same: to conjure up a vanished world of aristocratic ease and to elegize over its passing. And the peculiar situation that characterizes so many Southern narratives, of a male protagonist obsessed with a woman who is simultaneously 'there' (in the sense that she dominates his thoughts and vision) and 'not there' (in that she is hardly present physically, if at all); this is surely an imaginative way, and a powerful one at that, of dramatizing this elegiac impulse, the belief that everything that made life worth living has somehow and irrevocably gone with the wind.

And then there is the fact that Madeline Usher is Roderick's sister; as many critics have observed, on one level the feelings nourished between the two are latently incestuous. Incest is, in fact, a recurrent preoccupation of Southern writers; or, if one thinks of books like *The Sound and the Fury*, *Sanctuary*, and *Absalom, Absalom!*, perhaps it would be more accurate to describe it as an obsession. There are several probable reasons for this. In the first place, intense family feelings, particularly between brother and sister, seem to have been a significant feature of life in the Old South. A recent major book on the region, *Southern Honor* by Bertram Wyatt-Brown, analyses the situation at some length: arguing that 'the close association of brother and sister . . . may have stemmed from the general character of isolated family-bound plantation life', and from 'the deep antinomies' inherent in the patriarchal family structure. 'The intensity of the brother-sister relation', Wyatt-Brown concludes, was 'an island of comfort in a sea of misapprehension and dread of dependency upon mother's love and father's good favor, both often withheld'.[27] In the second place, incestuous feeling was a key element in the collective myth of the region, the cultural fantasy that Southerners wove out of their historical experience. 'The Southern family romance', Richard H. King observes, 'was the South's dream', '. . . the region was conceived of as a vast metaphorical family, hierarchically organized and organically linked by [pseudo-] ties of blood'.[28] Such a fantasy set up a number of erotic tensions and generational conflicts; and, in particular, it turned every potential relationship between men and women into a version of sibling intimacy. Simplifying things a little, we could say that, within the terms of this collective myth, every young white woman became a 'sister', a member of the clan, whose purity and honour had to be protected. Hence the *generalized* force of the racist question, 'Would you let your sister marry one?' And hence the (not always successful) attempt to dissociate the 'Southern belle'—as well as the 'Southern plantation mistress'—from sexuality, and to assign the sexual function, mythically, to black women. For if this were not done, then the threat of incest inherent in the Southern family romance would be more or less unavoidable.

So in one sense what stories like 'The Fall of the House of Usher' do is develop and dramatize the intensity of certain relationships common in the life of the Old South, and turn the metaphorical incest inherent in the Southern family romance into something literal, occupying the foreground. 'Every culture lives inside its own dream', said Lewis Mumford,[29] and all that writers like Poe and Faulkner do is examine that dream, imaginatively, and reveal its darkest edges. Not unrelated to all this is the fact that, in terms of Freudian theory, incest is closely linked with a desire to retreat to the womb. As a result, it can act as a convenient paradigm of an aspect of Southern culture mentioned already: the tendency to resist change and growth—the pressures visited on any group by history—and to yearn for the recovery of some Golden Age. Incest is also linked to narcissism, since it implies a longing to be united with oneself, or at least one's own mirror image, to come apart from the world and be separate. And as an increasingly closed society, preoccupied with idealized self-images, particularly of its own past, the Old South certainly leaned towards narcissism, receding from the rest of the nation—first in intellectual and imaginative terms, and then politically. On this level, Roderick Usher is rather more successful than many Southern heroes. Sealing himself off within his fantasies, his self-centred image of perfection, he does finally reunite with his own reflection and, at the moment that he does so, the phenomenal world simply disappears.[30]

The third dominant figure in 'The Fall of the House of Usher' is, of course, the house itself: a characteristically bizarre version of those mansions, intended to look old even when they were new, that Southern planters built as monuments to their own ambitions. Perhaps nothing more grandiloquently expressed the aristocratic pretensions of the Old South than these structures, often more façade than substance (wood, for example, was painted to look like marble); and Poe simply takes these dream palaces and makes them dreamier still—the House of Usher actually seems, not only decaying, but substanceless. The house, in fact, is as much mind as matter; inextricably attached to the nightmarish visions and haunted consciousness of its owner, it eventually dissolves with him into aboriginal nothingness. And it is, too, as much of a mirror as Madeline Usher is: a reflection of the obsessions, not only of Roderick himself, but of its imaginative creator, the author of the tale. As Poe has the narrator observe, 'Usher' is 'a quaint and equivocal appellation'[31] in that it refers to both the house and the family. But it is so in another sense as well—in that it has become a convenient, shorthand way of referring to the story, and so serves to remind us just how inextricably connected house and tale are.

Roderick Usher creates his own imagined world within 'Usher' the house, and so does Poe within 'Usher' the tale—a world into which he draws us, along with the narrator. From daylight reality, further inwards towards ever darker, more hidden and subterranean levels; the structure of the narrator's journey as he moves into 'Usher' the house corresponds exactly to our own journey as readers ever further into 'Usher' the fiction. Roderick Usher uses his arts to transform his guest's minds and expectations; so also does Poe, with his imaginative guests. And at the moment of revelation—when, so it is hoped, the full truth of the solipsistic vision is revealed—both 'Usher' the house and 'Usher' the tale disintegrate, disappear, leaving the narrator and the reader alone with their own personal thoughts and surmises. In sum, 'The Fall of the House of Usher' is pre-eminently self-reflexive; every feature of the tale refers us back to the actual process of creative production, by its author, and re-production, by us, its readers. And while self-reflexiveness is by no means a characteristic peculiar to Southern writing, it is obviously not at odds with the regional tendency towards narcissism and nostalgia. In this sense, too, Poe's story stands at the beginning of a long line of Southern narratives, whose distinguishing characteristics include an extraordinary inwardness, a stifling sense of claustrophobia, a scarcely concealed hysteria, and the habit of looking backwards, not only for comfort, but for meaning and the means of salvation.

'Jesus, the South's fine, isn't it?', observes a character in that greatest of all Southern novels, *Absalom, Absalom!* 'It's better than the theatre, isn't it.'[32] In his own fashion, the histrionic Mr. Poe seems to have recognized and appreciated this, and determined to play a part—and a central part, at that—in the regional drama. Some ways in which he performed his rôle were, as I have tried to show, fairly obvious, even flamboyant, but they were none the less significant for that, no less symptomatic of his inmost needs and desires. And others entered his life and texts in circuitous ways, with the result that many of the distinguishing marks of his regionalism can only be caught aslant; they have to be seen, as it were, through a glass darkly. Of course, Poe was not *simply* a Southern writer, any more than Faulkner was; the province of his imagination was not just the territory below the Mason-Dixon line. Nevertheless, 'Southernness' is often there in his writing even when it remains unacknowledged, a habit of seeing rather than the object of vision—a structure of feeling, more than the thing to be felt. At such times (and they are frequently the most important, as far as this regional dimension is concerned), the South is very much an absent presence in his work, like something Poe himself might have invented. It is rather like one of his own strange, ethereal female characters, in fact: an image inscribed on the imagination since childhood, a familiar ghost haunting the darker recesses of the mind (Poe's, and ours), intangible and yet inescapable.

NOTES

1. *The Letters of Edgar Allan Poe*, edited by John Ward Ostrom, 2 vols. (Cambridge, Mass., 1948), I, 170. To Frederick W. Thomas, June–July, 1841.
2. J. V. Ridgely, *Nineteenth-Century Southern Literature* (Lexington, Ky., 1980), p. 24; Edward Rans and Andrew Hook, 'The Old South', in *Introduction to American Studies*, edited by Malcolm Bradbury and Howard Temperley (London, 1981), p. 103.

3. Marshall McLuhan, 'The Southern Quality', *Sewanee Review*, LV (1947), 371, and 'Edgar Allan Poe's Tradition', *Sewanee Review*, LII (1944), 25. See also, Harry Levin, *The Power of Blackness: Hawthorne, Poe, Melville* (1958; New York, 1960 edition), p. 120; Jay B. Hubbell, *The South in American Literature: 1607–1900* (Durham, N.C., 1954), p. 528.

4. 'Among the many parts he was to play in life, that of Southern gentleman was the earliest and the one to which he adhered most consistently.' Julian Symons, *The Tell-Tale Heart: The Life and Works of Edgar Allan Poe* (London, 1978), p. 15. See also, Arthur H. Quinn, *Edgar Allan Poe: A Critical Biography* (New York, 1941), pp. 204, 249; David Sinclair, *Edgar Allan Poe* (London, 1977), p. 56.

5. See, e.g., John Hope Franklin, *The Militant South* (Cambridge, Mass., 1956); David Donald, 'The Southerner as Fighting Man', in *The Southerner as American*, edited by Charles G. Sellers (Chapel Hill, N.C., 1960); J. Sherwood Williams et al., 'Southern Subculture and Urban Pistol Owners', in *Perspectives on the American South: Volume 2*, edited by Merle Black and John Shelton Reed (New York, 1984).

6. *Letters*, I, 8. To John Allan, 19 March 1827.

7. *Letters*, I, 256. To James Russell Lowell, 2 July 1844.

8. 'Marginalia', *Democratic Review*, November 1844, in *The Complete Works of Edgar Allan Poe*, edited by James A. Harrison (1902; New York, 1965 edition), XVI, 3.

9. Ibid., XVI, 13.

10. J. M. Huizinga, *The Waning of the Middle Ages* (New York, 1954), p. 39.

11. See, e.g., Michael O'Brien, *The Idea of the American South: 1920–1941* (Baltimore, Md., 1979); Daniel Joseph Singal, *The War Within: From Victorian to Modernist Thought in the South, 1919–1945* (Chapel Hill, N.C., 1982); Fred Hobson, *Tell About the South: The Southern Rage to Explain* (Baton Rouge, La., 1983).

12. Cited in O'Brien, *Idea of the American South*, p. 215.

13. *Southern Literary Messenger*, II (June 1836), 460. Cited in Sidney P. Moss, *Poe's Literary Battles: The Critic in the Context of His Literary Milieu* (Durham, N.C., 1963), pp. 52–3. See also, p. 33.

14. *Broadway Journal*, 1 November 1843, in *Complete Works*, XIV, 11. See also, Michael Allen, *Poe and the British Magazine Tradition* (New York, 1969), p. 51; review of *A Fable for Critics*, *Southern Literary Messenger*, March 1849, in *Complete Works*, XIV, 172.

15. Review of *The Wigwam and the Cabin*, *Godey's Lady's Book*, January 1846, in *Complete Works*, XIV, 95.

16. Review of *Georgia Scenes*, *Southern Literary Messenger*, March 1836, in *Complete Works*, VIII, 259. For some of the more general matters referred to here see, e.g., Charles S. Sydnor, *The Development of Southern Sectionalism, 1819–1848*, Vol. V (1948) in *The History of the South*, edited by Wendell Holmes Stephenson and E. Merton Coulter, 10 vols. (Baton Rouge, La., 1947–67).

17. Perry Miller, *The Raven and the Whale: The War of Words and Wits in the Era of Poe and Melville* (New York, 1956), pp. 116, 268.

18. Killis Campbell, *The Mind of Poe, and Other Studies* (1933; New York, 1962 edition), p. 115. Campbell also cites Stedman's argument, referred to here.
19. *The Complete Tales and Poems of Edgar Allan Poe* (Harmondsworth, Middx., 1982), p. 546. All references to the tales will be to this easily available edition.
20. James Henry Hammond, 'Hammond's Letter on Slavery', in *The Pro-Slavery Argument: As Maintained by the Most Distinguished Writers of the Southern States* (Charleston, S.C. 1852), p. 104.
21. Edward Sapir, *Selected Writings in Language, Culture, and Personality* edited by David G. Mandelbaum (Berkeley, Calif., 1949), p. 162.
22. 'The Journal of Julius Rodman', in *Complete Works*, IV, 84. The review of *Slavery in the United States* included in the *Complete Works* was, in fact, written by Beverley Tucker.
23. *Complete Tales*, p. 854.
24. See Chapter IV of William R. Taylor, *Cavalier and Yankee: The Old South and American National Character* (London, 1963). See also, *Complete Tales*, p. 234.
25. W. J. Cash, *The Mind of the South* (1941; New York, 1967 edition), p. 89.
26. Thomas Nelson Page, *On Newfound River* (London, 1891), p. 2. See also, William Byrd of Westover, *History of the Dividing Line Betwixt Virginia and North Carolina*, in *The Prose Works of William Byrd of Westover*, edited by Louis B. Wright (Cambridge, Mass., 1966), p. 279, and *The London Diary and Other Writings*, edited by Louis B. Wright and Marion Tinling (New York, 1958), p. 38; John Randolph, letter to J. Quincy, 12 March 1814, cited in Russell Kirk, *Randolph of Roanoke: A Study in Conservative Thought* (Chicago, 1951), p. 189. Also, Lucinda H. MacKethan, *The Dream of Arcady: Place and Time in Southern Literature* (Baton Rouge, La., 1980).
27. Bertram Wyatt-Brown, *Southern Honor: Ethics and Behaviour in the Old South* (New York, 1982), pp. 251–52.
28. Richard H. King, *A Southern Renaissance: The Cultural Awakening of The American South, 1930–1955* (New York, 1980), pp. 26–7.
29. Cited in King, *A Southern Renaissance*, p. 26.
30. In this connection see, Robert D. Jacobs, 'Faulkner's Tragedy of Isolation', in *Southern Renascence*, edited by Louis D. Rubin and Robert D. Jacobs (Baltimore, Md. 1955), p. 174.
31. *Complete Tales*, p. 232. On the architecture of the period see, e.g., Richard Beale Davis, *Intellectual Life in Jefferson's Virginia, 1790–1830* (Chapel Hill, N.C., 1964), pp. 205–52.
32. *Absalom, Absalom!* (1936; London, 1937 edition), p. 217.

10

Poe in France:
A Myth Revisited

by JOHN WEIGHTMAN

The Poe Myth is, by now, one of those teasing problems of literary history, like the Origins of Courtly Love or the Rise of Sensibility after 1700, that successive generations of inquirers have investigated in detail, and often brilliantly, but whose central core of mystery has never quite been broached. Why should Baudelaire, at the age of 27 and after reading one or two of Poe's tales in translation, have become so obsessed with the American as to champion his cause in France with unparalleled fervour? Why should he, himself a creative writer and chiefly a poet, have persisted, during sixteen years of a relatively short and notoriously difficult existence, in the laborious task of transposing Poe's prose works into French? The case is surely unique; no other major figure has ever been known to perform such a sustained act of piety towards a fellow author.

The phenomenon would be more comprehensible if Poe were, by common consent, a writer at least equal to—or markedly better than—Baudelaire. But this, of course, has never been a view current among the *literati* on the Anglo-American side, especially those who admire Baudelaire. In America and England, Poe's literary position has always been uncertain. His *Tales* rank as a popular classic, but there is no consensus about the level on which they operate; are they genuinely archetypal, or half-spontaneous, half-contrived exploitations of the clichés of Gothic horror? His most famous poem, 'The Raven', is more notorious than seriously admired. Literary historians credit him with being one of the originators of the detective story and the science-fiction fantasy, and have recognized his verve as a critic and polemical prose-writer. The secondary literature about the problems of his life and the possible meanings of his symbolism is now immense, but no English-language critic has ever claimed absolute status for him as a great writer.

Indeed, some of the most authoritative Anglo-American figures—Henry James, Aldous Huxley, Yvor Winters, T. S. Eliot, etc.[1]—have kept asking, either directly or by implication: why should a great European writer have become so enamoured of a debatable American author, who is at best 'three-fifths genius . . . two fifths fudge'?[2] In short, it is only in France, since the second half of the nineteenth century and despite one or two discordant voices, that Poe has been considered a peerless genius, a touchstone, a unique point of reference.

The evidence to this effect is full of surprising details. Baudelaire, in a moment of great emotional stress, determined to pray to Poe as an intercessor between himself and God. Mallarmé, perhaps with a touch of poetic licence, said that he went to England to learn English (and thus determined the subsequent course of his workaday career) only so that he could read Poe in the original. Valéry, as a young man, committed himself to the view that 'Poe is the only impeccable writer; he was never mistaken.' André Gide reports Paul Claudel as asserting: 'Baudelaire and Poe are the only modern critics.' The actor-producer Aurélien-François Lugné, later to become the famous director of Le Théâtre de l'Oeuvre, actually invented a fictitious blood-relationship with the American and turned himself into Lugné-Poe, sometimes spelt and pronounced Lugné-Poë. This is perhaps another unique, though minor, phenomenon in literary history, even more curious than Cecily Fairfield's borrowing of the name 'Rebecca West' from *Rosmersholm*; she did not go so far as to style herself Fairfield-Ibsen.

Nor did Poe's vogue disappear with the turn of the century. As late as 1926, Camille Mauclair, out-Baudelairing Baudelaire, published a dithyrambic volume entitled *Le Génie d'Edgar Poe*, which rejected the concept of Poe as being in any way a 'decadent' writer and asserted the supreme healthiness and objectivity of his mind and art. Could Poe have foreseen this, he might have been gratified, but his sense of romantic grandeur would have been still more flattered, had he known that in 1933, shortly before the centenary of his death, a real-life European princess, albeit of an upstart line, would make him the subject of an admiring and exhaustive Freudian study; Marie Bonaparte's *Edgar Poe, étude psychanalytique*, accepts him unquestioningly as a writer of the first world rank. The fact that her interpretation is diametrically opposed to Mauclair's only adds to the richness of the Poe theme as it has blossomed in France, and continues to blossom, although now mainly in academic circles. Contemporary French specialists have made Poe the subject of elaborate thematic analysis, and Claude Richard's monumental thesis, *Edgar Allan Poe, journaliste et critique* (1978), hails him as the true ancestor of *la nouvelle critique*.[3]

Two separate issues are involved: what did Baudelaire see in Poe in the first place, and why did later generations of Frenchmen share his enthusiasm and even, in some instances, carry it a stage further?

Baudelaire went some way towards explaining his interest in Poe in general terms, but, to the surprise of more than one literary historian, he never said anything very specific. Among his critical essays, there is no analytical study of Poe either as poet or prose-writer. His longest comments are the prefaces to the two volumes, *Histoires Extraordinaires* (1856) and *Nouvelles Histoires Extraordinaires* (1857). The first is largely a summary of Poe's life, depending on the American sources then available, and presenting him as a suffering, misunderstood genius, isolated in a philistine world—that is, exactly the sort of persecuted artistic figure Baudelaire sees himself as in 'Bénédiction', the initial poem of the 'Spleen et Idéal' section of *Les Fleurs du Mal*. The second preface amplifies this point, with the addition of slightly more detailed remarks about Poe's theories. He is praised for being a believer in the pure ideal of art, divorced from any vulgar concern with didacticism. His insistence on the conscious technique of poetic composition is contrasted favourably with the more slovenly belief in facile inspiration. His use of alcohol and opium is defended as a possible means of achieving those higher states necessary for the perception of the Ideal, a point which corresponds, if not to Baudelaire's own practice, at least to an attitude he expresses in *Les Petits Poèmes en prose*—'*Il faut être toujours ivre!*'—and to his sympathetic account of De Quincey's opium addiction in *Les Paradis Artificiels*. Finally, Poe is commended for his understanding of the tragic character of existence and the flawed nature of man, an aristocratic insight greatly superior,˙ it is asserted, to the naïve, bourgeois faith in progress. In all this, Baudelaire seems to be painting Poe in his own image, rather than seeing his complexities objectively as they are, and appreciating his works in detail.

We might be tempted to conclude, then, as T. S. Eliot does in his *Hudson Review* article of 1948, 'From Poe to Valéry', that Baudelaire was impressed by the general image of '*le poète maudit*' (*avant la lettre*, of course, since Verlaine had not yet invented the expression), 'the personality of the man' . . . 'the continental figure of the myth of Byron'. This is no doubt true enough in its way, but it still leaves us wondering why Baudelaire became so excited about an American example. The plight of isolated literary genius had been a major Romantic theme, to which Alfred de Vigny, in particular, gave full paranoiac expression in *Chatterton* and *Stello*. Art versus didacticism and meticulous care in composition were tenets of the Art-for-Art's-sake movement, which predated Poe, and to whose leading figure, Théophile Gautier, Baudelaire dedicated *Les Fleurs du Mal*. Gérard de Nerval, a poet and story-writer almost exactly contemporary with Poe, could have provided a French instance of a *poète maudit*. There is something apparently gratuitous about Baudelaire's concentration on Poe. Racking our brains, we could perhaps suggest that, for publicity reasons, he may have thought it more dramatic to use a remote, little-known, foreign figure as a stick with which to beat the French philistines, and to cast aspersions—as he does in the second preface—on the didactic element in the work of Victor Hugo, the dominant living French poet. But while such an impulse might have prompted an article or two, it would hardly have been enough to carry him through years of translation work.

Other critics, and notably P. F. Quinn, the author of *The French Face of Poe* (1957), explain Baudelaire's fascination by dwelling on the curious parallels between the personalities and family situations of the two men. Both had nervous temperaments, characterized by a brittle tension between analytical intelligence and hysterical imbalance. Both were remarkably incapable of conducting their everyday lives with any success, and stumbled from one psychological and financial crisis to another; to adapt the phrase from *L'Albatros* by means of which Baudelaire put the best possible interpretation on this disability, *leurs ailes de géant les empêchaient de marcher*. Both retained a certain dandyistic composure in spite of their mishaps. Both were fatherless and, in late adolescence, fell foul of their stern, efficient step-fathers, John Allan and General Aupick. Both had a mother-fixation, Poe on his two mother-substitutes, Frances Allan and Maria Clemm, and Baudelaire on his real mother, whom he clung to all his life, in spite of his involvements with other women. Baudelaire was aware of this resemblance with Poe, because he conceived, by transference, a great attachment to Maria Clemm. The only serious difference between the two men seems to have been in relation to sex; the evidence suggests—and has been accepted by most critics—that Poe was impotent, that he contracted a *mariage blanc* with the tubercular Virginia and never experienced a consummated relationship with any woman. Baudelaire, on the other hand, notwithstanding the early disaster of syphilis, evidently enjoyed some moments of fulfilment, which he transposed into great love poems. But, generally speaking, it can be agreed that they had enough in common to make it plausible for Baudelaire eventually to look upon Poe almost as an *alter ego*, already happily ensconced in the haven of the next world, and thanks to whom he could, as it were, see himself in a tragic, yet glorious and comforting, perspective, through a sort of narcissism at one remove.

I say 'eventually', and the reservation is important because, when Baudelaire was first attracted to Poe through coming across his stories, he as yet knew little or nothing about the American's life and personality. He describes the *coup de foudre* in a letter to his mother, written in 1853:

> The first time I opened one of his books [research seems to show that it was not a book, but a review or newspaper containing a translation of *The Black Cat*] I saw, with terror and delight, not only subjects I had dreamed of, but sentences that I had thought of and that he had imitated twenty years before.

He repeats the statement, almost in the same terms, to another correspondent in 1860, but in neither context does he mention what these subjects were, nor which sentences, so the reader is left guessing. If his assertion is true, why did he never try his hand at the sort of tale for which Poe is most famous? He produced only two short stories, *La Fanfarlo* and *Le Jeune Enchanteur*, which might, at a pinch, be seen to bear some resemblance to Poe's less typical, ironical pieces, such as *The Spectacles* or *Some Words with a Mummy*. Here and there, in his other prose writings, we can note possible points of contact. A few sadistic touches in *Les Petits Poèmes en prose*—e.g. in *Le Mauvais Vitrier*—are reminiscent of *The Imp of the Perverse*, and it seems clear that the confessional fragment, *Mon coeur mis à nu*, was directly inspired by paragraph XLI of *Marginalia*. However, none of this amounts to much and, in any case, Baudelaire's reputation has always rested on his achievement as a poet, not on anything he wrote in prose, in spite of the respect often accorded to his critical writings.

As regards Poe's poetry, a certain doubt hangs over Baudelaire's attitude towards it. He obviously devoted far less time to the verse than to the tales. He made a plain, prose translation of 'The Raven' and, according to his friend Asselineau, would recite the poem with enthusiasm, but whether in the original English or in his own version is not recorded. He kept to prose in translating the pieces of verse in the tales. Perhaps he rightly sensed that the attempt to transpose poetry, as such, from one language to another, is, for clearly demonstrable linguistic reasons, like trying to square the circle; at any rate, he states in the preface to *Nouvelles Histoires Extraordinaires* that the idea of translating Poe's poems can never be more than a fondly cherished dream. But it is curious that he should never have said anything very relevant about the poetry itself, except to claim, again in a letter to his mother, that he felt an affinity with the American in this area too:

> What is rather peculiar, and impossible for me not to notice, is the close, though not positively marked, resemblance between my own poems and those of this man, allowance having been made for differences of temperament and climate.

This remark is, in itself, so hedged about with qualifications as to be unenlightening. It is true that nostalgia, which is virtually Poe's only poetic subject, is also an important theme with Baudelaire, but he was in no sense necrophiliac like Poe, and his best poems contain a wealth of varied emotion, some of it positive to the point of ecstasy, which makes them quite different from Poe's generally melancholy and monotonous verse. He certainly could not have subscribed to Poe's extreme statement, inspired no doubt by a series of poignant bereavements, that the most poetic subject in the world is the death of a beautiful woman, although, in *Une Charogne*, a poem about the prospective death of the beloved, he dealt with precisely this theme, but in a very powerful and totally un-Poe-like way. I assume that it is unnecessary to labour the point that, in spite of the unevenness of quality in *Les Fleurs du Mal*, Baudelaire, the poet, is in a quite different category from Poe. In suggesting a sort of equivalence between them, he is doing the American too great an honour, and is probably being moved by a sense of kinship not strictly related to poetry. This is the nub of a perhaps insoluble problem. I can only suppose that the sense of kinship had something to do with tales, before it was reinforced by knowledge of Poe's life. Could it be that, because of his richly neurotic temperament, of which there is ample evidence in his correspondence, Baudelaire had within him a tangle of complexes that were not completely resolved in his poetry, and that he was unable to express directly in prose? Even more than most poets, he kept complaining of writer's block, and the Poe translations were, in fact, the only fairly regular work he ever did. P. F. Quinn goes so far as to suggest that they occupied a more important place in his life than his own poetry. I cannot believe this, and the idea would certainly seem shocking to all French admirers of Baudelaire. But it is possible that the translation of Poe's vividly symbolic prose-writings became a form of self-expression by proxy, a *dérivatif* or partial therapy, and all the more effective through the symbols being sufficiently mysterious and indefinite not to have any precise meaning that might hinder their operation. This hypothesis would explain the doggedness with which Baudelaire pursued his task, and his personal identification with the texts as he produced them. If Poe were, for him, a means to phantom or substitute creation, an elaborate false pregnancy in prose, the mechanism of which he himself did not fully understand, this would also explain why, in 1865, two years before his death, he felt a sort of revulsion at what had happened. He wrote to a correspondent, in connection with another translation project:

> I am afraid of that kind of drudgery. I have wasted a lot of time translating Edgar Poe, and the great benefit I have gained from doing so is that some kind souls have said that I borrowed *my* poems from Poe, although they had been written ten years before I became acquainted with Poe's work. I regard translation as a lazy man's way of minting money.

The last sentence is obviously untrue, since his earnings had been negligible in relation to the effort expended. Nor would he have been so obsessive, had money been his only concern. It seems likely that he had some unexplained, and perhaps unconscious, motivation, of the kind I have suggested.

My hypothesis may, or may not, be valid. However, one thing of which we can, I think, be certain, is that Poe owes his exceptional fame in France primarily to Baudelaire's standing *as a poet*, not simply to the fact that Baudelaire translated the tales. Had Baudelaire been a translator pure and simple, the situation would have been quite different. Poe's reputation in France is, in this respect, not at all comparable to Proust's reputation in the English-speaking world. Proust came across because of the inherent richness of his work, in spite of the many inaccuracies in Scott-Moncrieff's good, but uneven, translation. Poe was worshipped *a priori* and taken completely on trust, because Baudelaire had professed such admiration for him. Since *Les Fleurs du Mal* was a sacred text for the literary generations of the second half of the nineteenth century, Poe too became holy writ, to be interpreted reverently, even if only in snatches. The apostolic succession is quite clear: Poe/Baudelaire > Mallarmé > Valéry. Mallarmé worshipped

Baudelaire and Poe; Valéry worshipped Mallarmé and was therefore prejudiced in favour of Poe and Baudelaire. Mallarmé, as it happened, was a particularly strong link in the chain, because his famous evening receptions for young writers and artists—*les mardis de la rue de Rome*—helped to surround Poe with a religious awe that prompted imitative expressions of enthusiasm, often difficult to relate to Poe's actual writings. For instance, what Verlaine, Claudel and Albert Samain say about Poe belongs more to the realm of phatic approval than of critical assessment. Among the writers connected with Symbolism, only Remy de Gourmont appears to have kept his critical balance while commenting on Poe. As for Camille Mauclair's indiscriminate paean of praise, although anti-decadent in bias, it seems to be a last extreme echo of the special, late nineteenth-century atmosphere. We may also wonder if Poe would ever have come to the notice of Marie Bonaparte as a likely subject for Freudian analysis, had he not been carried along on the general cultural prestige of Baudelaire, Mallarmé and Valéry; her incidental remarks about the supposed 'realism' of Zola and Maupassant, which she contrasts unfavourably with the imaginative depth of Poe's writing, show that she had no great awareness of literary critical problems. Even the recent academic works, such as Claude Richard's thesis, seem to begin from a position of spontaneous reverence for Poe, because of the weight of the Baudelairean tradition.

Mallarmé mentions Poe's tales, especially 'The Fall of the House of Usher', with respect, but only in passing, and there is no evidence to suggest that he paid particular attention to them. He was concerned, in the first place, with the Baudelairean conception of the poet as martyred hero of a Higher Cause (hence the magnificent sonnet celebrating the erection of the Poe monument in 1875), then with the poetry itself, a proportion of which he translated and commented on, and lastly with some aspects of Poe's literary theories. But, in the first two connections at least, strict relevance to the discernible reality of Poe is not a marked feature of his interest.

The 'Tombeau d'Edgar Poe', great poem though it is, must rank as hagiography. The unforgettable opening, *Tel qu'en lui-même enfin l'éternité le change*, now one of the best-known lines in the whole of French literature, is inaccurate in the sense that 1875 did not mark the entry of Poe, the poet, into an ensured eternity of fame; his poetic position is, if anything, more dubious than before. The splendid image of Poe as avenging angel or divine legislator, giving a purer meaning to the words of the cowering tribe of American philistines, is sheer hyperbole. Further, it is simplistic to suggest that the contemporary public attributed Poe's talent merely to drink; in spite of Griswold's maliciousness after his death, in life he benefited from a fair degree of tolerant understanding, as did Dylan Thomas, a somewhat similar case within living memory. Finally, the poem is slightly marred by what seems to be a technical slip; the wonderful expression designating the monument as a meteorite—*calme bloc ici-bas chu de quelque désastre obscur*—should perhaps not stand in apposition to *ce granit*, since granite is an igneous earth-rock. However, none of this seriously affects the musical and emotional beauty of the sonnet as a lyrical vindication of poetry in general, of which Poe himself is only, as it were, the accidental occasion.

This brings us to the question of how far Baudelaire, Mallarmé or any other of the French enthusiasts were really equipped to evaluate Poe's verse in the original. The answer is: hardly at all. Baudelaire had acquired a smattering of English in childhood from his mother, who had spent some time in England, and although he improved his knowledge later, it presumably remained bookish rather than oral. Mallarmé, who was officially an *angliciste*, never mastered the language properly, as the inspectors' reports on his teaching regretfully repeat, and as *Thèmes anglais*, his eccentric excursion into English philology, sadly confirms. Neither had a sensitive enough knowledge of English to be aware of the crudities of Poe's verse, so devastatingly analysed by Aldous Huxley in the essay 'Vulgarity in Literature', by Yvor Winters in 'A Crisis in American Obscurantism' and by T. S. Eliot in the *Hudson Review* article already referred to.

Nevertheless, they may have been stimulated in certain ways by Poe's poems. As Eliot remarks:

> It is certainly possible, in reading something in a language imperfectly understood, for the reader to find what is not there;

and when the reader is himself a man of genius, the foreign poem read may, by a happy accident, elicit something important from the depths of his own mind, which he attributes to what he reads.

This is convincing as a general principle; the difficulty is to see what Baudelaire, Mallarmé, Valéry, etc. may have got indirectly out of Poe's verse, since such creative misreading would, by definition, be hard to detect. However, in the case of Mallarmé, we can tell how far he misread Poe in a straightforward way from the prose versions he made of some of the poems, and from the accompanying *scolies* or commentaries. Minor mistakes of interpretation occur here and there but, above all, his dithyrambic appraisals elevate Poe to a level that no American or English critic would claim for him. Also, oddly enough, Mallarmé seems to think that by producing literal, and slightly un-French, renderings, which he refers to as *calques* (i.e. exact, traced copies), he can remain tolerably faithful to the rhythmical nature of the originals; in fact, his prose inevitably eliminates the heavy beat of the poems and so softens one of their main characteristics.[4]

The one area in which a definite connection can be established between Mallarmé and the reality of Poe is that of poetic theory. Mallarmé began by admiring and imitating several French poets, including Hugo. Then he discovered Baudelaire, and became so obsessed with him as to produce one or two poems that are uncannily Baudelairean. Through Baudelaire, he came across Poe and seems gradually to have transferred his theoretical allegiance to the American, so that we find him, at the age of 24, writing to a friend: '. . . the further I go, the more faithful I will be to the strict ideas bequeathed to me by my great master, Edgar Poe.' A little later, he expresses his hope of making *Hérodiade* 'a poem worthy of Poe and unsurpassed even by his'. Since, in fact, *Hérodiade*, like all his typical works, is hermetic, as Poe's verse never is, and far denser than any poem by the American, he is not following Poe's actual practice but developing suggestions contained in Poe's three essays, 'The Poetic Principle', 'The Philosophy of Composition' and 'The Rationale of Verse', and also, perhaps, *obiter dicta* from *Marginalia*.

212

Poe in France: A Myth Revisited

Poe's poetic doctrine has been very effectively criticized by both Yvor Winters and T. S. Eliot in the essays already mentioned. Winters dismisses it out of hand as a series of paradoxes and mis-statements, leading to poetry characterized by an immediate, shallow emotionalism and an otherworldly nostalgia, perversely alien to general human truth. This is certainly one way of looking at it, and Winters' strictures are borne out by the tinniness and monotony of most of Poe's verse. Eliot, while almost as critical of Poe's theories, takes the more tolerant line that his various assertions—about the impossibility of the long poem, the need for the poem to create a single, whole effect, carefully calculated by the poet, the non-poetic nature of Truth as opposed to Beauty, etc.— although all individually debatable, had the positive effect of encouraging French writers, from Mallarmé onwards, to aim at distilling a poetic essence, *la poésie pure*, as far removed as possible from the discursiveness of prose. He consequently argues that the French found in Poe a stimulus that American and English writers missed; Poe himself may have arrived at his ideas by borrowing and exaggerating principles first enunciated by Coleridge, but he deserves credit as the catalyst who made Symbolism possible; the aspiration towards *la poésie pure* was a valid direction in which literature could go at the time and, although it has now spent its force through the realization that poetry, if absolutely pure, would refine itself out of existence, it resulted in good work with which Poe's name will remain justifiably associated.

One or two French critics, on the other hand, have maintained that Mallarmé, elaborating on the more concentrated poetry already produced by Baudelaire in reaction against the rhetorical abundance of Hugo, would have developed in the same way, had he never heard of Poe. It is impossible to decide absolutely between the two hypotheses, but I think Eliot's is probably the correct one, and all the more so since he himself, as a poet, owed more than a little to Baudelaire and Mallarmé, and obviously knew how paradoxically and unexpectedly such influences may work. Out of a doubtful theory, used as a prop to support creation, good effects may sometimes come. Mallarmé varies a little in his attitude towards Poe's doctrine of total consciousness; in one context, he takes Poe's description of the writing of 'The Raven' quite seriously; in another, like Baudelaire, he sees it rather as a legitimate *jeu d'esprit* directed against the believers in facile inspiration. But he accepted the importance of conscious control, and put his trust in the relatively short poem, entirely poetic in its effect, and in the superiority of suggestiveness over direct statement. One can only suppose that he was acquainted with *Marginalia* (CCXV), where Poe, in praising Tennyson, makes the following remark:

> I *know* that indefiniteness is an element of the true music [of poetry] . . . a suggestive indefiniteness of meaning with a view to bringing about a definiteness of vague and therefore of spiritual effect.

This is practically identical in its implications with Mallarmé's famous principle, enunciated in 1891:

> *To name* an object is to destroy three quarters of the poetic pleasure, which arises from guessing little by little: *to suggest* the object, that is the ideal. It is the perfect manipulation of this mystery which constitutes the symbol: gradually conjuring up an object to illustrate a mood [*état d'âme*], or, conversely, choosing an object and deducing a mood from it through a series of decodings.

The sentence which immediately follows shows how Mallarmé makes the transition from Poe's indefiniteness to his own hermeticism: 'Poetry must always be enigmatic, and the aim of literature—it can have no other—is to conjure up [*évoquer*] objects.'

This is not the place to discuss whether or not, in some of their works, Mallarmé and Valéry carried the indefiniteness of hermeticism to such a peak that the flickering play of ambiguities defeats its own purpose by straining language beyond comprehension. The relevant point is that Poe's ideas, if indeed they were essential for Mallarmé and Valéry, helped the two Frenchmen, when at their best, to produce major poems greatly superior to anything that Poe himself was capable of, and far removed from his thin Idealism. *L'Après-midi d'un faune* represents a brilliant fusion of carnality and spirituality that Poe might well have disliked, while *Le Cimetière marin* and *Ebauche d'un serpent* restate, with magnificent linguistic felicity and originality, two ancient 'content' or 'Truth' themes, firmly rooted in this world: the mystery of life and death and the insolubility of the problem of evil.

It is not certain whether Valéry derived his obsession with poetic technique more from direct acquaintance with Poe's writings than, at second hand, from Mallarmé. The only Poe text he discussed publicly was *Eureka*, for which he wrote a preface, when Baudelaire's translation was reissued in 1921. The piece has been taken seriously by some Poe specialists, but it is very much *une oeuvre de circonstance*; Valéry recalls his early enthusiasm for Poe, gets himself into something of a knot over the key-term 'Consistency' through not realizing that Baudelaire's rendering of the word as *Consistance* is a mis-translation, and is polite about the general thesis of *Eureka*, while plainly hinting that it is a logical fantasy alien to his sceptical mind. Had he not been inhibited in regard to Poe by a sense of obligatory piety (as he was not, for instance, when he launched his famous attack on Pascal), he could have pointed out the absolute contradiction between the excellent, indeed pre-Valerian, paragraph of *Marginalia* (CXII):

> . . . there is something in the vanity of logic which addles a man's brains. Your true logician gets, in time, to be logicalized, and then, so far as regards himself, the universe is one word . . . He deposits upon a sheet of paper a certain assemblage of syllables, and fancies that their meaning is riveted by the act of deposition . . .

and the text of *Eureka*, which is just such a deposition, a purely verbal, therefore human, argument—a theodicy, in fact—purporting to prove the unprovable, namely that the universe is a manifest 'plot of God'.

But Valéry's early correspondence with André Gide, as well as his posthumous *Cahiers*, show that, in his youth, he had at least looked into a number of Poe's works. He praises Poe's originality in attempting to supply a theoretical foundation for literature, and credits him with having rejected 'mixed poetry' (*la poésie mêlée*). And it is no doubt significant that the twenty-eight volumes of the *Cahiers*, as well as various fragments published in his life-time, contain an extensive, though inter-mittent, meditation on the nature of poetry, which is like an immensely refined and sophisticated reconsideration of various points that Poe touches on rather hastily and dogmatically.

What is more important, perhaps, is the statement, in the *Cahiers*, that Poe provided him, at the age of 20, with a general intellectual stimulus through the galvanizing effect of a few isolated sentences or ideas. He refers, in particular, to an incidental remark in 'The Domain of Arnheim'—'I believe that the world has never seen . . . that full extent of triumphant execution, in the richer domain of art, of which the [*sic*] human nature is capable'—which does not seem very striking in itself, but was apparently an inspiration for him.

Curiously enough, in *Marginalia*, there are also several remarks which could have a direct application to Valéry, especially CXVIII:

> It is the curse of a certain order of mind that it can never rest satisfied with the consciousness of its ability to do a thing. Not even is it content with doing it. It must both know and show how it was done.

The fact is that the central preoccupation of Valéry's life was not poetry, with which he was concerned during only two, widely separated phases of his career, but the incessant process of intellectual analysis, covering all areas of activity, that he carried on daily in his *Cahiers*. In the first stage of his career, he represented this process, in symbolic form, in the eponymous hero of *Monsieur Teste*, the almost mystic hero of cerebration, who may, to some extent, be a sublime transposition of Poe's maniacally ratiocinative characters, such as Legrand in 'The Gold Bug' and the amateur detective Dupin. If so, here again, through reading Poe in a spirit of adoration, Valéry refined and intensified elements that were present, in a much cruder form, in the American. But it is impossible to be sure of the degree of Poe's influence in this respect because, in other contexts, Valéry also lays great stress on the importance of Leonardo da Vinci's *Notebooks* in starting him on his great intellectual quest, the sceptical conclusion of which he again symbolized in old age by means of the eponymous hero of *Mon Faust*. Still, it is a further posthumous honour for Poe to be mentioned in parallel with Leonardo.

We see, then, that each of the three main agents of Poe's

fame in France, despite some overlapping, reacted to him in a rather different way, and that Mallarmé and Valéry, even more than Baudelaire, magnified him out of all recognition. Considering the transmogrification certain elements in his writings underwent in their hands, we might be tempted to say: *Tel qu'il n'était que très peu en lui-même la France l'a changé.* So much so that the French attitude has no doubt, for better or for worse, encouraged the American academic public, at least, to treat Poe more reverently than it might otherwise have done, and to create the modern Franco-American Poe industry, of which Claude Richard's thesis is such an imposing product.

Thanks to the prestige of his three great advocates, Poe has continued to be referred to with respect in the French literary world but, after his intense, *fin-de-siècle* vogue, when he certainly contributed something to the decadent dandyism of Des Esseintes and Axël, the now dated heroes created by Huysmans and Villiers de l'Isle-Adam, it is not obvious that he had, or still has, any direct importance for creative writers. In an early Franco-American thesis, *The Influence of Edgar Allan Poe in France* (New York, 1927), C. P. Cambiaire claimed to find resemblances to, or echoes of, Poe in scores of French authors, but I think he was carried away by too credulous an enthusiasm.

As regards more recent literature, it might be possible to discern something Poe-like in the fantastic short-stories of Noël Devaulx or Michel Tournier, although, if I am not mistaken, neither has admitted any debt to the American. Tournier, it is true, has paid tribute to the formative influence of Gaston Bachelard, and Bachelard, in his phenomenological studies, such as *La Terre et les Rêveries du Repos* and *L'Eau et les Rêves*, refers warmly to Poe, but only in passing and in disappointingly vague and general terms. Also, it is conceivable that the *nouveau roman*, as practised by Alain Robbe-Grillet, with its highly contrived and therefore rationalistic arrangement of irrational elements, could be seen as ultimately neo-Poesque; however, if it is, the influence has been mediated through other authors, because Robbe-Grillet makes no mention of Poe in his autobiography and, in any case, his refrigerated compulsiveness seems to be rather different from the manic drive of Poe's most characteristic tales.

As far as my knowledge goes, undoubtedly the most fascinating and creative consequence of the Poe myth in the twentieth century has been Marie Bonaparte's Freudian study, which even a reader lukewarm about Poe himself can find profoundly entertaining, whether or not he agrees with the basic thesis. Starting from the premise that Poe was indelibly marked at the age of 3 by the incestuous desires aroused by the sight of his mother's corpse (although there is no actual proof that he saw it), Princess Bonaparte argues that he replaced the vision of his dead mother by a succession of female figures, one of whom he 'married', but with none of whom, because of unconscious guilt, he could ever conclude 'a carnal embrace'. The Princess sees Poe's life as having been wholly governed by this circumstance; his frustrated instinct was channelled into his writings, the most successful parts of which are equivalent to pure Freudian dreams, ringing the changes on sadonecrophiliac imagery; his displays of manic ratiocination are attempts to keep insanity at bay, or a compensation for unsatisfied sexual curiosity. His work in general was 'a way of "nobly" fleeing from temptation safely in intense, sublime absorption. But even that left him insecure and then he fled to drink and to his drinking cronies.' She adds that Poe, like all writers, wrote what his unconscious dictated', but was very exceptional in that his unconscious expressed itself so elaborately and so clearly.

This view makes short work of Poe, the conscious artist, but it allows the Princess to display the most admirable ingenuity in interpreting 'The Murders in the Rue Morgue', 'The Fall of the House of Usher' and various other tales, as well as *Eureka*. She sees them all as the products of a mind warped in childhood and permanently unable to overcome its disability. She admits, incidentally, that a relationship with 'a normal, healthy woman' might have proved Poe's 'salvation'. This is tantamount to saying that the mainspring of his creativity was his 'perversion' which, as she admits, remains monotonously the same, however varied the disguises his unconscious finds for it. Nevertheless, the Princess continues to make lavish use of the term 'genius', without apparently realizing that what she is proving is not Poe's universal validity as a great writer but rather the highly idiosyncratic nature of his pathological case.

And so, this last great French apotheosis of Poe, insofar as we can find it credible, amounts, paradoxically, to his quasi-demolition as a serious literary figure.

NOTES

1. Henry James, 'Charles Baudelaire', *French Poets and Novelists* (London: Macmillan, 1878); Aldous Huxley, 'Vulgarity in Literature', *Music at Night and Other Essays* (London: Chatto & Windus, 1930); Yvor Winters, 'Edgar Allan Poe: A Crisis in the History of American Obscurantism', *American Literature*, VIII, January 1937, 379–410; T. S. Eliot, 'From Poe to Valéry', *Hudson Review*, II, August 1949, 327–43.
2. James Russell Lowell, *A Fable For Critics* (1848).
3. Claude Richard, *Edgar Allan Poe, journaliste et critique* (Librarie C. Klincksieck, 1978). This latest French study contains as up-to-date and complete a bibliography as exists.
4. In a letter to Valéry, written in French and dated 16 March 1929, Huxley, after repeating the point about the vulgarity of Poe's versification, remarks: 'En le traduisant, Mallarmé a transfiguré "The Raven" à peu près comme Beethoven a transfiguré dans ses grandes variations la valse de Diabelli. . . . le grand poème manqué anglais est devenu le chef d'oeuvre français.' This is a wild exaggeration, prompted no doubt by cross-Channel politeness. Mallarmé's version is a delicate piece of writing, but it cannot possibly stand comparison with Beethoven's metamorphosis of the trite Diabelli waltz into a wealth of different musical modes.

Notes on Contributors

HAROLD BEAVER is Professor of American Literature at the University of Amsterdam. He has contributed five editions of Melville and Poe to the Penguin English Library and his *The Great American Masquerade* (1985) has recently appeared in the Critical Studies Series.

ROBERT GIDDINGS is Senior Lecturer in English and Media at Dorset Institute of Higher Education, and author of *The Tradition of Smollett* (1967), *You Should See Me in Pyjamas* (1981) and (with Alan Bold) *True Characters: Real People in Fiction* (1984), *The Book of Rotters* (1985) and *Who Was Really Who in Fiction* (1986). For the Critical Studies Series he has edited *J. R. R. Tolkien: This Far Land* (1983), *The Changing World of Charles Dickens* (1983) and *Mark Twain: A Sumptuous Variety* (1985).

ARNOLD GOLDMAN is Assistant Chief Officer of the Council for National Academic Awards, having previously taught at the Universities of Manchester, Sussex and Keele. He is the author of two books on James Joyce, editions of Dickens and Scott Fitzgerald and essays on a number of major American authors.

RICHARD GRAY is Reader in Literature at the University of Essex. He has edited two anthologies of American poetry, a collection of essays on Robert Penn Warren and (in the Critical Studies Series) *American Fiction: New Readings* (1983). He is the author of *The Literature of Memory: Modern Writers of the American South* as well as essays on American poetry and fiction.

JAMES H. JUSTUS, Professor of English at Indiana University, has written on such American authors as Charles Brockden Brown, Hawthorne, Hemingway, Faulkner and other twentieth-century writers of the American South. His most recent book is *The Achievement of Robert Penn Warren* (1981).

MARK KINKEAD-WEEKES was until recently Professor of English at the University of Kent at Canterbury. He is the author (with Ian

Gregor) of *William Golding: A Critical Study* (1967, rev. edn., 1983), *Samuel Richardson, Dramatic Novelist* (1973) and has written extensively on aspects of the English novel and on African and Caribbean literature. A scholarly edition of *The Rainbow* is forthcoming in the Cambridge 'Collected Works of D. H. Lawrence' and he also heads a team that will be responsible for the new Cambridge Biography of Lawrence.

A. ROBERT LEE is Lecturer in American Literature at the University of Kent at Canterbury. He is editor of the Everyman *Moby-Dick* (1975) and six previous collections in the Critical Studies Series: *Black Fiction: New Studies in the Afro-American Novel Since 1945* (1980), *Nathaniel Hawthorne: New Critical Essays* (1982), *Ernest Hemingway: New Critical Essays* (1983), *Herman Melville: Reassessments* (1984), *Nineteenth-Century American Poetry* (1985) and *The Nineteenth-Century American Short Story* (1985). He is the author of B.A.A.S. Pamphlet No. 11, *Black American Fiction Since Richard Wright* (1983) and recent essays on Chester Himes, Richard Wright, Emily Dickinson, Stephen Crane, Mark Twain, Herman Melville and Robert Penn Warren.

ERIC MOTTRAM is Professor of English and American Literature at King's College in the University of London. He has published books on Kenneth Rexroth, Paul Bowles, Allen Ginsberg, William Burroughs and others, and, with Malcolm Bradbury, edited and contributed to the *Penguin Companion to American Literature*. His last three books of poetry were *Elegies, A Book of Herne* and *Interrogation Rooms*.

DAVID MURRAY is Lecturer in American Studies at the University of Nottingham and has written on Pound and the New York poets, as well as a B.A.A.S. pamphlet *Modern Indians* (1983), essays on critical theory and a forthcoming full-length study of American-Indian culture.

JOHN WEIGHTMAN is Professor Emeritus of French in the University of London and Honorary Research Fellow at Westfield College. He is the author of *On Language and Writing* and *The Concept of the Avant-Garde* and his many essays and reviews have appeared in *T.L.S.*, the *New York Review of Books, Encounter*, the *Observer*, the *American Scholar* and elsewhere.

Index